TAJIKI

AN ELEMENTARY TEXTBOOK

ЗАБОНИ ТОҶИКӢ

КИТОБИ ДАРСӢ

(ДАВРАИ МУҚАДДАМОТӢ)

VOLUME ONE

ҶИЛДИ ЯКУМ

Nasrullo Khojayori

Насрулло Хоҷаёрӣ

Library of Congress Cataloging-in-Publication Data

Khojayori, Nasrullo.

Tajiki : an elementary textbook / Nasrullo Khojayori.

p. cm.

Includes bibliographical references and index.

ISBN 978-1-58901-263-9 (pbk. vol. 1 : alk. paper) --

ISBN 978-1-58901-264-6 (pbk. vol. 2 : alk. paper) --

ISBN 978-1-58901-269-1 (pbk. reference grammar : alk. paper)

1. Tajik language--Textbooks for foreign speakers--English.

I. Title.

PK6973.K49 2009

491'.5782421--dc21

2008052593

This grammar book, as well as other language materials for Central Asian Languages produced by CeLCAR, Indiana University-Bloomington, is supported by a Title-VI grant from the Department of Education

TABLE OF CONTENTS

SCOPE AND SEQUENCE

Chapter	Topic	Grammar	Function
Chapter 1	Салом Алифбои тоҷикӣ	Pronunciation	-Greetings -The Tajiki alphabet and pronunciation
Chapter 2 Синф	Ашёи синф Одамон дар синф Рақамҳо Ифодаҳои синф	-Pronoun чӣ 'what?' Demonstratives -Verb аст 'is' -Pronoun кӣ 'who?' -Numbers 0-10, Plurals and classifiers -Commands, Definite direct object	-Classroom objects -People in the classroom -Tajiki numbers -Classroom expressions
Chapter 3 Салом ва ҳолпурсӣ	Салом, Шумо хубед? Шумо аз куҷоед? Ӯ кист?	-Personal pronouns -Predicate endings -Negative/interrogative equational sentences -Prepositions of place	-Greetings and farewells -Places of origin -Professions
Chapter 4 Шиносоӣ	Шиносоӣ Миллатҳо Муаррафӣ	-Possessive endings -Question words -Suffixes ӣ and истон, Izofat -Personal titles	-Introductions -Nationalities -Introducing others
Chapter 5 Обу ҳаво	Ҳаво хуб аст? Ҳаво чанд дараҷа гарм аст? Соат чанд?	-Past tense of будан 'to be' -Past time markers -Numbers above 10 -Ordinal numbers -Days of the week	-Weather in the past and present -Temperature -Telling the time
Chapter 6 Хонадон	Оилаи тоҷикӣ Дар хонадони ҳамсар Ӯро тасвир кунед	-Verb доштан 'to have' -Simple past tense -Comparatives and superlatives	-Family members -In-laws -Common adjectives for people
Chapter 7 Дар бозор	Мубодилаи асъор Қаторҳои бозор Чанд пул?	-Compound verbs -Verbs будан/шудан 'to be/become' -Demonstratives in аш	-Money -Fruit and vegetables -Asking prices

ACKNOWLEDGEMENTS

Як гули мақсуд дар ин бӯстон,
Чида нашуд бе мадади дӯстон.
— *Саъдӣ*

There is no flower in the garden of the goals
Which was not grown without help of a friend.
— Saadi

This textbook could not have been written without the assistance of many people. First, I am deeply grateful to the two scholars who brought me to the United States and gave me the opportunity to write this book: Dr. William Fierman, Director of the Inner Asian and Uralic National Resource Center, whose love of Central Asia, knowledge of its cultures, and appreciation of the role of the national languages in the formation of national identity make him an incomparable advocate in the United States for the study of their languages and cultures; and Dr. Bill Johnston for his excellent ideas and his deep understanding of second-language pedagogy, which have provided his students invaluable guidance in developing textbooks with authentic materials.

Second, sincere thanks to Dr. Paul Foster, Director of CeLCAR, for his support and dedication throughout this process and providing all the resources needed to complete this book.

Third, I offer deep thanks to Dr. Azim Baizoyev for editing the Tajiki text; to Mikael Thompson for editing the English text and giving help in all areas of the book's composition, from brainstorming new exercises and suggesting better treatment of the chapter topics to organization and sequencing of activities, and above all for better explaining Tajiki grammar to native English speakers; and last but far from least to my wife, Farzona Zehni, who was involved in all stages of the textbook and without whose help the book could not have been written. Also, the practical tasks of writing this book were greatly eased by the unstinting efforts of Alisher Davlatzoda, who transferred data, recordings, and written materials to and from Tajikistan, found all the people who recorded the audio and video portions of the book, coordinated the myriad activities associated with the project, and provided technical support of every kind. Finally, I would like to thank Tom Tudek, Jim Woods and Sukhrob Karimov for design and illustrations.

I am also very thankful to all my friends who helped me by providing pictures, videos, audios, and all other assistance. I am especialy grateful to Khiromon Baqozoda, Tohiri Safar, Abdulfattoh Shafiev, Nasiba Mirpochoeva, Chris Whitsel and Amin Shohmurodov.

Dr. Nasrullo Khojayori

Preface

Our goal in the development of *Tajiki: An Elementary Textbook* at the Center for Languages for the Central Asian Region (CeLCAR) at Indiana University was to create instructional materials that would make a difference in the classroom and provide instructors with wide array of activities to make their classes interactive. *Tajiki: An Elementary Textbook* offers a thematically organized and integrative approach to the Tajiki language and culture combined with current innovations in foreign language teaching. Some of these innovations include: a functional approach to grammar; an emphasis on integrated skills development; and extensive use of various authentic materials, especially videos filmed in the different regions of Tajikistan. We believe that the large number of activities provided in the textbook and the supplementary materials, such as the multimedia available through guptextbooks.com, will help students to develop strong speaking, listening, reading and writing skills.

Tajiki: An Elementary Textbook is distinguished by the following features:

- emphasis on communicative activities and tasks
- step-by-step development of language skills
- presentation of Tajiki culture, integrated into all activities
- opportunities for classroom practice

Besides emphasizing Tajiki culture, the textbook contains universal topics and contemporary themes that are meaningful to learners.

While developing activities, we kept in mind the idea that languages are best learned when real-world tasks become the focus of language activities. Therefore, we organized the sequence of our activities by providing students with:

- sources for gaining information in Tajiki, such as texts, listening materials, real-life dialogues and videos
- the linguistic tools for understanding those sources
- tasks, activities and questions to use their linguistics skills and evaluate their own progress

Overall, we hope that our materials will make a difference in your classroom and that you will enjoy many hours of teaching and learning Tajiki.

A Note for the Instructor

Tajiki: An Elementary Textbook is developed specifically for classroom use. Its purpose is to provide learners and their instructors with a wide selection of materials and task-oriented, communicative activities designed to facilitate development of the language skills of the learner. The textbook is divided into fourteen thematic chapters. These chapters cover topics commonly found in beginning textbooks, such as work, study, family, shopping and travel. Language learners who successfully complete *Tajiki: An Elementary Textbook* are expected to be able to read simple texts, engage in conversation about simple topics, and write short texts in Tajiki. All multimedia used in the textbook can be found through guptextbooks.com.

Organization of the Text

Each chapter is divided into three or four sections, each section focusing on a particular topic, and a glossary. Each section has seven parts, four of them emphasizing one of the four basic skills (listening, speaking, reading and writing), though all four skills will be practiced in the exercises; the first three parts introduce the topics and vocabulary in a given section, the next three parts provide further practice, and the last part ties the section together, allowing students to practice all four language skills with authentic video materials.

Part I: Сеҳри сухан

Part I includes new vocabulary that will be actively used throughout the chapter. The vocabulary items are introduced by audio, which the teacher should play in class so that all the students can practice out loud. This is followed by individual exercises and group activities intended to reinforce the vocabulary. If students are having trouble, the teacher should supplement the exercises in the book by pointing to various objects and asking students to name or describe them, for example.

Part II: Гуфтугӯ

This part focuses on speaking. The exercises are intended to lead students to practice the new grammatical structures in the section and understand them deductively.

Part III: Дастур

Part III explains new grammatical structures to make certain the structures practiced in Part II are clear.

Part IV: Хониш

Part IV focuses on reading skills. In this part authentic materials from magazines and newspapers are used as much as possible.

Part V: Гӯш кунед

Part V focuses on listening skills.

Part VI: Хат

This part of each lesson focuses on writing, often through exercises that call for students to write sentences and dialogues with each other.

Part VII: Тамошо кунед

Exercises based on short video clips filmed in Tajikistan. The purpose of these video clips is to introduce students to the authentic use of the Tajiki language while bringing together all the vocabulary and grammar covered in the section. The activities given in this section do not require the understanding of every single word or grammatical structure; instead students are encouraged to grasp the main idea and to be attentive to some non-linguistic features introduced in these videos. As the speakers use authentic language (dialogues were not scripted), it might be useful to revisit these video clips later in the course when students become more proficient in Tajiki.

Cultural notes

Every chapter includes notes describing elements of Tajiki culture, Барги Сабз. These notes are short; however, as an instructor, you might give further explanations regarding their content. Moreover, you may follow them up with short discussions that would encourage students to compare and contrast these cultural points with their own culture. Furthermore, the later chapters include some of the most commonly used proverbs and superstitions of Tajiki culture. The explanation of these proverbs is not provided, and it is hoped that this will create an interesting discussion between you and your students about the meaning and the use of these proverbs.

Introduction to Tajiki

Tajiki is a member of the Iranian family of languages, which includes Persian, Kurdish, Soghdian, and many other languages of Iran, Afghanistan, Tajikistan, and surrounding countries. (*Tajiki* is the name of the language, *Tajik* the name of the people.) Tajiki is one of the three varieties or dialects of Persian, the others being Farsi (Iran) and Dari (Afghanistan). The Iranian languages in turn make up part of one branch (the Indo-Iranian languages) of the Indo-European family of languages, which includes Greek, Latin, the Germanic languages (including English), the Slavic languages (including Russian), the Celtic languages, the Indian languages (such as Sanskrit and Hindi), Armenian, and others. That is, all of these languages are modern descendants of a much earlier language called Proto-Indo-European, which was never written down but which linguists can more or less reconstruct. Some Tajiki words are very close to the corresponding words (cognates) in English and the other Indo-European languages:

Tajiki	English	Latin	Greek
modar	mother	mater	matér
padar	father	pater	patér
bar-	bear (v.)	fer-	pher-

Other words have changed so much in the different languages that they are quite dissimilar—for example, Tajiki *zan* 'woman, wife' is cognate with English *queen*, Greek *gyné*, Russian *zhená*, and Irish *ban* (as in *banshee*, 'woman of the fairies').

Proto-Indo-European seems most likely to have been spoken in the steppes north of the Black Sea at the time it started spreading. The beginning of the breakup of Proto-Indo-European into its daughter languages cannot be dated exactly, but rough estimates can be made on the basis of archeological evidence and the absence of certain terms relating to agriculture and technology common to all the branches of Indo-European languages. Proto-Indo-European probably broke up no later than 5,000 to 6,000 years ago. After the language spread, it broke up into different dialects that increasingly diverged from each other as their speakers lost contact with each other. This gave rise to separate languages that in turn spread and diverged over the millennia to develop into the various languages of each of the branches of Indo-European family.

The people who spoke the ancestral form of the Indo-Iranian languages (Proto-Indo-Iranian) spread into the region south of the Black, Caspian, and Aral seas well before 1,000 BC. By the first millennium BC, Proto-Indo-Iranian had already separated out into distinct Indian and Iranian languages. The Iranian languages at this time (the Old Iranian languages) were spoken from the north shore of the Black Sea to west and northwest of China (making up the dominant language of the Scythians, a nomadic culture dominating the Eurasian steppes and including peoples speaking early Turkic and Mongolic languages), and further south in the Iranian plateau to the shores of the Persian Gulf. Numerous peoples spoke Old Iranian languages, including the Persians proper along the Persian Gulf, the Medes in the northwestern Iranian plateau, and various Central Asian peoples: Soghdians, Bactrians, Khwarezmians, Parthians, and others. The major linguistic division at this time was between the Western Iranian (Old Persian and Median) and Eastern Iranian languages (the others); the Western Iranian languages are further classified as Northwestern (Median) and Southwestern (Old Persian).

The Medes unified the region of the Iranian plateau and expanded to found an empire extending throughout much of modern-day Iran; its Persian successor states, the Persian empire of the Achaemenids (648-330 BC), the Parthian empire (170 BC-226 AD), and the Sassanid empire (226-650 AD), ensured the cultural and linguistic unity of the Western Iranian languages. The Eastern Iranian languages, on the other hand, were spoken in a much more fragmented region in which Soghdian served as a lingua franca (a common language of trade and administration) that coexisted with local languages which came to diverge much more from each other over this period than the Western Iranian languages did; the descendants of these languages (which are spoken throughout Afghanistan and Tajikistan) are much more distinct from Tajiki (and from each other) than Tajiki is from Farsi and Dari. Moreover, while the Persian empires were officially Zoroastrian (such religions as Judaism, Nestorian Christianity, Roman and Greek paganism, and Buddhism were usually tolerated, though Catholic Christianity was often persecuted under the Sassanids as the official religion of Persia's major enemy, Rome), Central Asia at the time was a cultural and religious stew in which Buddhism, Manichaeism, Nestorian Christianity, and Zoroastrianism coexisted. Indeed, each religious tradition used a distinct script to set itself apart from the others; however, these scripts were not limited to particular languages but rather adapted to the various local languages when that religion's scriptures were translated. Culturally, Central Asia was a network of city-states based on agriculture and trade linked by the various trade routes of the Silk Road surrounded by a sea of nomadic herding peoples, in which local leaders rarely became powerful enough to conquer their enemies and were often prey to the depredations of nomadic steppe empires and conquest by sedentary empires like Persia and China. This is the cultural background which even today shapes Tajik culture as much as Islam has.

After the conquest of Persia by the Arabs in 650, the Eastern Iranian languages went into decline as Islam was spread to Transoxiana (also known by its Arabic designation, Mawara' an-Nahr, "the land beyond the [Oxus] river"). The Persian of the time, written in Arabic script and enriched with a number of Soghdian loanwords, became the new common language of culture, trade, and administration throughout Central Asia and further west to the region around Nishapur; it was the form of Persian spoken in many of the great cultural centers of Central Asia: Bukhara, Samarkand, Balkh, Tashkent, and Khujand, for example. It was also the form of Persian spoken by many of the greatest Persian poets and philosophers after the Arab conquest of Persia, like Rudaki, Firdawsi, Omar Khayyam, Rumi, Attar, al-Farabi, ibn-Sina (Avicenna), and al-Ghazali. This preeminence was established by the first native Persian Islamic dynasty, the Samanids (819-999), whose capitals at Samarkand, Bukhara, and Herat are among the greatest cultural centers of Central Asia. At this time Persian was viewed as a unitary language called Dari, meaning "of the court"; regional differences in speech were unimportant compared to the uniformity of the written language, which has changed little since the 9th century.

However, with the rise of the Safavids in the early 16th century, this cultural unity was weakened. The Safavids, who expanded from Azerbaijan to rule Iraq, Iran, and much of Afghanistan, were staunch Shi'ites who warred constantly with the Sunni states on their borders (indeed, the dynasty was effectively ended in 1722 by the revolt of the Ghalzai, Afghan Sunnis whom the Safavids had tried to convert by force to Shi'ism).

Once the Persian cultural world was divided, the language of the two regions diverged, with that of Persia coming to be called *Farsi*; the term *Tajiki* for the eastern dialects is a 20th century innovation. (The older term for the language, *Darii Kobuli*, meaning "Persian of Kabul," is still used for the Persian spoken in Afghanistan.) Outside of language, the religious and cultural differences between the Safavids and Transoxiana accentuated the Central Asian orientation of Tajik culture. However, there is a tendency among scholars to call the common language Farsi regardless of national boundaries, much as American English is called English rather than American.

Finally, a century of Russian domination encouraged the spread of Western culture as refracted through Russian culture and Soviet ideology (including a significant influx of Russian loanwords, a major portion of which is common Greco-Latin terminology borrowed into Russian); in particular, the Czarist and Soviet policies towards minority nations inculcated western ideals of nationalism that are common to Central Asia but differ significantly from the view of nation and state in much of the rest of the Islamic world. In addition, in accordance with Soviet policy for minority languages, a new written standard of Tajiki was promulgated that was based heavily upon colloquial speech, which led to the elimination of many Arabic words common in literary Persian.

Besides Russian loanwords (many of which are being replaced by non-Russian words), Tajiki has also borrowed many words from Arabic and some (though far fewer) from the Turkic languages. Arabic words are especially common in the literary and intellectual levels of the language, very much as Greek and Latin words are especially frequent in these realms in English, but they are also quite common in the most commonplace levels of speech—thus, the Arabic word *ba'd* 'after' is at least as common as the native Persian word *pas*, and both prepositions are fully acceptable in speaking. Similarly, compound verbs based on *tavallud* (Arabic for 'birth') are as commonly used as the native Persian verb *zodan*. Turkic words are most common in vocabulary concerning livestock, herding, and steppe life, but even terms for body parts and kinship terms have been borrowed from the Turkic languages. In return Arabic and the Turkic languages have borrowed heavily from Persian. (It is said that throughout the Islamic world Arabic is the language of religion, Persian the language of administration and poetry, and Turkic the language of the military. More important for the beginning student of Tajiki, Arabic is also the language of grammar.) While most of these words will be unfamiliar to most speakers of English, there are a few Arabic words that have been borrowed into both Persian and English: *sifr* 'zero' goes with both *cipher* and *zero*, and *sharbat* 'juice' with *sherbet* and *sorbet*, for example. There are also a number of Persian words that have been borrowed into English (often through Arabic). Thus, *noranj* 'orange' goes with *orange* and *poijoma* goes with *pajama* (in Tajiki it refers to the light undertrousers worn by both sexes, from *poi* 'leg' and *joma* 'dress'). Similarly, *vizier* is the English form of Tajiki *vazir*, and by a circuitous route *divan* comes from the Persian word *divan* (Tajiki *devon*) for a document house or ministry. The Persian word was also used for the hall in which an administrator would hold public audiences, and then this was applied to the sofa where he sat. (The Persian word also referred to a collection of poems, a meaning occasionally also found in the West, as in Goethe's *Divan of West and East*, or *West-Östlicher Divan*.)

Боби **ЯКУМ**
CHAPTER **ONE**

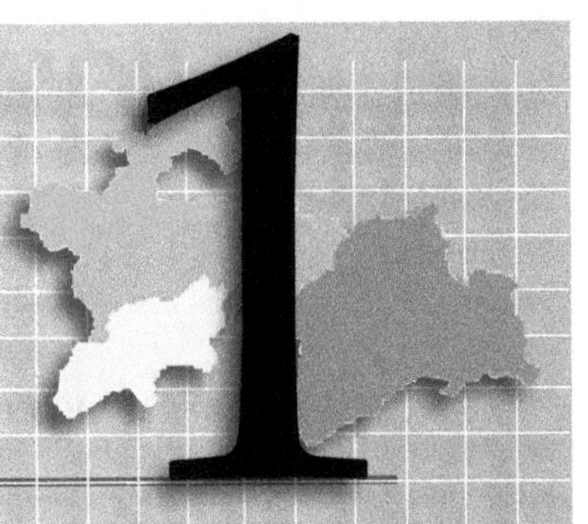

АЛИФБОИ ЗАБОНИ ТОҶИКӢ
TAJIKI ALPHABET

IN THIS CHAPTER

- **Салом** Greetings
- **Садонокҳо** Vowels
- **Ҳамсадоҳо** Consonants
- **Имло** Handwriting in Tajiki
- **Алифбои тоҷикӣ** Tajiki Alphabet
- **Луғатнома** Vocabulary

А. САЛОМ A. GREETINGS

1. СЕҲРИ СУХАН!

Машқи 1: Listen and practice.

Assalomu Alaykum!
Vaalaykum assalom!

Salom!
Salom!

Assalomu alaykum!
Salom!

A man and an old man
Assalomu alaykum, bobo!
Va alaykum assalom!

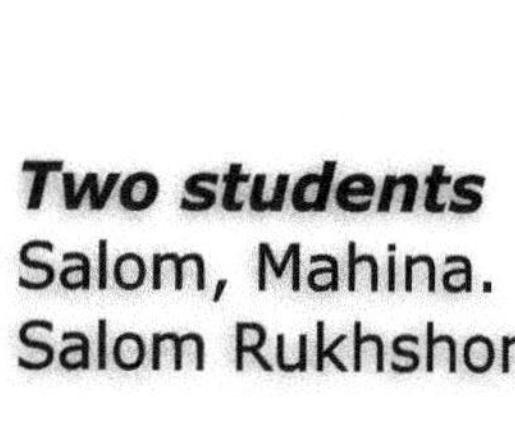

Two students
Salom, Mahina.
Salom Rukhshona.

Two teenagers
Assalom!
Salom!

A woman and a boy
Assalom!
Va alaykum assalom!

Машқи 2: Analyze the different situations pictured above. Which phrase is the formal form of greeting? Which is the informal one?

Машқи 3: Look at the pictures of the people below. How would you greet each one? Tell a classmate what you would say to each of these people. Now assume you are going to greet the following people. Write the proper greeting for each and tell how you will act when greeting them.

Compare your answers with a classmate. Did you come up with the same choices? If not, why might they differ?

2. ГУФТУГӮ

Машқи 4: Using what you have learned, work with a classmate and try to come up with a greeting (both phrases and actions) appropriate to these situations.

a) two high school students
b) two university professors
c) an adult and a child
d) two friends

Машқи 5: Go around the class and greet each other and your instructor. Use appropriate greetings based on what you have learned.

3. ТАМОШО КУНЕД

Машқи 6: You will watch videos in which different people greet each other. Pay close attention to what the people say and do in each example and write in Latin script their actions and words in the boxes provided:

Scene 1.

ACTIONS	PHRASES
1.	
2.	
3.	

Scene 2.

ACTIONS	PHRASES
1.	
2.	
3.	

Scene 3.

ACTIONS	PHRASES
1.	
2.	
3.	

Барги сабз

There are different ways of greeting people in Tajikistan. The formality of the relationship, the social setting, and the ages of the two people determine which greeting to use. Younger people should greet older people only verbally at first. The older person is expected to offer his hand first. When greeting an older person, the younger person should put his hand over his heart during the conversation; employees are expected to do the same when speaking with their boss.

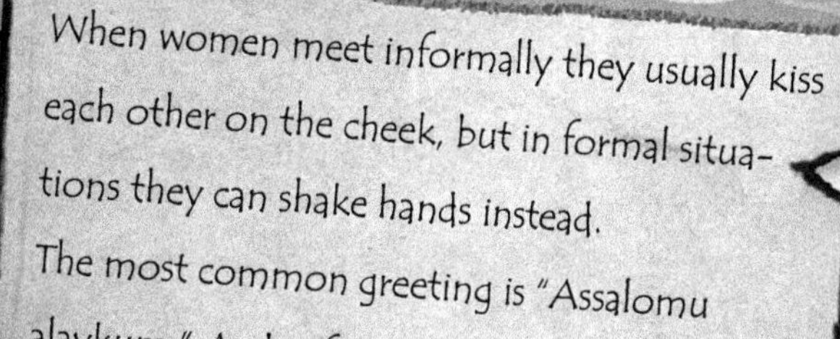

When women meet informally they usually kiss each other on the cheek, but in formal situations they can shake hands instead.

The most common greeting is "Assalomu alaykum," Arabic for "Peace to you" or "Peace be with you," to which one replies "Va alaykum assalom," Arabic for "And (I wish) peace to you." You can use "Assalomu alaykum" with everyone. With children, colleagues and people of the same age you can say "salom," Arabic for "peace." In literary language people can use the Tajiki word "durud" instead of "salom."

Б. САДОНОКҲО B. VOWELS

1. СЕҲРИ СУХАН!

Машқи 1: Listen to the audio and follow along as each letter is pronounced. Then listen to the audio a second time and repeat every sound you hear.

2. ГУФТУГӮ

Машқи 2: Listen to the 6 letters and write them on the lines below.

1. ______	4. ______
2. ______	5. ______
3. ______	6. ______

Машқи 3: Now take turns practicing saying the letters out loud with a partner. You may also choose to have your partner guess which letter you are saying.

3. ДАСТУР

Pronunciation:

VOWEL SOUNDS

There are six vowels in Tajiki

Аа --- [a]	as in **car -- асп** – horse; **лола** – tulip
Оо --- [o]	as in **boat** (pronounced "pure" without a final *w* sound) **-- об** – water
Ээ (Ее)- [e]	as in **met -- себ** – apple
Ии (й) - [i]	as in **ill -- ин** – this (**й** is used only at the end of words, and almost always indicates that the vowel is stressed; final **и** is unstressed)
Уу --- [u]	as in **root -- нур** – light
Ӯӯ --- [Э]	Pronounce the vowel in **cut** with rounded lips **-- ӯ** – he/she

VOWEL SPACE

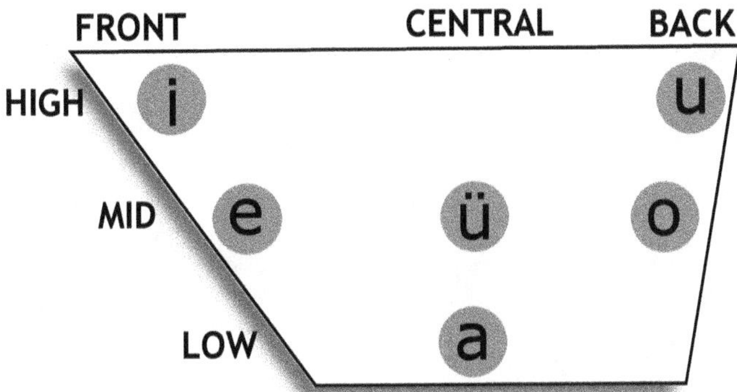

4. ГӮШ КУНЕД!

Машқи 4: Listen to the audio and decide which sound is being pronounced. Put 1 for **у** [u] and 2 for **ӯ** [ü].

к_ш	___	к_ш	___	ч_ш	___
н_ш	___	б_р	___	б_р	___
н_р	___	х_р	___	с_р	___

В. ҲАМСАДОҲО C. CONSONANTS

1. СЕҲРИ СУХАН!

Машқи 1: Here are words beginning with each of the consonants. Follow along as the voice on the audio says the consonant sounds and repeat them.

бобо	*'grandfather'*	**китоб**	*'book'*	**тарбуз**	*'watermelon'*
вақт	*'time'*	**қалам**	*'pencil'*	**фарзанд**	*'child'*
гап	*'speech'*	**лаб**	*'lip'*	**ҳамён**	*'wallet'*
ғор	*'cave'*	**модар**	*'mother'*	**хола**	*'aunt'*
даст	*'hand'*	**нон**	*'bread'*	**чашм**	*'eye'*
жола	*'hail'*	**пахта**	*'cotton'*	**ҷаҳон**	*'world'*
зан	*'woman'*	**роҳ**	*'road'*	**шакар**	*'sugar'*
йигит	*'a young man'*	**сар**	*'head'*	**маъно**	*'meaning'*

2. ГУФТУГӮ

Машқи 2: Listen as the voice on the audio says 16 letters and write them on the lines below.

1.	5.	9.	13.
2.	6.	10.	14.
3.	7.	11.	15.
4.	8.	12.	16.

What differences can you make out between the letters in each pair?

3. ДАСТУР

THERE ARE TWENTY-FOUR CONSONANTS IN TAJIKI

Бб – ***b*** as in ***book***
Вв – ***v*** as in ***very***
Гг – ***g*** as in ***good***
Ғғ – ***gh***; no direct correspondence (1)
Дд – ***d*** as in ***door***
Жж – ***zh*** as in ***pleasure***
Зз – ***z*** as in ***zoo***
Йй – ***y*** as in ***yes***
Кк – ***k*** as in ***clock***
Ққ – ***q***; no direct correspondence (2)
Лл – ***l*** as in ***little***
Мм– ***m*** as in ***many***
Нн – ***n*** as in ***new***
Пп – ***p*** as in ***pick***
Рр – ***r*** as in ***run***
Сс – ***s*** as in ***small***
Тт – ***t*** as in ***teacher***
Фф - ***f*** as in ***fog***
Хх – ***kh*** as in ***Bach***
Ҳҳ – ***h*** as in ***help***
Чч – ***ch*** as in ***church***
Ҷҷ – ***j*** as in ***just***
Шш – ***sh*** as in ***show***
Ъ – ***'*** no direct correspondence (3)

---

1. **Ғ** (gh) is pronounced like **Х** (kh) while allowing the vocal chords to vibrate.

2. **Қ** (q) is pronounced like **К** (k), only with the back of the tongue touching the roof of the mouth much closer to the throat. If you pay attention to the position of your tongue as you say "key" and "coo" carefully, you should find that your tongue is further back in the mouth in "coo"; to make **q** your tongue should touch the roof of the mouth even further back than that.

3. **Ъ** (') is pronounced like the "catch" in the throat (the glottal stop) in "uh-oh."

4. ГӮШ КУНЕД!

Машқи 3:

A. Follow along with the words and listen to how they are pronounced on the audio.

B. Listen again, and this time repeat the sounds.

C. Listen again, and this time write the letters in the blanks.

___орон	___ард	___ома	___оҳар
___арзиш	по___	___адар	___афта
___ул	___ор	___анг	___ой
___оз	___анд	___оат	___ой
___ар	___о___а	___ухм	___авҳар
ми___гон	___ӯй	___икр	шӯ___ла

Г. ҲАРФҲОИ ЙОТБАРСАР D. YOTED LETTERS

1. СЕҲРИ СУХАН!

Машқи 1:

A. Listen and practice.

яхмос	**ёр**
Яҳё	**дарё**
елим	**Юнон**
гӯед	**Каюмарс**

B. Now work with a partner. Write 2 words for each letter. One of you should read your list while the other writes your words down. Then change roles and check each other's writing.

2. ГУФТУГӮ

Машқи 2:

A. Listen as your teacher says the words and number them in the order they are spoken in the chart below.

ёқут		Каюмарс	
биёбон		Юнон	
ёд		донишҷӯе	
дарё		мегӯед	
ях		яхдон	

B. Work with a partner. One of you should say a word while the other writes its transcription and underlines the sounds indicated by the yoted letters. Take turns.

3. ДАСТУР

There are four letters in the Tajiki alphabet that stand for a sequence of two sounds. These letters are: ***Ее, Ёё, Юю, Яя***. The first sound in all of these letters is ***й (y)***.

Й + А = Я (ya) ***Й*** + Э = Е (ye)
Й + О = Ё (yo) ***Й*** + У = Ю (yu)

4. ГӮШ КУНЕД!

Машқи 3 : Listen and write the transcriptions of the following words.

яхмос	
биёбон	
сеюм	
Каюмарс	
Юнон	
ҳамсоя	
дароед	
намоед	
кушоед	
биёед	
донишҷӯе	
ёқут	
сиёҳ	
гиёҳ	
баёнот	
каён	
Нигерия	
лаёқат	

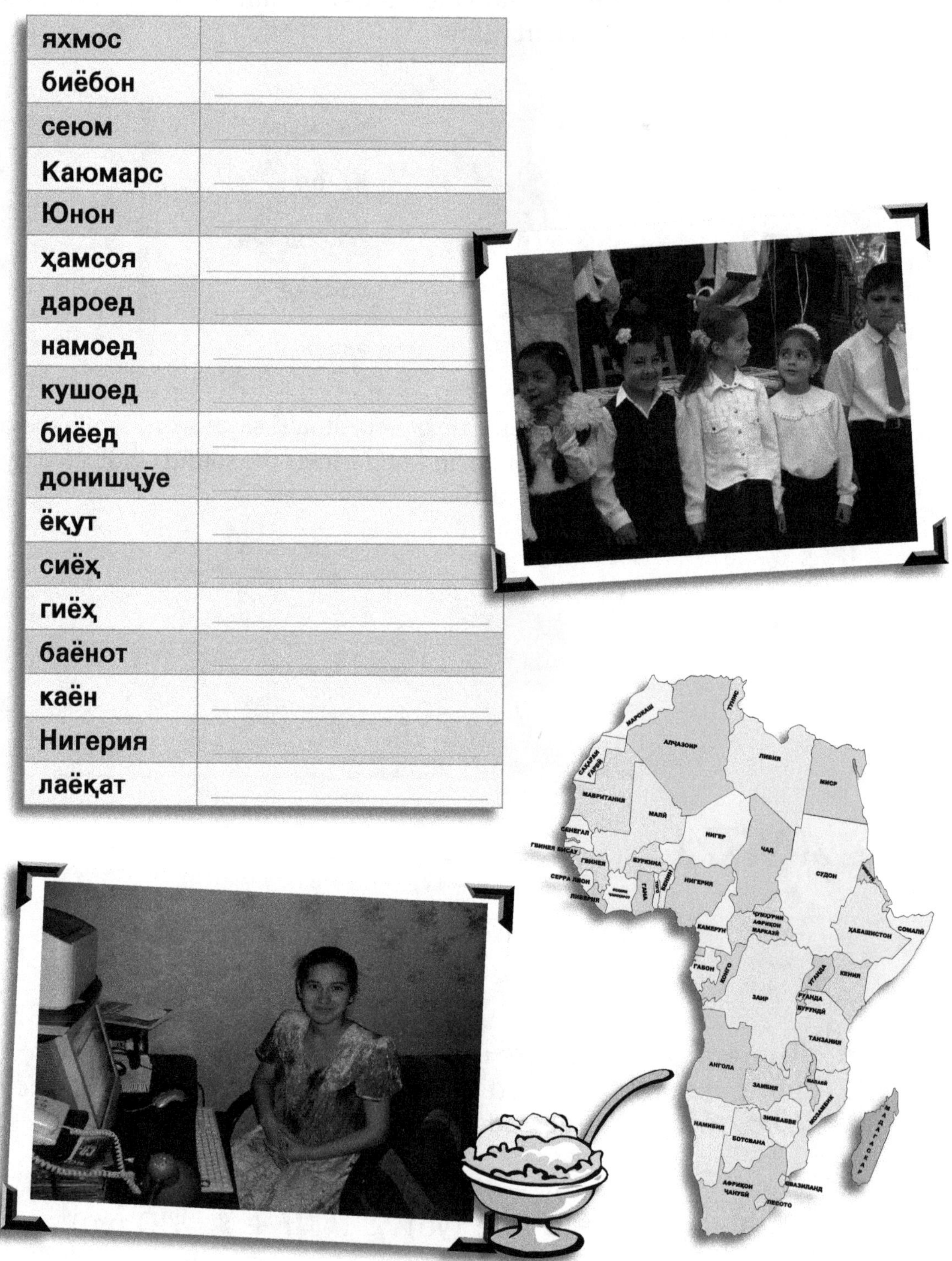

Машқи 4: Listen as the voice on the audio says the names of several cities as they are pronounced in Tajiki. Listen carefully and write them down as you hear them.

NAMES OF CITIES	WRITE	CHECK
Rome		
Paris		
Moscow		
Cape Town		
Vancouver		
Washington		
New York		
Seattle		
Los Angeles		
Rio de Janeiro		
Caracas		
Wellington		

Машқи 5: Now get together with your classmates and discuss your writing. Use the table of the alphabet on page 25 to check your spelling.

5. ХАТ

Машқи 6: Write the following words in Tajiki:

miyon	
sayohat	
meoyed	
yusuf	
duyum	
humoyun	
soya	

yor	
yak	
yelim	
yagon	
choye	
muyassar	
bisyor	

Д. ИМЛО E. HANDWRITING IN TAJIKI

1. СЕҲРИ СУХАН!

Машқи 1: Read the chart and write the English equivalents of each word in the row underneath.

Аа	*Амрико*	*Сахара*
Бб	*Боливия*	*Кӯлоб*
Вв	*Венгрия*	*Тува*
Гг	*Гана*	*Ҳамбург*
Ғғ	*Ғарм*	*Мағриб*
Дд	*Дания*	*Флорида*

Ее	Ереван	Копенҳаген
Ёё	Ёвон	Итолиё
Жж	Женева	Париж
Зз	Заир	Мозамбик
Ии	Исроил	Миср
ӣ	------	чинӣ
Йй	Йоркшир	Баҳрайн

Кк	Куба	Мексика
Ққ	Қирғизистон	Африқо
Лл	Лаос	Белгия
Мм	Молдова	Колумбия
Нн	Норвегия	Вашингтон
Оо	Осиё	Бонн
Пп	Полша	Аврупо
Рр	Россия	Белорус

Сс	Словения	Босния
Тт	Тоҷикистон	март
Уу	Украина	Туркия
Ӯӯ	Ӯротеппа	Чоркӯҳ
Фф	Фаронса	Исфаҳон
Хх	Хитой	Техас
Ҳҳ	Ҳинд	Теҳрон

Ҷҷ	Ҷакарта	Озарбойҷон
Шш	Шветсия	Бишкек
Ъъ	-------	Санъо
Ээ	Эрон	Венесуэлла
Юю	Юнон	Мюнхен
Яя	Ялта	Филаделфия

Notes:

(1.) Note that the cursive letters for l, m, and ya (л, м, я) are preceded by a small hook.

(2.) Lower case t and sh (т, ш) can be distinguished with a small horizontal line above and below the letter, respectively. This is commonly done when they occur next to such letters as i, g, and p (и, г, п) to prevent ambiguity.

Машқи 2: Read the words below and write their transliterations:

китоб	
қалам	
хома	
ҳамроҳ	
маҳ	
сафар	
асп	
донишҷӯ	
ҳаяҷон	
саҳифа	
чароғ	

Париж	
баҳор	
варақ	
гурба	
амрикоӣ	
Яғноб	
шимол	
хуш	
борон	
ӯзбак	
қазоқ	

Машқи 3:  Write the following words in cursive.

Душанбе	
Хуҷанд	
Вашингтон	
Монтана	
Ҳисор	
Суғд	
Бадахшон	
Флорида	
Қӯрғонтеппа	
Хатлон	
Индиана	
Чикаго	

Ню-Йорк	
Техас	
Ғарм	
Тоҷикобод	
Данғара	
Истаравшан	
Панҷакент	
Исфара	
Конибодом	
Мӯъминобод	
Помир	
Хоруғ	

The building of Union of Writers of Tajikistan. On the facade are monuments to the greatest poets of the Tajik people, such as Rudaki, Firdavsi, Abu Ali ibn Sino and others.

One of the buildings of Tajik Technical University.

Машқи 4: Read the list below with the help of your instructor and mark the words that are cognates.

об	*water*	о,б
нон	*bread*	н
шом	*evening*	
шаб	*night*	
лаб	*lip*	
камон	*bow*	
карам	*cabbage*	
қалам	*pencil*	
табақ	*plate*	
вақт	*time*	
расм	*picture*	
себ	*apple*	
модар	*mother*	
дӯст	*friend*	
мӯй	*hair*	
чой	*tea*	
чарх	*wheel*	
тундар	*thunder*	
роҳ	*road*	
ҳуҷра	*apartment*	
ҷамъ	*plus, total*	
таъмин	*supply*	

Мағриб	*West*	
зоғ	*raven*	
Яғноб	*Yaghnob*	
фалсафа	*philosophy*	
Юсуф	*Joseph*	
ёр	*friend*	
жола	*hail*	
Эрон	*Iran*	
бибӣ	*grandmother*	
абрӯ	*eyebrow*	
пахта	*cotton*	

Машқи 5: Did you notice that you keep learning new letters with each new word? Read the table again and in the last column write the new letter you learned with each word. The first two are done for you.

Хони наврӯзӣ
Navruz table

Тоҷикдухтарон
Tajik girls

Машқи 6:  Read the list below with the help of your instructor.

Булғор	**Қазоқистон**
Маҷористон	**Ҳиндустон**
Афғонистон	**Хитой**
Покистон	**Африқои Ҷанубӣ**
Тоҷикистон	**Шветсия**
Ӯзбакистон	**Юнон**
Эрон	**Чили**

Машқи 7: What are the capitals of the countries you named above? Look at the Tajiki maps in the appendices.

Машқи 8:  Match the countries with their capitals:

Америка	**Берлин**
Озарбойҷон	**Киев**
Фаронса	**Оттава**
Олмон	**Копенҳаген**
Украина	**Варшава**
Канада	**Исломобод**
Дания	**Париж**
Полша	**Вашингтон**
Покистон	**Боку**

Машқи 9: List the following countries in appropriate columns by continent.

Амрико	Аврупо	Африқо	Осиё

List of countries:
Покистон, Олмон, Чин, Япония, Алҷазоир, Канада, Чили, Боливия, Заир, Бангола, Муғулистон, Фаронса, Полша, Эрон, Миср, Зимбабве, Мексика, Нидерландия, Тайланд, Ҳиндустон, Арманистон, Сурия, Лубнон, Австрия, Люксембург, Туркия, Россия

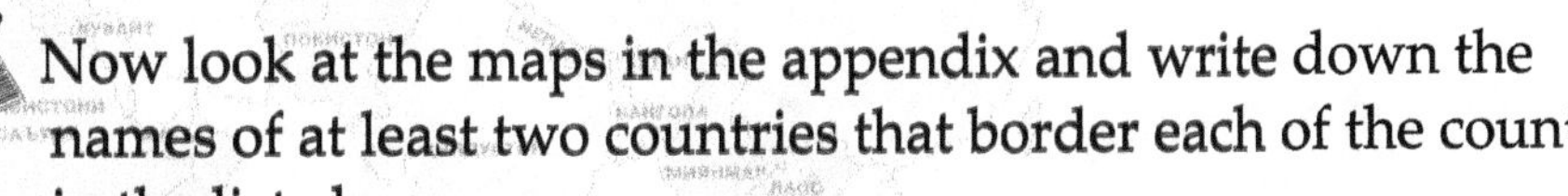

Машқи 10: Now look at the maps in the appendix and write down the names of at least two countries that border each of the countries in the list above.

Машқи 11: Working with a classmate, find the following words in the advertisement below:

1. The names of 3 countries	
2. An address	
3. A telephone number	
4. Some literary terms	
5. The names of two languages	
6. The names of 3 months	
7. The city where the advertiser is located	
8. A date	

Барои беҳтарин кори адабӣ дар байни донишҷӯёни макотиби олии ҷамоҳирии Тоҷикистон, Қиргизистон ва Қазоқистон озмун эълон менамояд.

ШАРТҲОИ ОЗМУН:

Асар бояд ба жанрҳои зерин навишта шавад. (ҳикоя, шеър, повест ва ғайра).

1. Лирика
2. Эпос
3. Драма

Мавзӯъ –озод

Забони асар–русӣ, тоҷикӣ

Ҳатман асар бояд бо ҳуруфи Times New, 14 компютер навишта шуда бошад.

Навиштани ному насаб, муассисаи таълимӣ, суроға, телефон ҳатмист.

Мӯҳлати охири қабули кор: 20.09.03

(июн, июл ва август бо E–mail)

Ғолибони озмун бо мукофоти пулӣ сарфароз карда мешаванд. Асарҳои беҳтарин дар маҷаллаи "Тавлиди шеър" соли 2003 (қисми 2) нашр мешавад.

Ба суроғаи зерин муроҷиат кунед: ш.Душанбе, маҳаллаи 102, кӯчаи Муҳаммадиев 17/6; ДДЗ, қисмати 1.ошёнаи 2–юм. тел. 32–87–30.

Based on the words you recognize, what do you think this is an advertisement for?

АЛИФБОИ ТОҶИКӢ Tajiki Alphabet

Машқи 12: Listen, read and memorize the chart.

	LETTER	LETTER NAME	TRANSCRIPTION	ITALIC FORMS	HANDWRITING
1	Аа	a	a	*Аа*	*Аа*
2	Бб	be	b	*Бб*	*Бб*
3	Вв	ve	v	*Вв*	*Вв*
4	Гг	ge	g	*Гг*	*Гг*
5	Ғғ	ghe	ğ	*Ғғ*	*Ғғ*
6	Дд	de	d	*Дд*	*Дд*
7	Ее	ye	ye	*Ее*	*Ее*
8	Ёё	yo	yo	*Ёё*	*Ёё*
9	Жж	zhe	zh	*Жж*	*Жж*
10	Зз	ze	z	*Зз*	*Зз*
11	Ии	i	i	*Ии*	*Ии*
12	Ӣӣ	i-zada-nok	i	*Ӣӣ*	*Ӣӣ*
13	Йй	yot	y	*Йй*	*Йй*
14	Кк	ke	k	*Кк*	*Кк*
15	Ққ	qe	q	*Ққ*	*Ққ*
16	Лл	le	l	*Лл*	*Лл*
17	Мм	me	m	*Мм*	*Мм*
18	Нн	ne	n	*Нн*	*Нн*

	LETTER	LETTER NAME	TRANSCRIPTION	ITALIC FORMS	HANDWRITING
19	Оо	o	o	*Оо*	Оо
20	Пп	pe	p	*Пп*	Пп
21	Рр	re	r	*Рр*	Рр
22	Сс	se	s	*Сс*	Сс
23	Тт	te	t	*Тт*	Тт
24	Уу	u	u	*Уу*	Уу
25	Ӯӯ	uh	ü	*Ӯӯ*	Ӯӯ
26	Фф	fe	f	*Фф*	Фф
27	Хх	khe	kh	*Хх*	Хх
28	Ҳҳ	he	h	*Ҳҳ*	Ҳҳ
29	ЧЧ	che	č	*ЧЧ*	Чч
30	Ҷҷ	je	j	*Ҷҷ*	Ҷҷ
31	Шш	she	š	*Шш*	Шш
32	Ъъ	alomati sakta	’	*Ъъ*	Ъъ
33	Ээ	e	e	*Ээ*	Ээ
34	Юю	yu	yu	*Юю*	Юю
35	Яя	ya	ya	*Яя*	Яя

Note:
The letter й is only used at the end of the word and the letter ъ is only used in the middle and final position.

VOCABULARY
ЛУҒАТНОМА

абрӯ	*n.* eyebrow
Аврупо	*n.* Europe
Австрия	*n.* Austria
Алҷазоир	*n.* Algeria
Америка	*n.* America; USA (=**Амрико**)
Амрико	*n.* America; USA (=**Америка**)
амрикоӣ	*adj.* American
Арманистон	*n.* Armenia
асп	*n.* horse
Афғонистон	*n.* Afghanistan
Африқо	*n.* Africa
Африқои Ҷанубӣ	*n.* South Africa
Бадахшон	*n.* Badakhshon (region of Tajikistan)
баёнот	*n.* expressions
Банғола	*n.* Bangladesh
баҳор	*n.* spring (season)
Берлин	*n.* Berlin
бибӣ	*n.* grandmother
биёбон	*n.* desert
биёед	*v.* come here!
бобо	*n.* grandfather
Боку	*n.* Baku
Боливия	*n.* Bolivia
борон	*n.* rain
Булғор	*n.* Bulgaria
бур	*v.* cut!
бӯр	*n.* chalk
вақт	*n.* time
варақ	*n.* (sheet of) paper
Варшава	*n.* Warsaw
Вашингтон	*n.* Washington
Венгрия	*n.* Hungary
гап	*n.* speech

гиёҳ	*n.* grass, herb
гурба	*n.* cat
Ғарм	*n.* Gharm
ғор	*n.* cave
Данғара	*n.* Danghara
Дания	*n.* Denmark
дарё	*n.* river
дароед	*v.* come in!
даст	*n.* hand
донишҷӯе	*n.* a student
Душанбе	*n.* Dushanbe (capital of Tajikistan)
дӯст	*n.* friend
ёд	*n.* memory
ёқут	*n.* ruby
ёр	*n.* friend
жола	*n.* hail
Заир	*n.* Zaire
зан	*n.* woman
Зимбабве	*n.* Zimbabwe
зоғ	*n.* raven
ин	*pro, adj.* this
Индиана	*n.* Indiana
Исломобод	*n.* Islamabad
Истаравшан	*n.* Istaravshan
Исфара	*n.* Isfara
йигит	*n.* young man
каён	*n.* ancient Persian kings
камон	*n.* bow (for arrows)
Канада	*n.* Canada
карам	*n.* cabbage
Каюмарс	*n.* Kayumars
Киев	*n.* Kiev
китоб	*n.* book
Конибодом	*n.* Konibodom
Копенҳаген	*n.* Copenhagen
куш	*v.* kill!, turn off! (the light, TV, etc.)

кушоед	*v.* open!
кўш	*v.* strive!, make effort!
қазоқ	*adj.* Kazakh
Қазоқистон	*n.* Kazakhstan
қалам	*n.* pencil
Қўрғонтеппа	*n.* Qurghonteppa (city of Tajikistan)
лаб	*n.* lip
лаёқат	*n.* talent
лола	*n.* tulip
Лубнон	*n.* Lebanon
Люксембург	*n.* Luxembourg
Мағриб	*n.* West
маҳ	*n.* moon, month (=**моҳ**)
машқ	*n.* exercise
маъно	*n.* meaning
мегўед	*v.* you will say
Мексика	*n.* Mexico
мижа	*n.* eyelash
Миср	*n.* Egypt
модар	*n.* mother
Монтана	*n.* Montana
Муғулистон	*n.* Mongolia
мўй	*n.* hair
Мўъминобод	*n.* Mu'minobod
намоед	*v.* seem!
Нигерия	*n.* Nigeria
Нидерландия	*n.* Netherlands
ном	*n.* name
нон	*n.* bread
нур	*n.* light
нўш	*v.* drink!
Ню-Йорк	*n.* New York
об	*n.* water
Озарбойҷон	*n.* Azerbaijan
Олмон	*n.* Germany
Осиё	*n.* Asia

Оттава	*n.* Ottawa
Панҷакент	*n.* Panjakent (major city of Tajikistan)
Париж	*n.* Paris
пахта	*n.* cotton
Покистон	*n.* Pakistan
Полша	*n.* Poland
Помир	*n.* Pamir (mountain range; region of Tajikistan)
расм	*n.* picture
роҳ	*n.* road
Россия	*n.* Russia
сар	*n.* head
сафар	*n.* journey, trip
саҳифа	*n.* page
себ	*n.* apple
сеюм	*adj.* third
сиёҳ	*adj.* black
Суғд	*n.* Sughd (region of Tajikistan)
сур	*n.* celebration
Сурия	*n.* Syria
табақ	*n.* plate
Тайланд	*n.* Thailand
тарбуз	*n.* watermelon
таъмин	*n.* supply
Техас	*n.* Texas
Тоҷикистон	*n.* Tajikistan
Тоҷикобод	*n.* Tajikabad
тундар	*n.* thunder
Туркия	*n.* Turkey
Украина	*n.* Ukraine
ӯ	*pro, n.* he/she
ӯзбак	*adj.* Uzbek
Ӯзбакистон	*n.* Uzbekistan
фалсафа	*n.* philosophy
фарзанд	*n.* child
Фаронса	*n.* France

Флорида	*n.* Florida
Хатлон	*n.* Khatlon (region of Tajikistan)
Хитой	*n.* China (=**Чин**)
хола	*n.* aunt
хома	*n.* pen (for writing)
Хоруғ	*n.* Khorugh
Хуҷанд	*n.* Khujand (major city of Tajikistan)
хӯр	*v.* eat!
ҳамён	*n.* wallet
ҳамроҳ	*n.* fellow traveler, companion
ҳамсоя	*n.* neighbor
ҳаяҷон	*n.* excitement
Ҳиндустон	*n.* India
Ҳисор	*n.* Hisor
ҳуҷра	*n.* apartment
ҳуш	*adj.* conscious
чароғ	*n.* lamp
чарх	*n.* wheel
чашм	*n.* eye
Чикаго	*n.* Chicago
Чилӣ	*n.* Chile
Чин	*n.* China (=**Хитой**)
чой	*n.* tea
ҷамъ	*n.* plus, total
ҷаҳон	*n.* world
ҷӯш	*v.* milk
шаб	*n.* night
шакар	*n.* sugar
Шветсия	*n.* Sweden
шимол	*n.* north
шом	*n.* evening
Эрон	*n.* Iran
Юнон	*n.* Greece
Юсуф	*n.* Joseph
Яғноб	*n.* Yaghnob
Япония	*n.* Japan

ях	*n.* ice
яхдон	*n.* refrigerator
яхмос	*n.* ice cream

Боби дуюм
CHAPTER TWO

СИНФ
CLASSROOM

IN THIS CHAPTER

- **Ашёи синф** Classroom Items
- **Одамон** People in the Classroom
- **Рақамҳо** Tajiki Numbers
- **Ифодаҳо** Classroom Expressions
- ***Луғатнома*** Vocabulary

А. АШЁИ СИНФ A. CLASSROOM OBJECTS

1. СЕҲРИ СУХАН!

Машқи 1: Listen and practice.

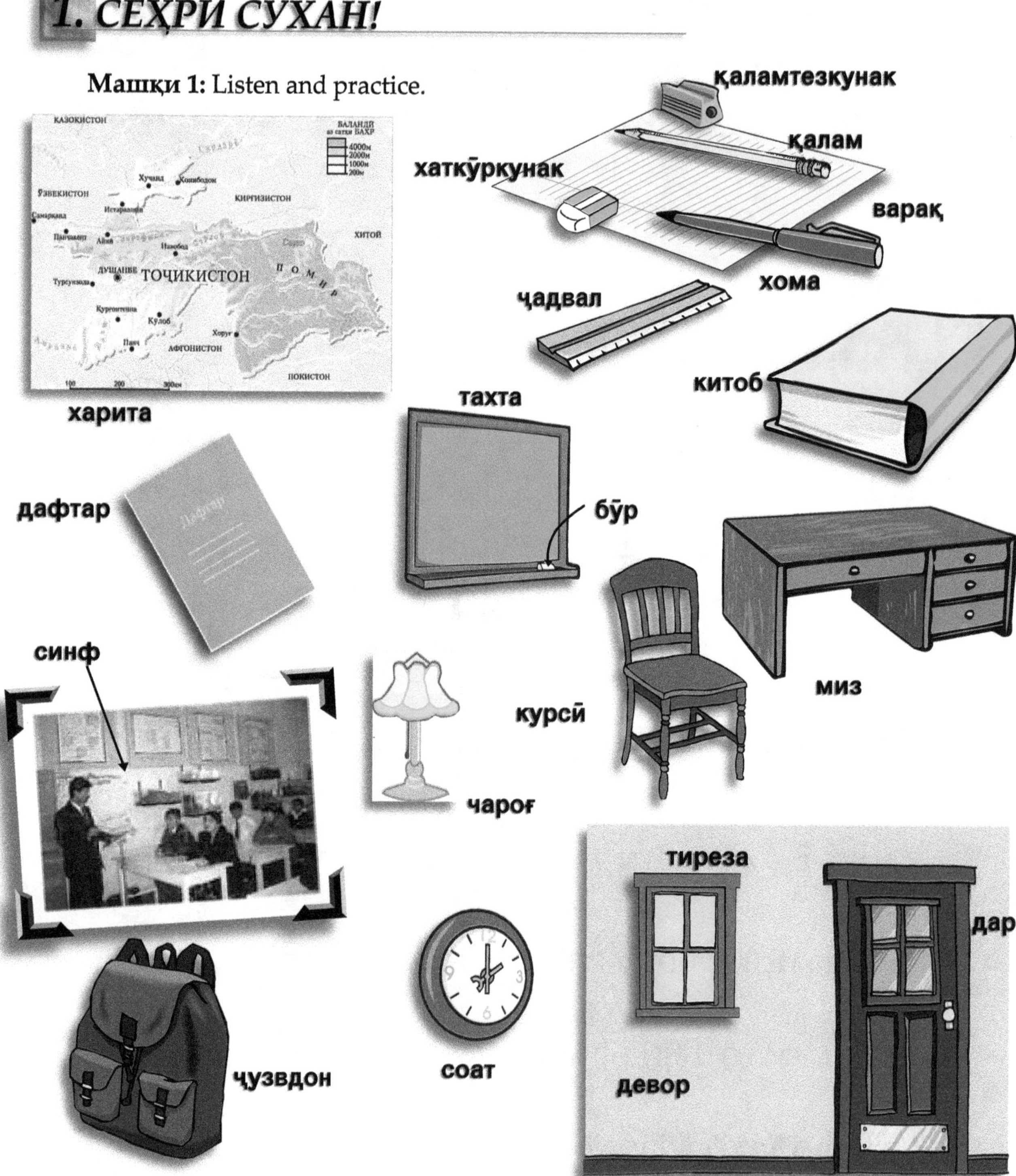

Машқи 2: Your teacher will point to some objects in the room. See how quickly you can identify those objects in Tajiki.

2. ГУФТУГӮ

Машқи 3: *Ин чист?* A. Listen to the conversation and fill in the blanks.

Зарина: ***Ӯҳӯ. Ин чист?***
Зулфия: **Ин ________ аст.**
Зарина: ***Зӯр. Ташаккур, Зулфия.***
Зулфия: **Намеарзад.**
Далер: *Акнун ин _____ ро кушо.*
Зарина: ***Хуб. Ӯҳӯ ин чист?***
Далер: *__________.*
Зарина: ***__________?***
Далер: *Ҳа. Зодрӯз муборак.*
Зарина: ***Як ҷаҳон ташаккур.***

B. ***Тахмини Шумо.*** Hold a small item out of sight in your hands. When your partner asks: **Ин чист? Калид?**, answer **Ҳа** or **Не**. Change roles.

Машқи 4: A. Listen and then practice with your classmate.

Ин чист? - Ин китоб аст.
Ин чист? - Ин қалам аст.
Ин чист? - Ин дафтар аст.
Ин чист? - Ин бӯр аст.

Он чист? - Он тахта аст.
Он чист? - Он дар аст.
Он чист? - Он тиреза аст.
Он чист? - Он соат аст.

B. Point to the items in the picture below and ask your partner what they are. Switch roles.

Машқи 5: ***Кор бо шарик.*** Point to something in your classroom and ask each other what it is.

Answer	Question?
Ин харита аст.	*Ин чист?*
Он дафтар аст.	*Он чист?*

тахта
қалам
ҷузвдон
соат
дар
тиреза
миз
курсӣ
харита
девор
парда
ҷаҳоннамо

3. ДАСТУР

1.1 Demonstrative pronouns

ин *this - something or somebody close by.*
он *that - something or somebody further away.*

You will also come across these forms:

ҳамин	*this, this one* **- synonymous with ин, but often more definite: this one here.**
ҳамон	*that, that one* **- more definite than он, often used to refer to something or somebody just mentioned.**
мана, ин	*this one here* **- while pointing at it.**
ана, он	*that one over there* **- while pointing at it.**

The pronouns **ин** 'this' and **он** 'that' take the suffix **-ҳо** to form the plural forms: **инҳо** 'these' and **онҳо** 'those':

Ин чист?	**Ин хома аст.**	*'What is this? This is a pen.'*
Инҳо чиянд?	**Инҳо китобанд.**	*'What are these? These are books.'*
	Инҳо қаламанд.	*'These are pencils.'*

Ин is also used as a simple pronoun meaning 'it.' Whether **ин** means 'it' or 'this' in a particular sentence is determined by context; if the sentence is pointing something out, **ин** means 'this,' but if it simply describes something that has already been mentioned, **ин** means 'it.'

1.2 VERB 'TO BE' - THIRD PERSON

Аст 'is' is a stative verb used to indicate the state of someone or something; it corresponds to the English verb 'to be' in the third person singular. We use **аст** to talk about someone or something's state of being. When it is used with a question word **чӣ?/кӣ?** it joins with the question word to form the contraction **чист?/кист?**

Ин миз аст.	'This is a table.'
Он курсӣ аст.	'That is a chair.'

For the third person plural 'they are,' **-анд/янд** is used. Unlike **аст, -анд** is not written as a separate word but is instead attached to the preceding word:

Инҳо мизанд	'These are tables.'
Онҳо курсиянд	'Those are chairs.'

Note:
In Tajiki verbs always come at the end of the sentence:

Ин чӣ аст?	*Инҳо чиянд?*
Ин китоб аст.	*Инҳо дафтаранд.*

In colloquial language the verb to be is always omitted:

Ин чӣ?	*Инҳо чӣ?*
Ин китоб.	*Инҳо дафтар.*

Машқи 6: Look at these objects. Make a conversation with a partner.

Намуна:

1. A: Ин чист? A: Онҳо чиянд?
   B: Ин телефон аст. B: Онҳо ________.

телефон

айнак

ҳисобгар

ҳамён

магнитофон

калид

Машқи 7: Find out some things that your classmate has. Ask him/her questions about them. Then change roles.

Машқи 8: Complete these conversations. Then practice with a partner.

1. A: Ин чист?
   B: Ин қалам аст.
2. A: Инҳо чиянд?
   B: Инҳо дафтаранд.
3. A: ________ чи ____?
   B: ________ дафтар(ҳо) ______.
4. A: ________ чи ____?
   B: ________ ҳамён(ҳо) ____.
5. A: ________ чи ____?
   B: ________ қалам ____.
6. A: ________ чи ____?
   B ________ хаткӯркунак ______.

4. ХОНИШ

Машқи 9: A. Read the following sentences. Find out which of the objects mentioned in them are in your classroom.

Ин синф аст. Ин дар аст. Онҳо тирезаанд. Ин девор аст. Инҳо мизанд. Мана, ин тахта аст. Ин бӯр аст. Инҳо китобанд. Онҳо дафтаранд. Ана, он харита аст. Мана, ин соат аст. Инҳо қаламанд. Инҳо хомаанд. Ин қаламтезкунак аст. Он хаткӯркунак аст. Мана, инҳо калиданд. Ана, он айнак аст. Онҳо курсиянд. Ана, онҳо чароғанд.

B. Make three true and three false statements based on your answers. Report them to the class, who will listen and answer, **Ҳа, дуруст** or **Не, нодуруст.**

5. ГӮШ КУНЕД

Машқи 10: Listen to the audio. Then check the sentences that you heard.

Мана, ин дафтар аст.		Ана, онҳо чароғанд.	
Ин қаламтезкунак аст.		Онҳо харитаанд.	
Ин бӯр аст		Ин соат аст.	
Инҳо мизанд.		Онҳо тирезаанд.	
Ин девор аст.		Он дар аст.	

6. ХАТ

Машқи 11: List the objects you see in your classroom. Say their Tajiki names and write them down, both printed and in cursive.

китоб	*китоб*		

7. ТАМОШО КУНЕД!

Машқи 12: A. Watch the video with the sound off and write down the names of the items that the student has.

B. Watch the video a second time with the sound on and check your answers.

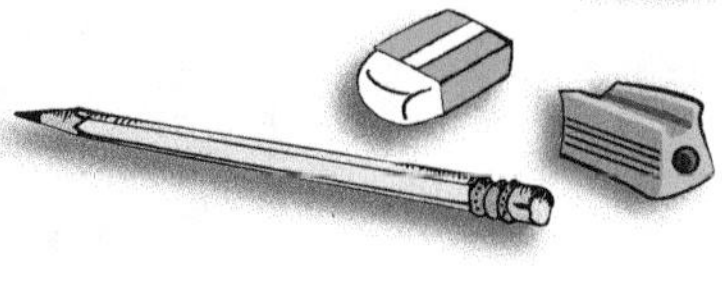

Б. ОДАМОН B. PEOPLE IN THE CLASSROOM

1. СЕҲРИ СУХАН!

Машқи 1: Listen and practice.

мард

зан

духтар

донишҷӯ

муаллим

писар

Машқи 2: Following the pattern above, work with a partner. Ask questions in Tajiki about different people in your class.

2. ГУФТУГӮ

Машқи 3: *Ӯ кист?* Listen to the conversation and fill in the blanks.

Фирӯза: Салом, _____ ҳо кистанд?

Беҳрӯз: Ин __________ аст. Вай донишҷӯ.

Фирӯза: Фаҳмо. Ин кӣ?

Беҳрӯз: Ин __________ аст.

Фирӯза: Номи ______ чист?

Беҳрӯз: Номаш Нилуфар.

Фирӯза: Номи зебо.

Беҳрӯз: _____, хеле зебо.

Машқи 4: ***Кор бо шарик.*** Ask a partner who the other people are in your class. Then change roles.

Намуна: *А:* ***Ин кист?*** *В: Ин донишҷӯ аст.*

А: Вай кист? *В: Вай мард аст.*

3. *ДАСТУР*

The question **кӣ аст?/кист?** (Who is ...?) in Tajiki, as in English, is only used for people.

Ин кист?	**Ин мард аст.**
Онҳо киянд?	**Онҳо муаллиманд.**

Машқи 5: Complete these conversations, then practice with a partner.

А: Ин кист ______________?
В: Ин муаллим ______________.

А: Онҳо ки ______________?
В: Онҳо донишҷӯ______________.

А: Инҳо чи______________?
В: Инҳо қалам ______________.

А: Он ки______________?
В: Он духтар______________.

Машқи 6: Look at these pictures. Find out who and what are in them and try to tell who or what they are in Tajiki.

Намуна: *Ин синф аст.*

Машқи 7:  Read this list of Tajik names. Match the names in Cyrillic script with their Latin equivalents.

а) Male names - *Номҳои мардона:*

Ҷамшед	1	**Zafar**	
Зафар	2	**Ardasher**	
Комрон	3	**Jamshed**	
Бахтиёр	4	**Shuhrat**	
Илҳом	5	**Surush**	
Шӯҳрат	6	**Komron**	
Рустам	7	**Suhrob**	
Сӯҳроб	8	**Bakhtiyor**	
Суруш	9	**Ilhom**	
Ардашер	10	**Rustam**	

в) Female names - *Номҳои занона:*

Аниса	1	**Gulru**	
Бунафша	2	**Lola**	
Гулрӯ	3	**Parvin**	
Гулчеҳра	4	**Malika**	
Дилбар	5	**Bunafsha**	
Парвин	6	**Nilufar**	
Малика	7	**Sabohat**	
Нилуфар	8	**Dilbar**	
Сабоҳат	9	**Anisa**	
Лола	10	**Gulchehra**	

5. ГӮШ КУНЕД

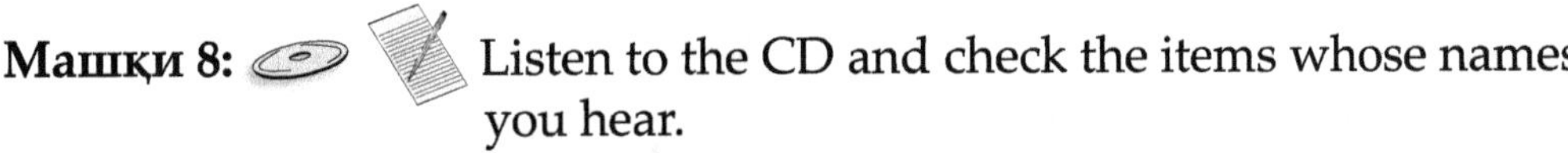

Машқи 8: Listen to the CD and check the items whose names you hear.

дафтар	харита	муаллим
хома	мард	қалам
хаткӯркунак	тиреза	порчаи шеърӣ
рафи китоб	гулдон	чароғ
бӯр	духтар	писар
зан	китоб	тахтаи синфӣ
варақ	ҷевон	донишҷӯ
курсӣ	миз	соат

6. ХАТ

Машқи 9: Write 5 sentences about the things in your classroom and about your classmates.

Намуна: *Ин писар аст. Инҳо китобанд.*

7. ТАМОШО КУНЕД!

Машқи 10: A.Watch the video with the sound off and check the names of the items you see.

китоб		хома	
луғат		қалам	
донишҷӯ		сурат	
духтар		муаллим	
писар		бӯр	

B. Now watch the video with the sound on and check the names of the items you hear.

китоб		хома	
луғат		қалам	
донишҷӯ		сурат	
духтар		муаллим	
писар		бӯр	

C. Descibe what you have in your bag.

Намуна:
A: Ман дар ҷузвдонам дафтару китоб дорам. Ту чӣ?
B: Ман дафтару китобу қалам дорам.

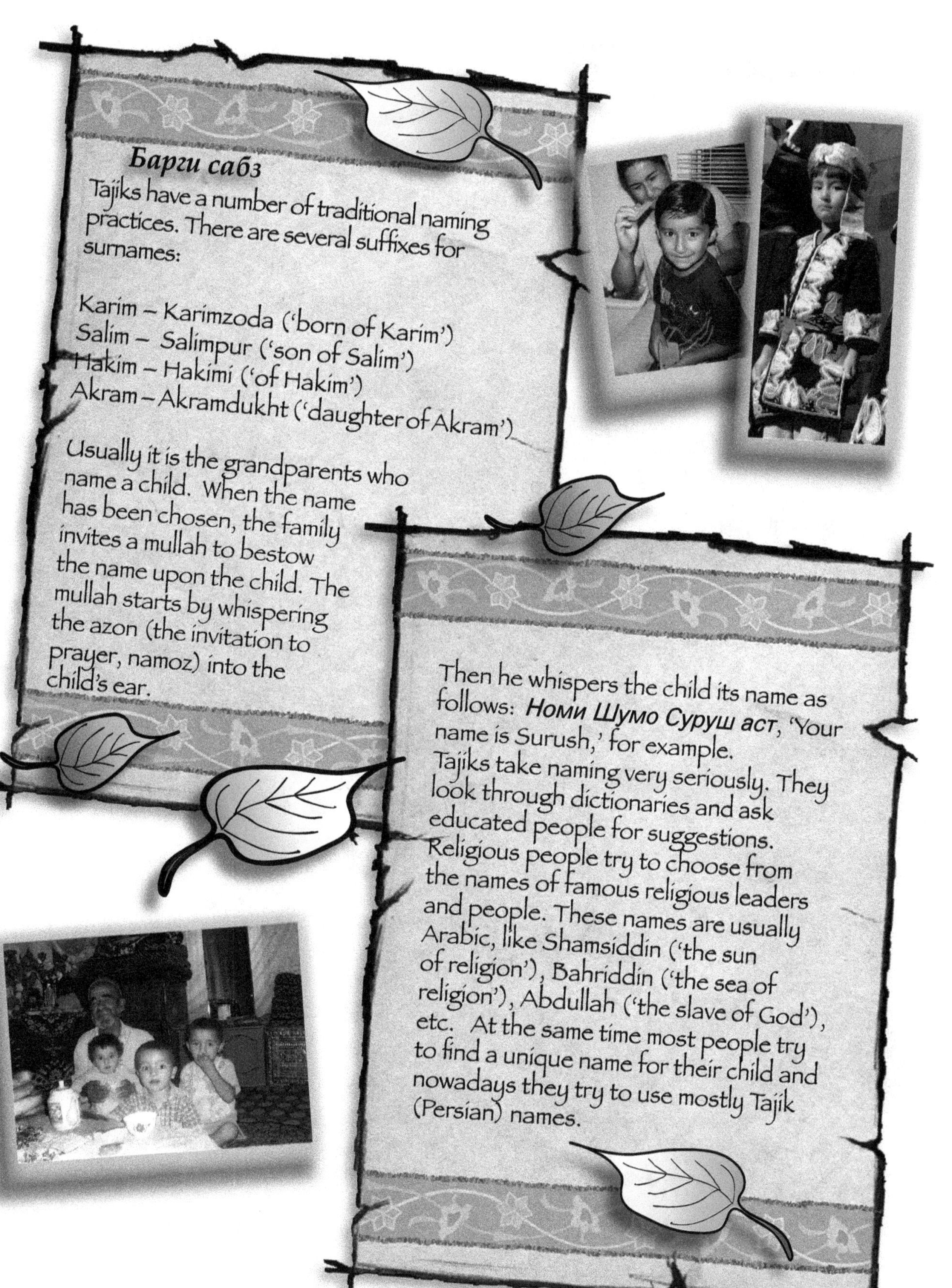

Барги сабз

Tajiks have a number of traditional naming practices. There are several suffixes for surnames:

Karim – Karimzoda ('born of Karim')
Salim – Salimpur ('son of Salim')
Hakim – Hakimi ('of Hakim')
Akram – Akramdukht ('daughter of Akram')

Usually it is the grandparents who name a child. When the name has been chosen, the family invites a mullah to bestow the name upon the child. The mullah starts by whispering the azon (the invitation to prayer, namoz) into the child's ear.

Then he whispers the child its name as follows: **Номи Шумо Суруш аст**, 'Your name is Surush,' for example.
Tajiks take naming very seriously. They look through dictionaries and ask educated people for suggestions. Religious people try to choose from the names of famous religious leaders and people. These names are usually Arabic, like Shamsiddin ('the sun of religion'), Bahriddin ('the sea of religion'), Abdullah ('the slave of God'), etc. At the same time most people try to find a unique name for their child and nowadays they try to use mostly Tajik (Persian) names.

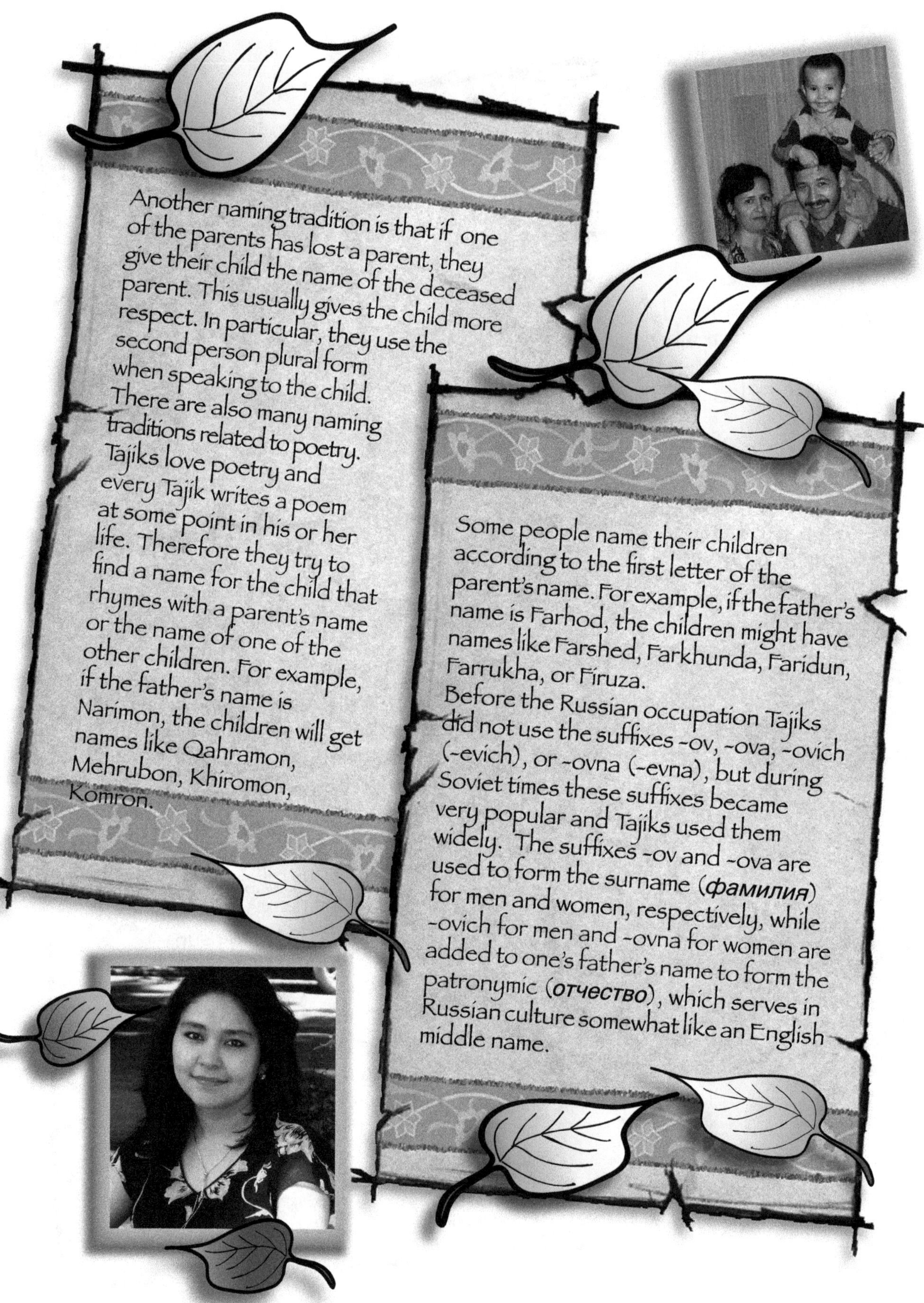

Another naming tradition is that if one of the parents has lost a parent, they give their child the name of the deceased parent. This usually gives the child more respect. In particular, they use the second person plural form when speaking to the child.

There are also many naming traditions related to poetry. Tajiks love poetry and every Tajik writes a poem at some point in his or her life. Therefore they try to find a name for the child that rhymes with a parent's name or the name of one of the other children. For example, if the father's name is Narimon, the children will get names like Qahramon, Mehrubon, Khiromon, Komron.

Some people name their children according to the first letter of the parent's name. For example, if the father's name is Farhod, the children might have names like Farshed, Farkhunda, Faridun, Farrukha, or Firuza.

Before the Russian occupation Tajiks did not use the suffixes -ov, -ova, -ovich (-evich), or -ovna (-evna), but during Soviet times these suffixes became very popular and Tajiks used them widely. The suffixes -ov and -ova are used to form the surname (**фамилия**) for men and women, respectively, while -ovich for men and -ovna for women are added to one's father's name to form the patronymic (**отчество**), which serves in Russian culture somewhat like an English middle name.

В. РАҚАМҲО C. TAJIK NUMBERS

1. СЕҲРИ СУХАН!

Машқи 1: Listen and practice.

сифр (нол)	0	панҷ	5
як	1	шаш	6
ду	2	ҳафт	7
се	3	ҳашт	8
чор	4	нӯҳ	9
		даҳ	10

Note:

In regular speech we do not pronounce "t" in "ҳафт" and "ҳашт" or "h" in "нӯҳ" and "даҳ."

Машқи 2: Now count tables, chairs, windows and other things in your classroom. Find out how many men and women are in your class.

2. ГУФТУГӮ

Машқи 3: ***Чандто донишҷӯ?*** Listen to the conversation and fill in the blanks.

Фаррух: Каримҷон, дар синфи ту чандто донишҷӯст?
Карим: Мо ____ донишҷӯем.
Фаррух: Чандто писар ва чандто духтар?
Карим: _____ писар ва _____ духтар. Ту чандто қалам дорӣ?
Фаррух: Ман ___ қалам дорам. Ба ту қалам лозим аст?
Карим: Ҳа, ман қаламамро фаромӯш кардам.
Фаррух: Мана, қалам.
Карим: Ташаккур.

Some words: ***дорӣ*** *- you have*
фаромӯш кардаам *- I have forgotten*
қаламамро *- my pencil*

Машқи 4:  Practice your numbers by writing out and then saying the following with another student:

a) ______________	your telephone number
b) ______________	your zip code
c) ______________	your house or apartment number

Машқи 5: ***Риёзиёт*** (Math in Tajiki). How well can you read equations in Tajiki?

Look at the words below for some helpful vocabulary. Then, working with a classmate, make up some equations and test how well you can solve each other's equations. Read an equation in Tajiki to your partner, then have your partner answer in Tajiki. Switch roles.

MATH VOCABULARY

+	**ҷамъ**	plus	:	**тақсим**	divided by
-	**тарҳ**	minus	=	**баробар**	equals
		* **зарб** multiplied by			

Note: Each of these terms is followed by the izofat -и, which indicates possession. Thus, "2+2=4" is "**Ду ҷамъи ду баробари чор.**"

Follow the given example:

Намуна:

7+2=9 You ask: "**Ҳафт ҷамъи ду?**"
Your partner answers: "**Нӯҳ**"

6–3=3 Your partner asks: "**Шаш тарҳи се?**"
You answer: "**Се**"

1) 3 + 2 =	____	6) 4 x 2 =	____
2) 8 ÷ 2 =	____	7) 2 x 5 =	____
3) 3 x 3 =	____	8) 10 - 7 =	____
4) 9 - 4 =	____	9) 10 ÷ 5	____
5) 7 + 1 =	____	10) 9 - 3 =	____

3. ДАСТУР

3.1. Plural form in Tajiki

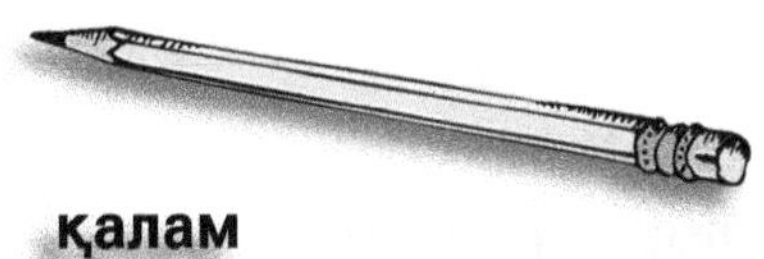

қалам

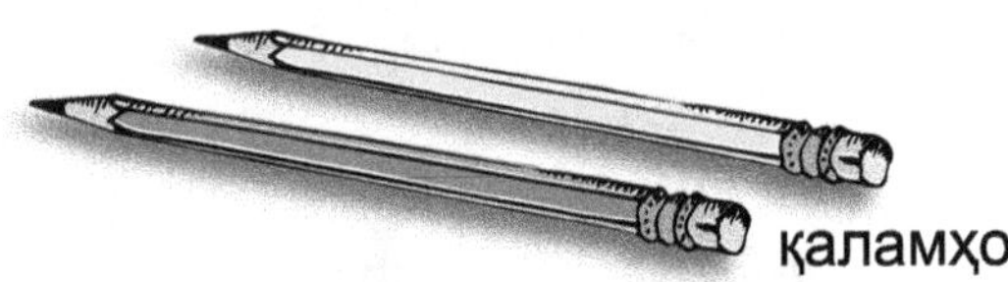

қаламҳо

зан

занҳо

калид

калидҳо

Машқи 6: Write the plurals of the following words:

a. китоб	
b. дар	
c. варақ	
d. тиреза	
e. бӯр	
f. ҷадвал	

3.2. NUMBERS IN TAJIKI

When the plurality of the noun is shown by a numeral (for example, "two pencils"), the suffix **-ҳо** is not needed, as the number already shows the plurality of the noun. Numerals are usually followed by a "classifier" chosen according to the type of noun. For people the classifier are **кас** and **нафар**, and for animals it is **сар**. For inanimate nouns **дона** is common. The generic classifier **то (та)** can be used for all countable nouns. The classifier is added to the stem of the numeral. Nouns for divisible things always take a classifier, which is usually a unit of measure: **се кило шакар** 'three kilos of sugar,' **ду метр атлас** 'two meters of silk,' **се бандча кабудӣ** 'three bunches of herbs.' However, classifiers are not always necessary with other nouns: **се дона дафтар** or **се дафтар** 'three notebooks.' In particular, you usually do not use a classifier with people: **ду духтар** 'two girls,' **ду муаллим** 'two teachers.'

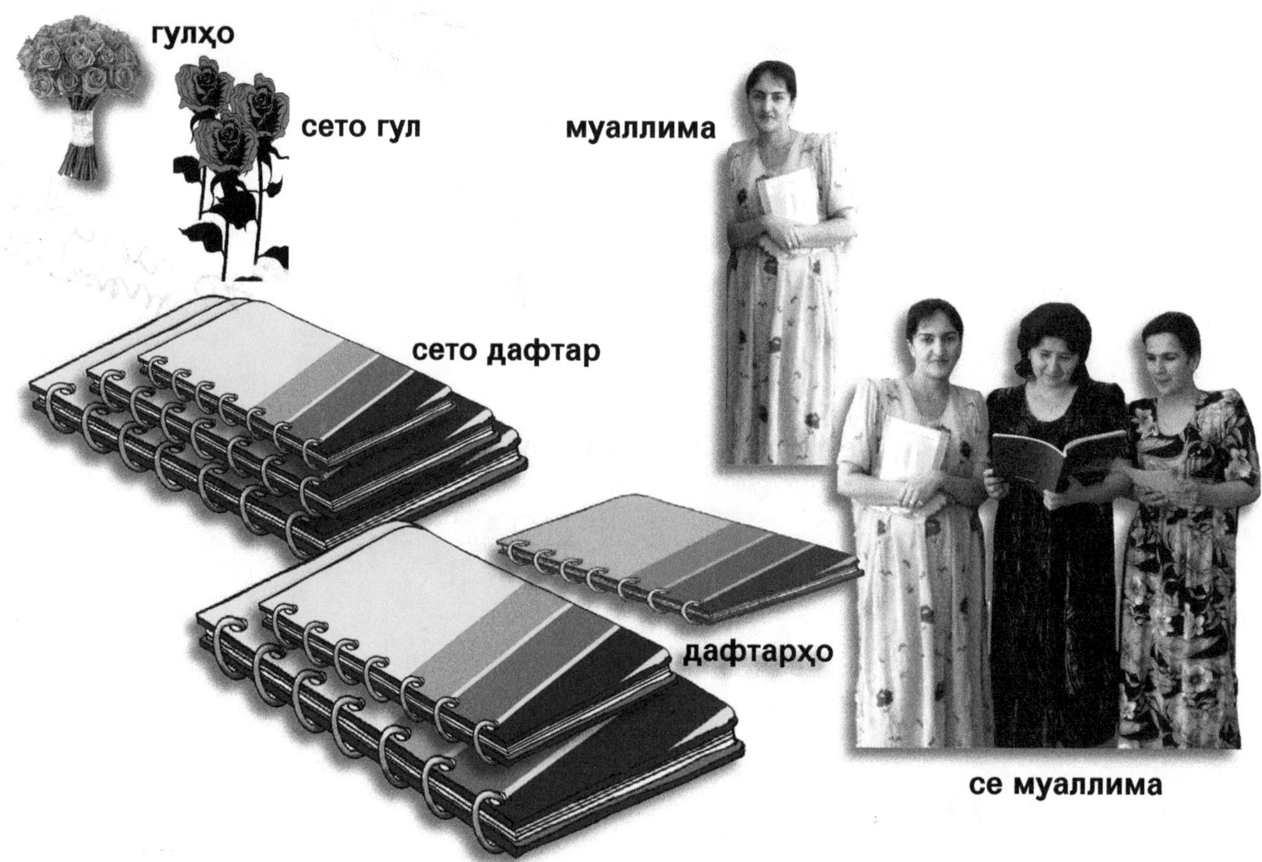

Машқи 7: Read the following phrases and decide if they are ***дуруст*** "correct" or ***нодуруст*** "incorrect."

	ДУРУСТ	НОДУРУСТ	CORRECT FORM
дуто зан			
панҷто қалам			
дуто мард			
ҳафтто дафтар			
нӯҳто писар			

Машқи 8: Put the following words in order so as to indicate plurality.

	CORRECT FORM
хома / 2	*хомаҳо/ дуто хома*
бӯр / 3	бӯрҳо/се бӯр
духтар / 5	духтарҳо/панҷ
писар / 9	Но писар
мард / 7	Хафт мард
ҷадвал /10	Да ҷадв
муаллим / 3	

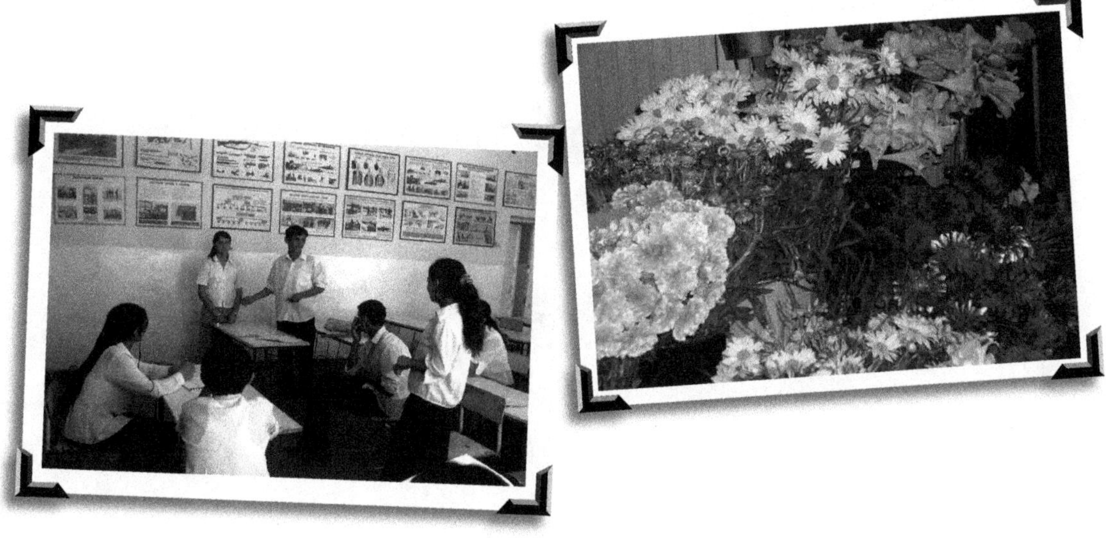

Машқи 9: Help the sellers at the market inventory their stalls. Look at the pictures below. How many of each item does the seller still have? Fill in the blanks with the word for the number of items.

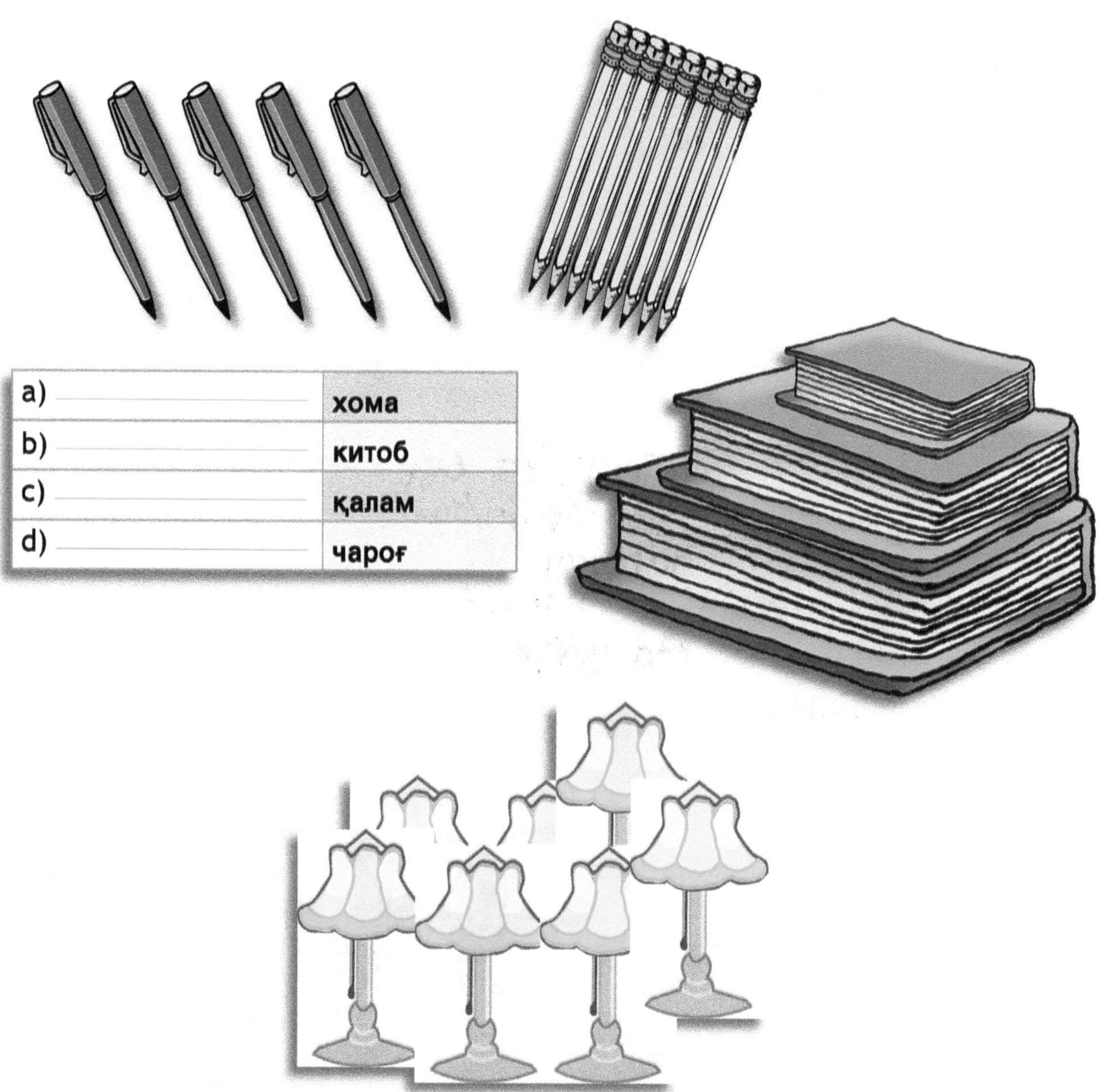

a) ______________________	хома
b) ______________________	китоб
c) ______________________	қалам
d) ______________________	чароғ

4. ХОНИШ

Машқи 10: Look at the somoni – Tajik currency. Read the serial numbers out loud with a classmate.

Машқи 11: Read the telephone and other numbers on the business cards below digit by digit.

БОНКИ МИЛЛИИ ТОҶИКИСТОН

Ҷаъмахон Хусайнов

Сардори идораи хизматрасон

734025, Ҷумҳурии Тоҷикистон
ш.Душанбе,
хиб. Рудаки 23/2

Тел: (992 372) 21-22-87
Сотка: 5-61
E-mail: J_Husainov@natbank.tajnet.com

ХОҶАГИ САИД АЛИЙ ХАМАДОНӢ
НОХИЯИ КУЛОБ

ЗАРДИЕВ
Абдуҷаббор Абдурахимович
Раис

Ҷумҳурии Тоҷикистон
ш. Душанбе, к. Чехов
2-юм гузоргох,
хуҷраи № 59

Тел.: 21-24-17; 21-13-57
Тел./факс: 21-24-17
дар Кулоб: 2-33-96; 3-42-45
Моб.: 70-03-18, 61-98-92

5. ГӮШ КУНЕД 

Машқи 12: Lola and Daler are making a list of the telephone numbers of their classmates. Listen and complete the chart:

НОМУ НАСАБ	РАҚАМИ ТЕЛЕФОН
Абдуррауф Муродӣ	63-64-78
Ҳумоюни Шаҳриёр	
Мирзои Салимпур	
Сурайё Латифӣ	
Парвинаи Акрамдухт	
Нодираи Хуршед	
Баҳманёри Қиёмпур	
Салими Аюбзод	
Манижаи Давлат	
Маҳина Каримзода	
Музаффар Раҳимӣ	
Латофат Халилӣ	

Машқи 13:  *Кор бо шарик.* Take turns with another student reading and writing the following numbers. As one student reads, the other should listen carefully and write down the correct number. Remember to read one digit at a time.

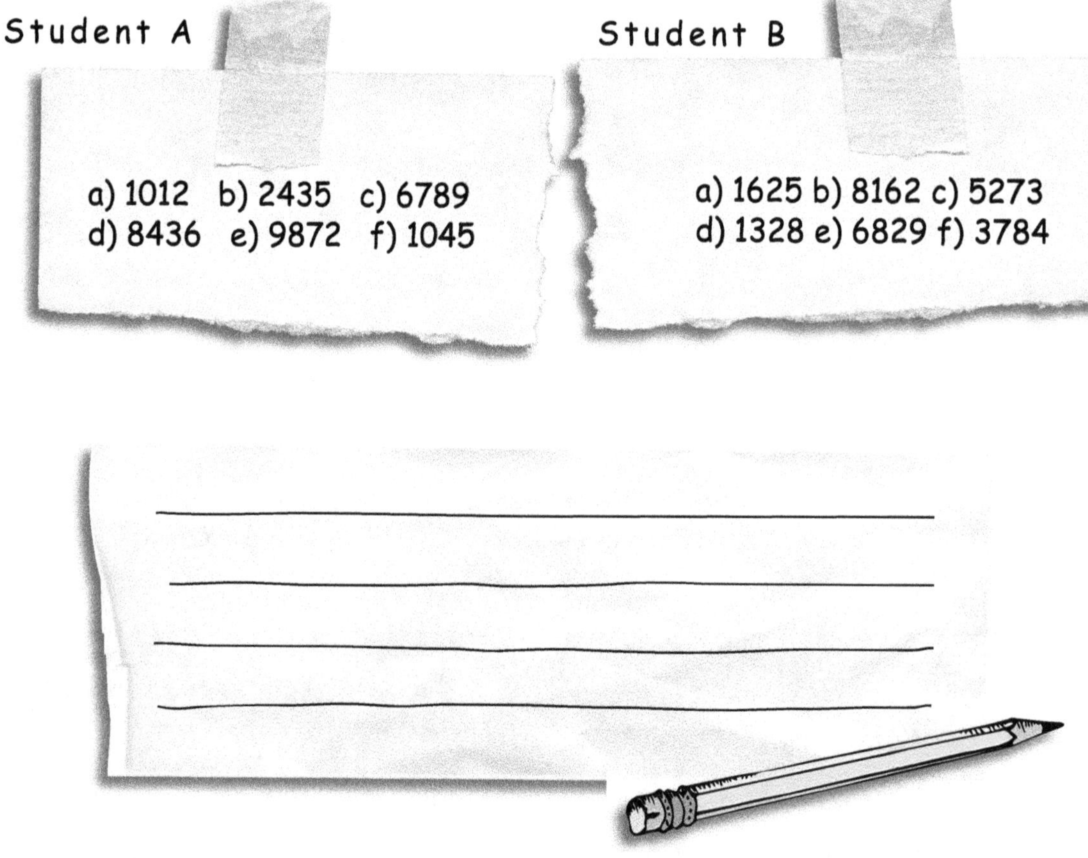

Машқи 14: Now challenge one of your classmates. Read your classmate a telephone number (either a real number you know or one from your cards) and see if he or she can write the number you read.

6. ХАТ

Машқи 15: Write the corresponding numerals under the number words and vice versa.

ҳафт	панҷ	се	ҳашт	ду
чор	шаш	нӯҳ	як	даҳ
7	3	9	1	8
4	5	10	2	6

Машқи 16: Solve the following math problems and write your answers in Tajiki. Use only words, not numerals. The first one is done for you.

4 ÷ 2 = 2	Чор тақсими ду баробари ду.
8 + 1 = ?	
(4 × 2) - 5 = ?	
(9 ÷ 3) + 4 = ?	
7- ? = 5	
(5 - 3) × 4 =	

7. ТАМОШО КУНЕД

Машқи 17: A.Watch the video with the sound on and repeat after the players.

B: Now solve the following problems and write next to each answer whether it is **тоқ** or **ҷуфт**.

1) 1 + 6 =	____
2) 4 ÷ 2 =	____
3) 3 x 3 =	____
4) 9 - 4 =	____
5) 7 + 1 =	____

6) 4 x 2 =	____
7) 2 x 5 =	____
8) 10 - 7 =	____
9) 10 ÷ 5	____
10) 8 - 3 =	____

Г. ИФОДАҲО D. CLASSROOM EXPRESSIONS

1. СЕҲРИ СУХАН!

Машқи 1: Listen and practice.

Шин/Шинед!

Хез/Хезед!

Навис/Нависед!

Хон/Хонед!

Кушо/Кушоед!

Пӯш/Пӯшед!

Гир/Гиред!

Гӯш кун/Гӯш кунед!

Нафаҳмидам!

Ташаккур!

Офарин!

Бубахшед

Лутфан, боз як бор гӯед.

Лутфан, бо тоҷикӣ гӯед.

Лутфан, такрор кунед!

Ҳа/Не

Speak LOUDER, please.

Лутфан, баландтар гап занед.

Is it clear?

Фаҳмо?

Speak slowly, please.

Лутфан, оҳистатар гап занед.

S-P-E-L-L I-T P-L-E-A-S-E!

Лутфан, ҳарф ба ҳарф гӯед

Word

Калима

The quick red fox jumped over the lazy brown dog.

Ҷумла

exCeLLent!

Ҳиҷо

THAT'S HOT!

Ибора

Машқи 2: What do you say when you:

- want to interrupt the teacher?
- want the teacher to repeat something?
- don't understand something?
- want to thank someone?
- can't hear what's being said?

2. ГУФТУГӮ

Машқи 3: ***Китобҳо.*** A. Listen to the conversation.

Мунира: **Дейвид, китобҳоро гиред.**
Дейвид: Лутфан, боз як бор гӯед.
Мунира: **Китобҳоро гиред.**
Дейвид: Ташаккур, шумо калимаи eraser-ро бо тоҷикӣ ҳарф ба ҳарф гӯед
Мунира: **Х-а-т-к-ӯ-р-к-у-н-а-к. Фаҳмо?**
Дейвид: Ҳа. Ташаккур.
Мунира: **Саломат бошед.**

B. Create a similar conversation with a partner and act it out. Switch roles.

Машқи 4:  ***Кор бо шарикон.***

A. Get into small groups. Take four small pieces of paper and write one command on each piece.
B. Put the cards in a pile and take turns drawing one card.
C. Read the command to the group. Pick one person from the group to act it out.

3. ДАСТУР

3.1. COMMANDS AND REQUESTS

Imperatives in Tajiki can be quite short (often just a single word), and as in English usually occur without a subject. A polite command or request is formed by adding the second person plural verb ending to the imperative, which is also the form used when speaking to more than one person:

хон – хонед. (In some dialects this form is used to indicate respect towards one person while the plural imperative is formed with **-етон**: **хон – хонетон.** This second form will not be used in this textbook.)

Шин / Шинед !

Хез / Хезед!

Хонед !

Нашин! / Нашинед!

Нахӯр! / Нахӯред!

Нарақсед!

3.2. DEFINITE DIRECT OBJECTS

In Tajiki it is important to be able to spot the direct object of a verb.The following commands do not have direct objects:

Дароед!	Come in!
Интизор шавед!	Wait!
Шинед!	Sit down!

These commands have direct objects:

Қаламро гиред!	Take the pencil!
Дарро кушоед!	Open the door!

Қаламро and ***дарро*** are the direct objects of the commands. They are the things upon which the action (taking, reading) is carried out. For direct objects, the particle ***-ро*** (which is never stressed) is added to the object if it is definite; in the corresponding English sentence, the direct object is preceded by 'the.' If the direct object is indefinite (for example, a pencil, some tea), then ***-ро*** is not used.

Чой нӯшед!	'Drink some tea.'
Чойро нӯшед!	'Drink the tea.'
Китоб гиред!	'Take a book.'
Китобро гиред!	'Take the book.'
Нома нависед!	'Write a letter.'
Номаро нависед!	'Write the letter.'

Машқи 5: Watch your instructor and repeat after him:

Китобро гузор!	**Хомаро гир!**
Дарро пӯш!	**Дар дафтар навис!**
Тирезаро кушо!	**Ҷумларо хон!**

Машқи 6: Now work in pairs and give commands to your partner, using classroom items.

4. ХОНИШ

Машқи 7: Read the text below. Underline the direct objects with one line and imperatives with two. Don't worry if you do not understand all the words.

Донишҷӯёни мӯҳтарам! Лутфан ба дарс дер накунед. Дар вақти дарс ба сухани муаллим бо диққат гӯш кунед. Агар шумо калима, ибора ва ё ҷумларо нафаҳмед, аз муаллим пурсед. Барои хуб ёд гирифтани забон ҳар рӯз дарсҳоро ду-се бор такрор кунед. Ба китобхона равед. Китоб хонед ва машқҳоро иҷро кунед. Дар вақти танаффус бо дӯстатон калимаҳоро такрор кунед ва ё ҳарф ба ҳарф гӯед. Лутфан танбал набошед ва шумо дар муддати кӯтоҳ бо забони тоҷикӣ гап мезанед.

5. ГӮШ КУНЕД

Машқи 8: Close your books and listen to the dialogue. Then listen again and fill in the blanks.

Муаллим: Ин ________________
Шаҳло: Мебахшед, лутфан, боз як бор ________________
Муаллим: Ин ________________
Шаҳло: Ташаккур ________________
Муаллим: Ин китоб аст. Китобро ________________
Шаҳло: Нафаҳмидам. Лутфан, ________________
Муаллим: Лутфан, китобро ________________
Шаҳло: Ташаккур!

Машқи 9: Now listen to the commands and check off the commands you hear.

- close the window
- open your book
- stand up
- go out
- sit down
- take this pen
- give that pencil
- clean the blackboard
- read the book

6. ХАТ

Машқи 10: Write commands using the direct object marker. Use the vocabulary given below. *Follow the example.*

Objects: **қалам, дафтар, дар, тиреза, парда, бӯр, ҷадвал, ҷумла**
Imperatives: **гир, деҳ, хон, пӯш, кушо, мон, навис, гӯй**

Намуна: Чароғро деҳ!

Машқи 11: Write the opposite command.

Дафтарро гиред	*Дафтарро нагиред*
Китобро хонед	
Калимаро нависед	
Сабр кунед	
Қаламро монед	
Гулро диҳед	
Пардаро пӯшед	
Машқро иҷро кунед	

7. ТАМОШО КУНЕД

Машқи 12: A.Watch the video with the sound off and write down the commands you think the students were given based on their actions.

B. Watch the video with the sound on and check your answers.

C. Watch the video with the sound on again and follow the commands yourself.

Барги сабз

Дар забони тоҷикӣ, одатан, ҳангоми ба касе бо супориш ва ё амре муроҷиат намудан калимаҳои туфайлии зиёд истифода мешаванд. Масалан:
Марҳамат, дароед.
Лутфан, такрор кунед.
Илтимос, ба ман занг назанед.
Хоҳиш мекунам, пас аз ду соат боз биёед.
Дар ҷавоби ин муносибати боэҳтиромона шахси дуюм низ бо калимаҳои туфайлии махсус ҷавоб медиҳад:

Хуб шудаст.
Фаҳмо.
Албатта.
Ба чашм (китобӣ).

Ҳангоми инкор ё рад кардани хоҳиш ва ё амр чунин калимаҳо истифода мешаванд:
Афсӯс, ман наметавонам.
Бубахшед ман имконият надорам.
Узр.

ЛУҒАТНОМА
VOCABULARY

айнак	*n.* eyeglasses
акнун	*adv.* now
ана, он	*pron.* that one
аст	*v.* is
атлас	*n.* atlas silk (silk from the atlas moth)
афсӯс	*interj.* alas
ашё	*n.* things, objects
бандча	*n.* bundle
баробар	*n.* equal
Ба Тоҷикистон биёед!	*phr.* Come to Tajikistan.
бубахшед	*interj.* sorry
бӯр	*n.* chalk
варақ	*n.* (sheet of) paper
гир	*v.* take (it)!
гул	*n.* flower
гулдон	*n.* vase
Гулро деҳед	*phr.* Give the flower!
гӯй	*v.* say!, tell!, speak!
гӯш кун	*v.* listen!
дар	*n.* door
дароед!	*v.* come in!
дарс	*n.* class
дафтар	*n.* notebook
даҳ	*num.* ten
девор	*n.* wall
Дер накунед!	*phr.* Don't be late!
деҳ	*v.* give!
донишҷӯ	*n.* student
ду	*num.* two
духтар	*n.* girl
зан	*n.* woman
зарб	*n.* multiplied by
зебо	*adj.* pretty

Зодрӯз муборак!	*n.* Happy birthday!
ибора	*n.* phrase
ин	*pron.* this
Интизор шавед!	*v.* Wait!
ист!	*v.* stop!
кабудӣ	*n.* greens
калид	*n.* key
калима	*n.* word
кило	*n.* kilogram
китоб	*n.* book
китобхона	*n.* library
кӣ	*pron.* who?
курсӣ	*n.* chair
кушо	*v.* open!
кӯтоҳ	*adj.* short
қалам	*n.* pencil
Қаламро монед	*phr.* Put the pencil (down)!
қаламтезкунак	*n.* pencil sharpener
қуттӣ	*n.* box
луғат	*n.* dictionary, glossary
лутфан	*adv.* please
Лутфан, баландтар гап занед!	*phr.* Speak louder, please.
Лутфан, боз як бор гӯед!	*phr.* Say it again, please.
Лутфан, бо тоҷикӣ гӯед!	*phr.* Say it in Tajiki, please.
Лутфан, оҳистатар гап занед!	*phr.* Speak slowly, please.
Лутфан, такрор кунед!	*phr.* Repeat, please.
Лутфан, ҳарф ба ҳарф гӯед!	*phr.* Spell it, please.
магнитофон	*n.* tape player
мана, ин	*pron.* this one
Мана, пулро гиред!	*phr.* Here, take the money!
мард	*n.* man

Машқро иҷро кунед!	*phr.* Do the exercise!
метр	*n.* meter
миз	*n.* table
мон!	*v.* put!
муаллим	*n.* teacher
навис!	*v.* write
Намеарзад.	*phr.* It was nothing, You're welcome.
насаб	*n.* last name
Нафаҳмидам!	*phr.* I did not understand.
не	*interj.* no
нӯҳ	*num.* nine
одамон	*n.* people
он	*pron.* that; he/she/it
Офарин!	*interj.* Excellent!
панҷ	*num.* five
парда	*n.* curtain
Пардаро пӯшед!	*phr.* Close the curtain!
писар	*n.* boy
порчаи шеърӣ	*n.* piece of poetry
пӯш	*v.* close (it)!
рад кардан	*v.* to refuse, deny
рақам	*n.* number
рақс	*n.* dance
рафи китоб	*n.* bookshelf
Сабр кунед!	*v.* Wait!
се	*num.* three
синф	*n.* classroom
сифр	*num.* zero
соат	*n.* clock
сомонӣ	*n.* somoni (currency of Tajikistan)
сурат	*n.* picture
сухан	*n.* speech
тақсим	*n.* divided by
Тамоку накашед!	*phr.* Don't smoke!
тарҳ	*n.* minus

тахта	*n.* board
тахтаи синфӣ	*n.* classroom blackboard
Ташаккур	*interj.* Thank you
телефон	*n.* telephone
тиреза	*n.* window
фаромӯш кардан	*v.* to forget
Фаҳмо?	*adj.* (Is it) clear?
харита	*n.* map
хаткӯркунак	*n.* rubber eraser
хез!	*v.* stand up!
хома	*n.* pen
хон!	*v.* read!
хоҳиш	*n.* wish
хӯр!	*v.* eat!
ҳа	*interj.* yes
ҳамин	*pron.* this one
ҳамон	*pron.* that one
ҳафт	*num.* seven
ҳашт	*num.* eight
ҳисобгар	*n.* calculator
ҳиҷо	*n.* syllable
чароғ	*n.* lamp
чӣ	*pron.* what?
чор	*num.* four
ҷадвал	*n.* table, ruler
ҷамъ	*n.* plus
ҷаҳоннамо	*n.* TV broadcast
ҷевон	*n.* shelf
ҷузвдон	*n.* bag
ҷумла	*n.* sentence
шакар	*n.* sugar
шаш	*num.* six
шин!	*v.* sit down!
як	*num.* one

Маҷлисгоҳи Донишгоҳи давлатии миллии Тоҷикистон

Боби **сеюм**
CHAPTER **THREE** 3

САЛОМ ВА ҲОЛПУРСӢ
GREETINGS

IN THIS CHAPTER

- **Салом, Шумо хубед?**
  Hello, are You Well?
- **Шумо аз куҷоед?**
  Where are You from?
- **Ӯ кист?** Who is He?
- **Луғатнома** Vocabulary

А. САЛОМ, ШУМО ХУБЕД? A. HELLO, ARE YOU WELL?

1. СЕҲРИ СУХАН!

Машқи 1: Listen and practice.

Ассалому алайкум!

Ассалому алайкум, Шумо хубед?
Ваалайкум ассалом. Ҳа, ман хубам.

Хайр, саломат бошед!

Салом, Шумо созед?
Салом, ташаккур.

- Хайр, то боздид!
- То боздид!
  Ё:
- Хайр, то дидан.
- То дидан.

- Ассалому алайкум, Шумо нағзед?
- Ташаккур, ман хубам. Аз Шумо пурсем?
- Ташаккур, ман ҳам хубам.

Машқи 2: ***Кор бо шарик.*** Go around the classroom. Practice saying hello and good-bye to your classmates and to your instructor.

2. ГУФТУГӮ

Машқи 3: ***Пурсупос.*** Listen and practice greetings.

1. **А: Салом, Ҷаъфар. Шумо чӣ хел?**
   В: Ташаккур. Хеле хуб. Аз Шумо пурсем?
2. **А: Субҳ ба хайр, ҷаноби Салимзода. Шумо хубед?**
   В: Ташаккур Сӯҳробҷон. Ман хубам.
3. **А: Салом, бобоҷон. Шумо чӣ хел?**
   В: Раҳмат, писарам. Ман хуб. Худат чӣ хел?
4. **А: Салом, хола. Ҳолатон хуб аст?**
   В: Ташаккур, духтарам. Худат чӣ хел?
5. **А: Салом, бибиҷон.**
   В: Духтарҷон, салом.

Машқи 4: Listen and then practice with your classmate.

1. **А: То боздид, Рустам.**
   В: То боздид, Музаффар.
2. **А: Хайр, то пагоҳ.**
   В: Хайр.
3. **А: То дидан.**
   В: То дидан.
4. **А: Хайр. Шаби хуш.**
   В: Ба Шумо ҳам.
5. **А: Хайр, барори кор.**
   В: Ба Шумо ҳам.
6. **А: Хайр, хуш бошед.**
   В: Паноҳи Худо, Шумо ҳам.

3. *ДАСТУР*

3.1. Personal pronouns

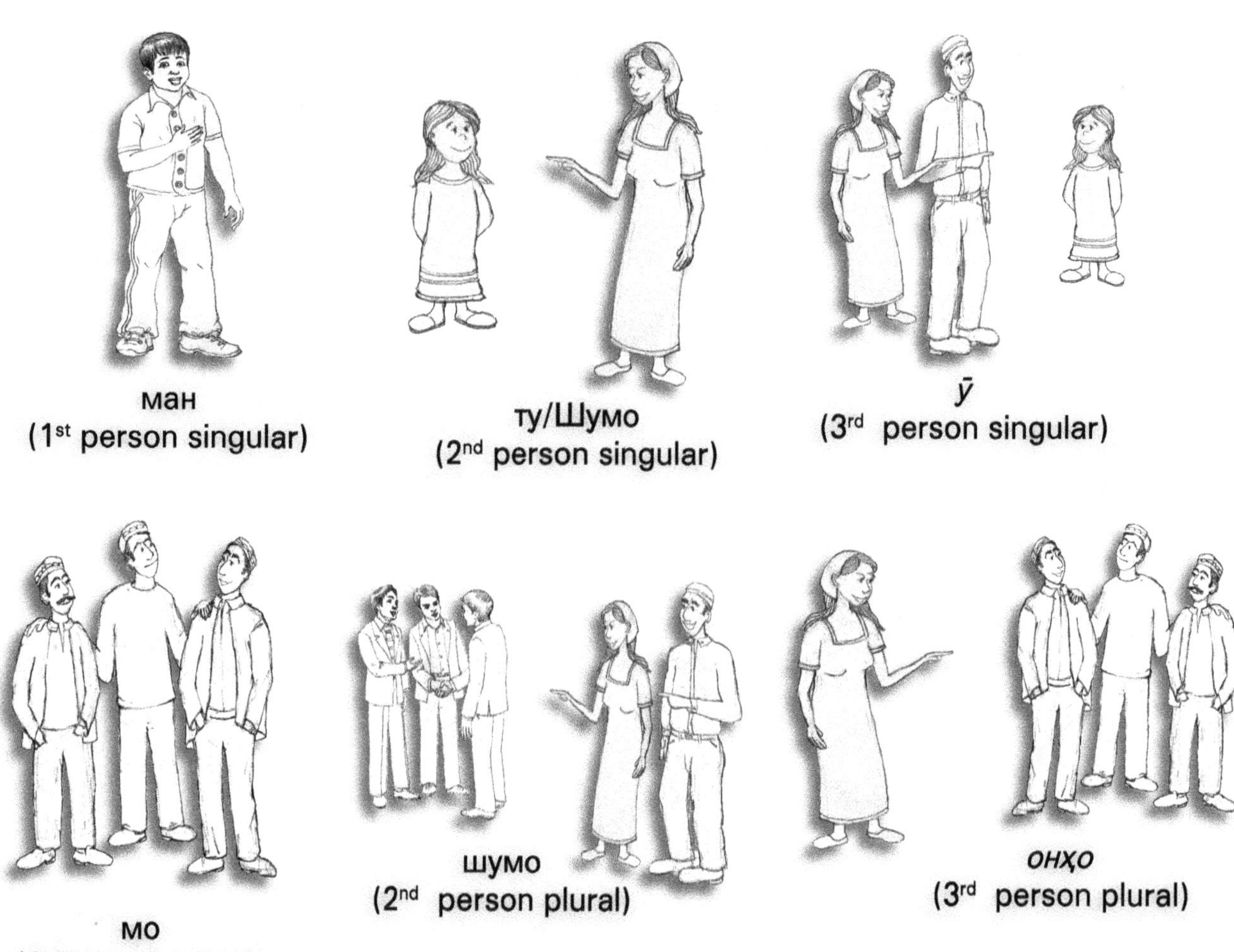

Note:
To be polite, instead of "ту" use "Шумо," which must be capitalized.

3.2. AFFIRMATIVE SENTENCES WITH VERB 'TO BE' (PREDICATE ENDINGS)

All words in Tajiki that are used as predicates (to identify or describe someone or something) must be marked with a personal ending to match the thing being talked about (the subject of the sentence).

Examples:

Ҷонишин Pronouns	Хабари номӣ Predicate nominal	Бандаки хабарӣ Predicate endings
Ман	муаллим / хаста	-ам
Ту	муаллим / хаста	-й
Ӯ (вай)	муаллим / хаста	аст
Мо	муаллим / хаста	-ем
Шумо	муаллим / хаста	-ед
Онҳо	муаллим / хаста	-анд

Машқи 5: Choose an adjective or noun and say something (it need not be true) about each of the pictures below.

3.3. INTERROGATIVE SENTENCES WITH THE VERB 'TO BE'

Questions with the verb 'to be' in Tajiki are shown by their intonation. The word order does not change.

Compare:

Affirmative sentence	Interrogative sentence
Ман донишҷӯям.	**Ман донишҷӯям?**

Short answers to such questions are expressed with the words **ҳа** 'yes' and **не** 'no.'

Look at these examples:

А: Шумо муаллимед? **B: Ҳа.**
А: Шумо беморед? **B: Не.**

Full answers are:

А: Шумо ташнаед? **B: Ҳа, ман ташнаам.**
А: Шумо хастаед? **B: Не, ман хаста нестам.**

Машқи 6: ***Кор бо шарик.*** Ask a partner questions about his or her moods. Then change roles.

Example:

Шумо гуруснаед? Ҳа, ман гуруснаам, 'Yes, I'm hungry.'

3.4. NEGATIVE OF THE VERB 'TO BE'

Look at the examples below and figure out how the negative of the verb 'to be' is formed in Tajiki:

Ман муаллим нестам	**Мо муаллим нестем**
Ту муаллим нестӣ	**Шумо муаллим нестед**
Вай муаллим нест	**Онҳо муаллим нестанд**

Машқи 7: Read the conversation. Then practice in pairs.

Озода: Бубахшед, Шумо Замира Баҳмандухт?
Нилуфар: Не, ман Замира нестам. Номи ман Нилуфари Сафарзода аст.
Озода: Оҳ, бубахшед.

Машқи 8: Class activity. Write your name on a slip of paper and put the slips in a pile. Take turns drawing slips and find the student whose name is on yours.

А: Бубахшед, Шумо Дилорои Меҳандухтед?
В: Не, ман Дилоро нестам.
А: Салом. Шумо Дилорои Меҳандухт?
С: Бале, ман.

3.5. CONJUNCTION BA 'AND'

In a series of objects or persons, **ва** is used only before the last noun:

> **Азим ва Комёр хастаанд,** 'Azim and Komyor are tired.'
> **Бунафша, Лола ва Шаҳло донишҷӯянд,**
> 'Bunafsha, Lola and Shahlo are students.'

The conjunction **ва**, which is borrowed from Arabic, is used rarely in spoken Tajiki. Its Tajiki equivalent is **у** (u), which is pronounced and written **ю** (yu) after vowels:

> **Кариму Шамшод хубанд,** 'Karim and Shamshod are fine.'
> **Лолаю Зебо ташна(й)анд,** 'Lola and Zebo are thirsty.'

4. ХОНИШ

Машқи 9: Read the antonyms and form negative statements.

бардам	хаста
тоза	чиркин
сер	гурусна
безеб	зебо
сиҳат	бемор
камбағал	бой
шод	хафа
нағз	ганда

тоза

сер

безеб

сиҳат

шод

нағз

бардам

камбағал

Машқи 10: *Кор бо шарик.* Read the conversation with a partner.

A: Салом, Ҳушанг.
B: Салом, Шодӣ. Ту чӣ хел?
A: Ташаккур, ман хубам. Ту хастай?
B: Не, ман хаста нестам. Ман бардамам.
A: Хайр, то дидан.
B: То дидан.

Машқи 11: *Шумо чӣ хел?* With your partner, make a conversation on the following scenarios.

1. Your partner looks ill. *Ask if he/she is OK.*
2. Student B looks tired. *Ask student C about him.*
3. You want to talk to student B. *Ask if he is busy.*
4. Someone in your class is beautiful. *Tell your partner about him/her.*

5. ГӮШ КУНЕД

Машқи 12: Listen to the following dialogue and guess what each part of it means.

Зан: Ассалому алайкум, Шумо хубед?
Мард: Ваалайкум ассалом. Ташаккур, хубам.
Зан: Бачаҳо хубанд?
Мард: Ҳа, Худоро шукр, хубанд.
Зан: Хайр, саломат бошед.
Мард: То боздид

Машқи 13: Listen and practice the following dialogue.

Нилуфар: **Шумо Замираи Баҳмандухтед?**
Замира: *Бале, ман Замираи Баҳмандухтам.*
Нилуфар: **Салом. Ман Нилуфари Сафарзодаам.**
Замира: *Салом. Шумо ҳамшаҳрии манед-а?*
Нилуфар: **Бале, дуруст аст.**
Замира: Аз дидоратон шодам.
Нилуфар: *Ман ҳам.*

6. ХАТ

Машқи 14:  Complete the conversation with the correct words in parentheses. Then practice with a partner.

Далер: **Салом Зевар. __________ чӣ хел? (Шумо/он)**
Зевар: Ман хуб__________. (й/ам) Ташаккур. Бубахшед, номи __________ чист?(онҳо/шумо)
Далер: **Номи ман Далер Салимзода.**
Зевар: Далер, ин кас Лола Аюби__________ (аст/анд). Ӯ ҳамсинфи ман __________(аст/ анд).
Далер: **Салом Лола. Аз дидори __________ шодам.(ман/шумо)**
Лола: *Ба фикрам, Шумо ҳамсояи ман __________.(ам/ед)*
Далер: **Дуруст. Ман бо Шумо ҳамсоя __________. (аст/ ам)**

Машқи 15: Use the proper predicate ending to form sentences from the words below.

1. Ман/духтар.	
2. Мо/гурусна.	
3.Ту/донишҷӯ.	
4. Шумо/хафа.	
5. Вай/ҷавон.	
6. Онҳо/писар.	

Машқи 16: *Шумо бемоtorед?* Are you sick?

A. Find out how everyone in your class is today. Fill in the chart with what you found out. Follow the example below.

A: Шумо беморед?
B: Не.
A: Шумо хастаед?
B: Ҳа.

НАМУНА

Ном	Савол/Ҷавоб

B. Now summarize your survey. How many students are feeling good, bad or ill?

Намуна: *Матин ва Шерзод хастаанд. Насим ва Гулрӯ хубанд.*

7. ТАМОШО КУНЕД

Машқи 17: A. Watch the video with the sound off and note the non-verbal behavior of the participants.

Speakers	Actions
First man	___
	___
	___
Second man	___
	___
	___

B. Look at this list of expressions heard in the video clip. Now watch the video with the sound on and number the expressions 1 through 16 to show the order in which the participants used them.

___	*Ассалому алейкум.*
___	*Саломат бошед.*
___	*Ака, чӣ хелӣ?*
___	*Коро чӣ хелай?*
___	*Созӣ.*
___	*Саломатӣ нағзай?*
___	*Не?*
___	*Ҳо.*
___	*Ташаккур.*
___	*Шукр, мешавад.*
___	*Не?*
___	*Корои Шумо нағзай? Тинҷ.*
___	*Саломатӣ?*
___	*Ҳа.*
___	*Ваалайкум.*
___	*Саломат бошед.*

C. Watch the video again and match the expressions on the left with the responses on the right.

Expressions		Response
1. Ассалому алайкум.	___	Ташаккур.
2. Саломатӣ нағзай?	___	Шукр, мешавад.
3. Саломатӣ?	___	Ваалайкум ассалом.
4. Саломат бошед.	___	Тинҷ.
5. Ака, чӣ хелӣ?	___	Саломат бошед.

Барги сабз

Ҳарчанд масоҳати Тоҷикистон чандон бузург нест, дар вилоятҳои кишвар тарзҳои гуногуни муроҷиат ба якдигар мавҷуданд. Масалан, дар қисми ҷанубии Тоҷикистон, шахси гӯянда ба ҳамаи одамон, новобаста аз синну соли онҳо, ҳангоми муроҷиат ҷонишини шахси дуюми танҳо - "ту"-ро истифода мекунад. Яъне гӯянда ҳам ба шахси аз худ калонтар ва ҳам ба шахси аз худ хурдтар "ту" мегӯяд. Танҳо ҳангоме ки ин

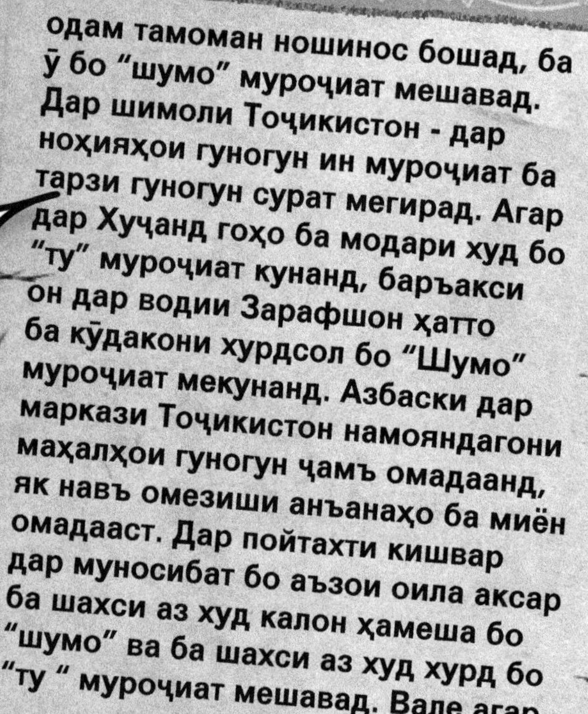

одам тамоман ношинос бошад, ба ӯ бо "шумо" муроҷиат мешавад. Дар шимоли Тоҷикистон - дар ноҳияҳои гуногун ин муроҷиат ба тарзи гуногун сурат мегирад. Агар дар Хуҷанд гоҳо ба модари худ бо "ту" муроҷиат кунанд, баръакси он дар водии Зарафшон ҳатто ба кӯдакони хурдсол бо "Шумо" муроҷиат мекунанд. Азбаски дар маркази Тоҷикистон намояндагони маҳалҳои гуногун ҷамъ омадаанд, як навъ омезиши анъанаҳо ба миён омадааст. Дар пойтахти кишвар дар муносибат бо аъзои оила аксар ба шахси аз худ калон ҳамеша бо "шумо" ва ба шахси аз худ хурд бо "ту " муроҷиат мешавад. Вале агар

ин одам бегона бошад, ҳангоми
шиносоӣ ҳамеша бо “шумо”
муроҷиат мешавад. Дар сурати
зиёд будани фарқияти синнусол,
масалан, дар муносибати муаллим
бо шогирд ва ё ҳамкорони
наслҳои гуногун, насли калонсол
метавонад бо “ту “ муроҷиат
намояд. “Шумо”-гӯӣ нишонаи
одоб ва эҳтироми шахси гӯянда
нисбат ба шахси дигар аст.

В. ШУМО АЗ КУҶОЕД? B. WHERE ARE YOU FROM?

1. СЕҲРИ СУХАН

Машқи 1: Listen and practice.

Машқи 2: A. Practice these questions with your teacher. Then ask your partner.

1. Ассалому алайкум. Шумо чӣ хел?	
2. Шумо аз куҷоед/куҷо?	
3. Шумо аз кадом деҳаед?	
4. Шумо аз кадом шаҳред?	
5. Шумо аз кадом мамлакатед?	
6. Шумо аз кадом қитъаед?	

B. Tell the class about your partner using what you learned above.

Машқи 3: Find your country on the map. Then ask your classmates where they are from and where they have visited and circle all the places on the map.

ҚИТЪАҲОИ ОЛАМ

Report your findings to the class.

Машқи 4: *Кор дар гурӯҳ.* Name two more countries in each region. Compare your charts.

Аврупо	Африқо	Амрикои Ҷанубӣ	Амрикои Шимолӣ	Осиё

А: Чилӣ дар Амрикои Ҷанубӣ аст.
В: Бразилия ҳам дар Амрикои Ҷанубӣ аст

НАМУНА

2. ГУФТУГӮ

Машқи 5: *Шумо аз куҷоед?* Listen and practice the dialogue. Then make your own.

A: Ассалом. Ман Насрин.
B: Салом, ман Терри.
A: Шумо аз куҷоед?
B: Ман аз Чинам. Аз шаҳри Пекин. Шумо чӣ?
A: Ман аз шаҳри Машҳади Эронам.
B: Насрин, аз дидоратон шодам.
A: Ташаккур ман ҳам.

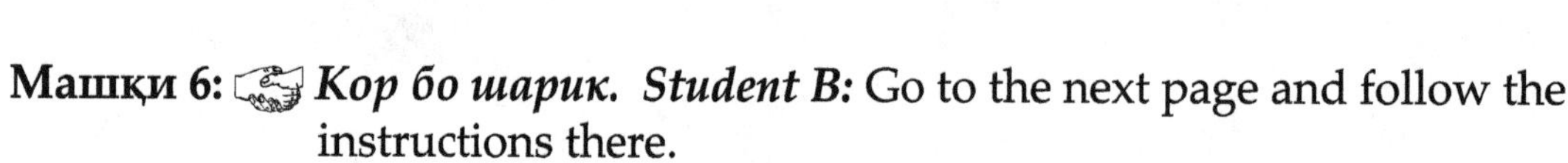

Машқи 6: *Кор бо шарик. Student B:* Go to the next page and follow the instructions there.
Student A: Ask your partner questions to fill in the blanks in chart A. Then answer your partner's questions based on chart B.

A: Мурод аз Россия аст?
B: Не, Мурод аз Россия нест.

A

1. Мурод аз Россия	
2. Ӯ аз Осиё	
3. Ӯ аз шаҳр	
4. Ӯ аз ҷазира	
5. Ӯ аз деҳа	

B

1. Сиёвуш аз Тоҷикистон аст.	
2. Ӯ аз шаҳр аст.	
3. Ӯ аз деҳа нест.	
4. Ӯ аз кӯҳ нест.	
5. Ӯ аз Аврупо нест.	

Student B: Ask your partner questions to fill in the blanks in chart B. Then answer your partner's questions based on chart A.

B: Сиёвуш аз Тоҷикистон аст?
А: Ҳа, Сиёвуш аз Тоҷикистон аст.

A

1. Мурод аз Россия нест.	
2. Ӯ аз Осиё аст.	
3. Ӯ аз шаҳр нест.	
4. Ӯ аз ҷазира нест.	
5. Ӯ аз деҳа аст.	

B

1. Сиёвуш аз Тоҷикистон _____.	
2. Ӯ аз шаҳр _________.	
3. Ӯ аз деҳа _________.	
4. Ӯ аз кӯҳ _________.	
5. Ӯ аз Аврупо _________.	

Машқи 7: Survey your classmates and fill in the chart below.

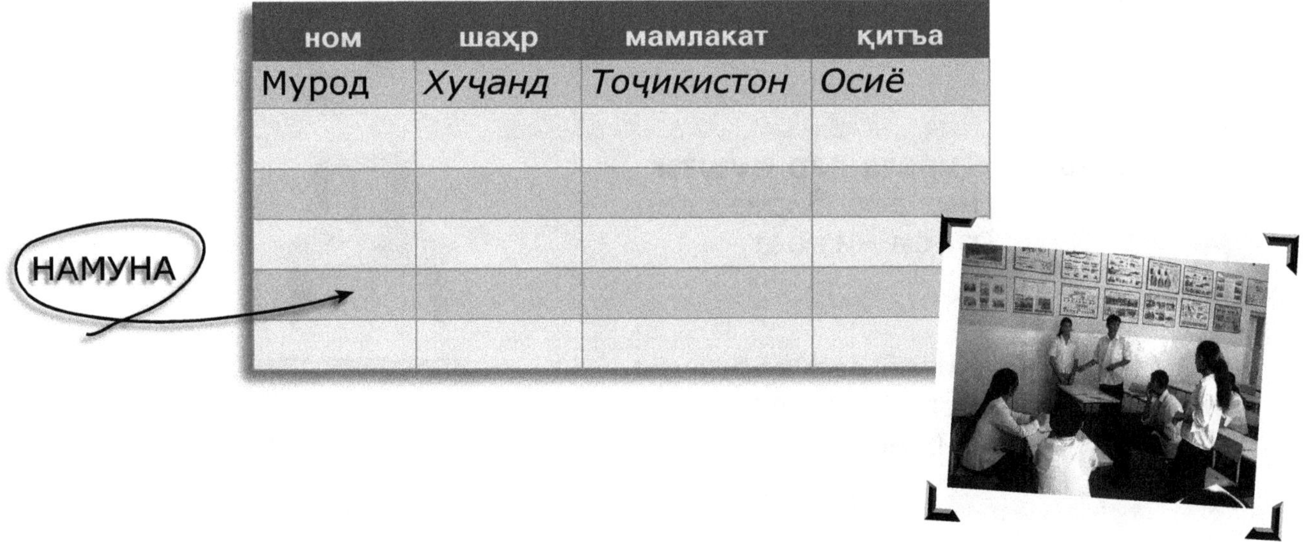

ном	шаҳр	мамлакат	қитъа
Мурод	*Хуҷанд*	*Тоҷикистон*	*Осиё*

Now, based on your survey make three true and three false statements for the class, who will respond ***Ҳа, дуруст аст*** or ***Не, дуруст нест./Не, нодуруст.***

Намуна:

A: Мурод аз Ӯзбакистон аст.
B: Не, нодуруст. Мурод аз Ӯзбакистон нест, вай аз Тоҷикистон аст.
A: Дуруст, Мурод аз Тоҷикистон аст.
A: Мурод аз Осиё аст.
B: Ҳа, дуруст.

3. *ДАСТУР*

3.1. Prepositions of place

The Tajiki equivalents of many English prepositions of place are formed by adding a noun of place after ***дар****.*

байн (миён)	Писар дар **байни** дарахтон аст. Писар дар **миёни** дарахтон аст.	
боло	Соат дар **болои** миз аст.	
атроф	Дар **атрофи** соат доира кашед.	
пас (пушт)	Тиреза дар **пушти** миз аст. Тиреза дар **паси** миз аст.	
зер (таг)	Китоб дар **зери** миз аст. Китоб дар **таги** миз аст.	

паҳлӯ	Соат дар **паҳлӯи** тиреза аст.	
аз	Писар **аз** хона омад.	
дарун	Писар дар **даруни** хона аст. Pesar dar daruni xona ast.	
назд *пеш*	Курсӣ дар **назди** миз аст.	
ба	Писар **ба** хона меравад.	
тарафи рост	Гулдон дар **тарафи рости** миз аст.	
тарафи чап	Гулдон дар **тарафи чапи** миз аст.	

Машқи 8: ***Бозӣ.*** Ask each other questions about the locations of classroom objects.

Намуна:

А: Китоб дар куҷост?

В: Китоб дар болои миз ва дар зери дафтар аст.

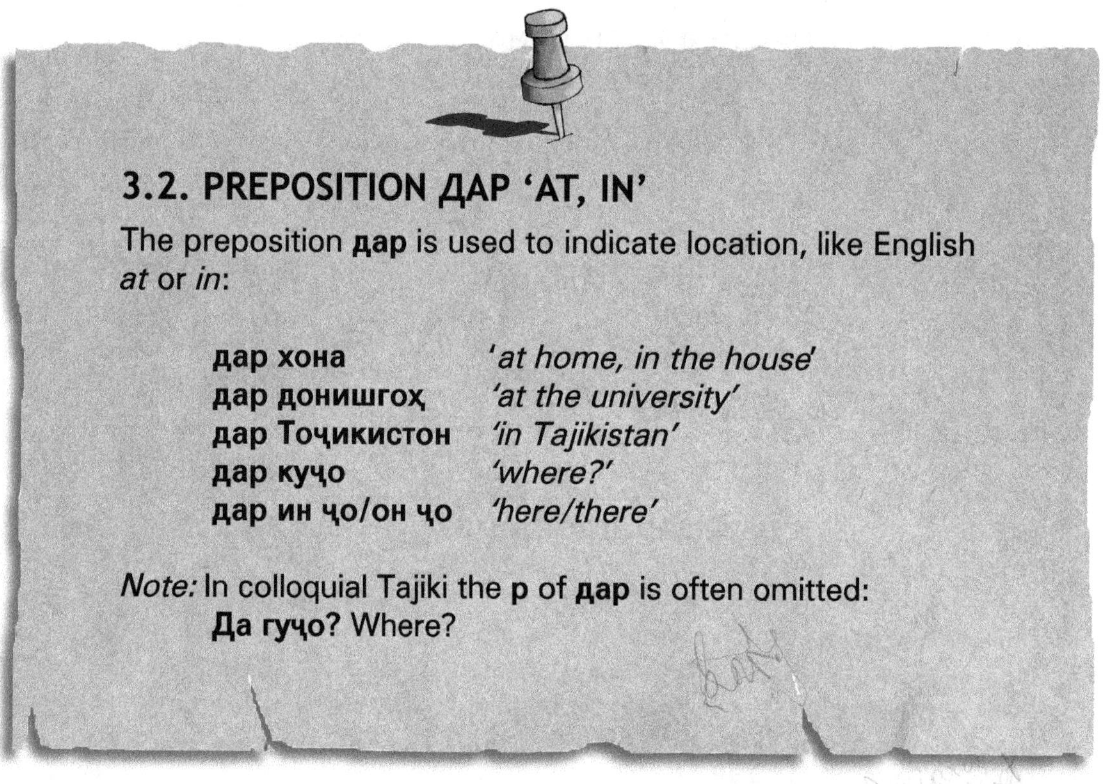

3.2. PREPOSITION ДАР 'AT, IN'

The preposition **дар** is used to indicate location, like English *at* or *in*:

дар хона	*'at home, in the house'*
дар донишгоҳ	*'at the university'*
дар Тоҷикистон	*'in Tajikistan'*
дар куҷо	*'where?'*
дар ин ҷо/он ҷо	*'here/there'*

Note: In colloquial Tajiki the **р** of **дар** is often omitted:
Да гуҷо? Where?

Машқи 9: Lola is searching for her things in her house. Where are they? Look at the picture and match each thing with its location.

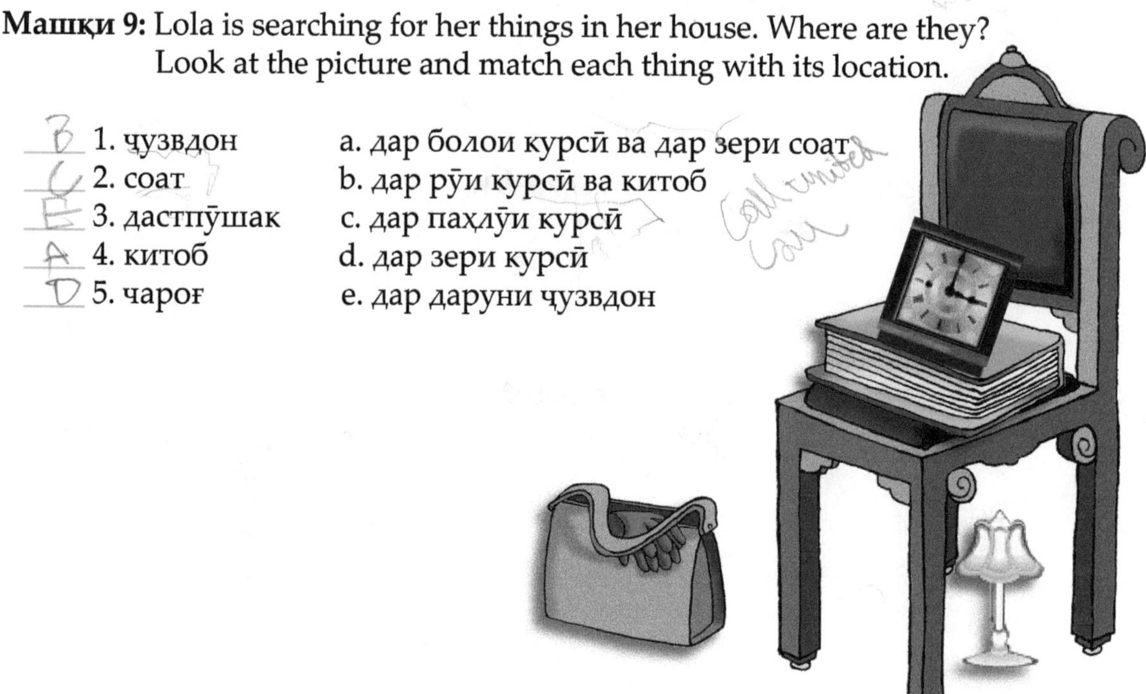

___ 1. ҷузвдон	a. дар болои курсӣ ва дар зери соат
___ 2. соат	b. дар рӯи курсӣ ва китоб
___ 3. дастпӯшак	c. дар паҳлӯи курсӣ
___ 4. китоб	d. дар зери курсӣ
___ 5. чароғ	e. дар даруни ҷузвдон

3.3. PREPOSITION АЗ - 'FROM'

The basic meaning of **аз** is motion away from or out of; that is, it indicates the source of motion or an action:

аз хона *'out of the house,'* **аз Салим** *'from Salim.'*

It is also used to indicate the time something started, **аз зимистон** *'from winter,'* and possession:

Ин китоб аз ман аст, *'This book is mine.'*

In colloquial Tajiki the letter **з** is generally omitted and the preposition is pronounced **а** in the North: **а хона** *'from home,'* **а мағоза** *'from the store,'* and as **ай** in the South: **ай хона** *'from home,'* **ай мағоза** *'from the store.'*

Дар and **аз** are often used with *'to be.'* In very informal speech, the predicate ending is often omitted.

Шумо аз Душанбе?	Не, ман аз Душанбе нестам. Ман аз Хуҷандам.
Ҷон аз Италия аст?	Не, ӯ аз Италия нест. Ӯ аз Ингилистон аст.
Онҳо аз Қазоқистонанд?	Не,онҳо аз Қазоқистон нестанд. Онҳо аз Тоҷикистонанд.
Волидайни Шумо дар Амрикоянд?	Не, волидайни ман дар Амрико нестанд. Онҳо дар Тоҷикистонанд.

3.4. COMPOUND PREPOSITIONS

Simple prepositions like **дар** and **аз** often occur in combination with words for spatial relationships to indicate more detailed shades of location or motion; most English prepositions (*beside, in front of, behind, inside, outside*, etc.) correspond to compound prepositions in Tajiki. Compound prepositions with **дар** indicate location; **аз**, motion away from; and **ба** 'to, towards,' motion towards:

дар хона	'in/at the house'
дар пеши хона	'in front of the house'
дар шаҳр	'in the city'
дар беруни шаҳр	'outside the city'
аз хона	'from the house'
аз паҳлӯи хона	'from beside the house'
аз деҳа	'from the village'
аз байни деҳа	'from the middle of the village'
ба хона	'to the house'
ба даруни хона	'into the house'

Машқи 10: Look at the picture and complete the sentences.

Муаллима ________ аст.	___	дар рӯи миз	а
Китоб, глобус ва гулдон ________ анд.	___	дар болои тахта	б
Духтар ________ синф аст.	___	дар тарафи чапи гулдон	в
Гулдон дар рӯи миз аст. Он ________ аст.	___	дар байни китоб ва глобус	г
Глобус дар болои миз аст. Он ________ аст.	___	дар паси муаллима	д
Талабагон ________ анд.	___	дар назди миз ва пеши тахта	е
Тахта ________ аст	___	дар тарафи рост	ё
Навиштаҷот ________ аст.	___	дар рӯбарӯи муаллима	ж

4. ХОНИШ

Машқи 11: Read the sentences below and find something in your classroom whose location you can describe with each preposition.

Себ дар рӯй(боло)-и миз аст.
Тахта дар пас(қафо)-и миз аст.
Ҷомадон дар зер(таг)-и миз аст.
Қалам дар назди китобу дафтар аст.
Китоб дар байни дафтар ва қалам аст.

Қайчӣ дар даруни миз аст.
Ахлотдон дар паҳлӯи миз аст.
Дафтар дар тарафи чапи себ аст.
Қалам дар тарафи рости себ аст.
Дар атрофи тахта хати сафед ҳаст.

Машқи 12: *Ин шаҳр дар куҷост?* Where are these cities? Match the cities to the countries.

НАМУНА

Токио	Амрико
Мехико	Англия
Сеул	Аргентина
Ню Йорк	Бангладеш
Бомбай	Бразилия
Ҷакарта	Индонезия
Қоҳира	Кореяи Ҷанубӣ
Манила	Мексика
Қарочӣ	Миср
Маскав	Нигерия
Шанхай	Покистон
Буэнос Айрес	Россия
Дҳака	Туркия
Рио де Жанейро	Фаронса
Лондон	Филиппин
Теҳрон	Ҳиндустон
Истанбул	Чин
Лагос	Эрон
Париж	Япония

Машқи 13: Choose something in the classroom. Using what you have learned so far, take turns guessing what each of you chose by asking questions about its location.

5. ГӮШ КУНЕД

Машқи 14: Listen and practice.

A: Калидҳо дар куҷоянд?
B: Онҳо дар даруни сумкаанд.

A: Қалам дар куҷост?
B: Қалам дар рӯйи миз аст.

A: Шумо аз куҷоед?
B: Ман аз Фаронсаам.

A: Ҷеф ва Крис аз куҷоянд?
B: Онҳо аз Амрикоянд.

Машқи 15: ***Чӣ чиз дар куҷост?*** Listen and match the words.

себ		миз	а
китобҳо		девор	б
муаллим		ҷузвдон	в
курсӣ		тахта	г
харита		компютер	д

6. ХАТ

Машқи 16: A. Guess the country. Work with a partner. Write sentences about a country's location, using the prepositions дар байни, дар назди, дар тарафи рости, дар тарафи чапи and дар. Read the sentences to your partner, who must guess the country. Use the map below.

Намуна:

Мамлакат дар байни Қазоқистон ва Тоҷикистон аст. Он дар паҳлӯи рости Ӯзбакистон ва дар тарафи чапи Чин аст.

Қазоқистон
Мугулистон
Баҳри Хазар
Ӯзбакистон
Қирғизистон
Туркманистон
Тоҷикистон
Хитой
Эрон
Афғонистон
Покистон
Ҳиндустон

СУҒД
Навоҳии тобеи марказ
БАДАХШОН
ХАТЛОН

B. Read "Барги сабз" and find the names of major Tajik cities and provinces.

7. ТАМОШО КУНЕД

Машқи 17: A. Watch the video and find out the names of the girls.

1. Name	

2. Name	

B. Watch the video again and indicate where they are from.

1. Girl		**1.** Марди 1	
2. Girl		**2.** Марди 2	

C. Now work with a partner to create a similar dialogue and act it out.

Барги сабз

Дар Тоҷикистон се вилоят мавҷуд аст. Дар шимоли кишвар вилояти Суғд - марказаш шаҳри Хуҷанд ҷойгир аст, ки ба марказҳои қадимии мардуми тоҷик шаҳрҳои Самарқанд ва Бухоро ва водии Фарғона наздик буда, мардумаш тарзи зисту анъанаҳои қадимии аҳолии шаҳрнишинро хуб медонад. Вилояти Хатлон - марказаш шаҳри Қӯрғонтеппа дар ҷануби кишвар ҷойгир аст. Бо вуҷуди таърихи қадим доштанаш мардуми вилоят тақрибан то нимаҳои қарни XX бо сабаби набудани шароити ҳамлунақл ва роҳҳои хуб бо марказҳои қадимӣ алоқаи нисбатан камтар дошт. Вилояти Кӯҳистони Бадахшон - марказаш шаҳри Хоруғ, чуноне ки аз номаш маълум аст, дар минтақаи кӯҳистон ҷойгир аст. Мардумаш бо забонҳои гуногуни помирӣ сухан мегӯянд, ҳамчунин забони тоҷикиро низ хуб медонанд. Бинобар тафовутҳои зикршудаи муҳити зист, инчунин бар пояи фарқиятҳои шеваҳои ҷанубӣ ва шимолии забони тоҷикӣ, дар байни тоҷикон одате ба миён омадааст, ки ҳангоми вохӯрӣ ду тоҷик гоҳо “аз куҷо?” будани ҳамсӯҳбаташро мепурсад. Аксар куҷой будани ҳамсӯҳбат аз рӯи сухангӯияш маълум мешавад.

В. Ӯ кист? C. What is he?

1. СЕҲРИ СУХАН

Машқи 1: Listen and practice.

сароянда

фурӯшанда

парастор

харидор

рассом

чӯпон

ошпаз

нависанда

дуредгар

милиса муфаттиш духтур

Машқи 2: Choose five close friends and write down their names and occupations. Then work with a partner and ask each other what your friends do.

А: Хадича кист?
В: Вай муаллима аст.

В: Толиб кист?
А: Ӯ рассом аст.

2. ГУФТУГӮ

Машқи 3: Listen to the dialogue and practice it with a partner.

А: Ассалому алайкум, Сӯҳроб.
В: Ваалайкум ассалом, Мадина.
А: Шумо чӣ хел? Хубед?
В: Ташаккур, ман хубам.
А: Сӯҳроб, ин кист?
В: Ин Фараҳноз. Ӯ аз Душанбе аст.
А: Ӯ кист?
В: Ӯ духтур аст.

Машқи 4: *Кор бо шарик.* Look at these pictures and ask a partner questions, then change roles.

Шамсия

Азим ва Амир

Зариф

Сурайё

3. ДАСТУР

SUFFIXES -OP AND -АНДА

a. Suffix -op forms nouns from the past stems of verbs

харид 'to buy' - харидор 'buyer'
гуфт 'to say' - гуфтор 'speech'
дид 'to see' - дидор 'meeting'

b. Suffix -анда forms nouns from the present stems of verbs

гир 'to take' - гиранда 'taker'
хон 'to read' - хонанда 'reader'
фурӯш 'to sell' - фурӯшанда 'seller'
гӯй 'to tell - гӯянда 'speaker'

4. ХОНИШ

Машқи 5: Look at this picture and read the text. Guess who is who and write their names in the boxes.

Ин Назокат. Ӯ фурӯшанда аст. Ӯ дар байни Латофат ва Шарофат аст. Ин Муҳаббат. Ӯ духтур аст. Ӯ дар тарафи рости Латофат аст. Латофат рассом аст. Ӯ каме хаста ва хафа аст. Ин Адолат аст. Адолат парастор аст. Ӯ гул дорад ва шод аст. Адолат дар тарафи чапи Шарофат аст. Шарофат муфаттиш аст. Онҳо дугонаанд. Онҳо аз Душанбеанд. Онҳо дар Тоҷикистонанд. Онҳо зебоянд.

5. ГӮШ КУНЕД

Машқи 6: Listen and practice.

A: Салом, ту аз кучо?
B: Салом, ман аз Душанбе.
A: Ту муфаттишӣ?
B: Не, ман рассомам. Ту чӣ?
A: Ман нависандаам.

A: Ассалому алайкум Даврончон, Шумо чӣ хел?
B: Худоро шукр, ман хубам.
A: Дар назди дар кист?
B: Ин Парвиз, ӯ сароянда аст.
A: Ҳа, фаҳмидам.

Машқи 7: Listen and match the names with their occupations.

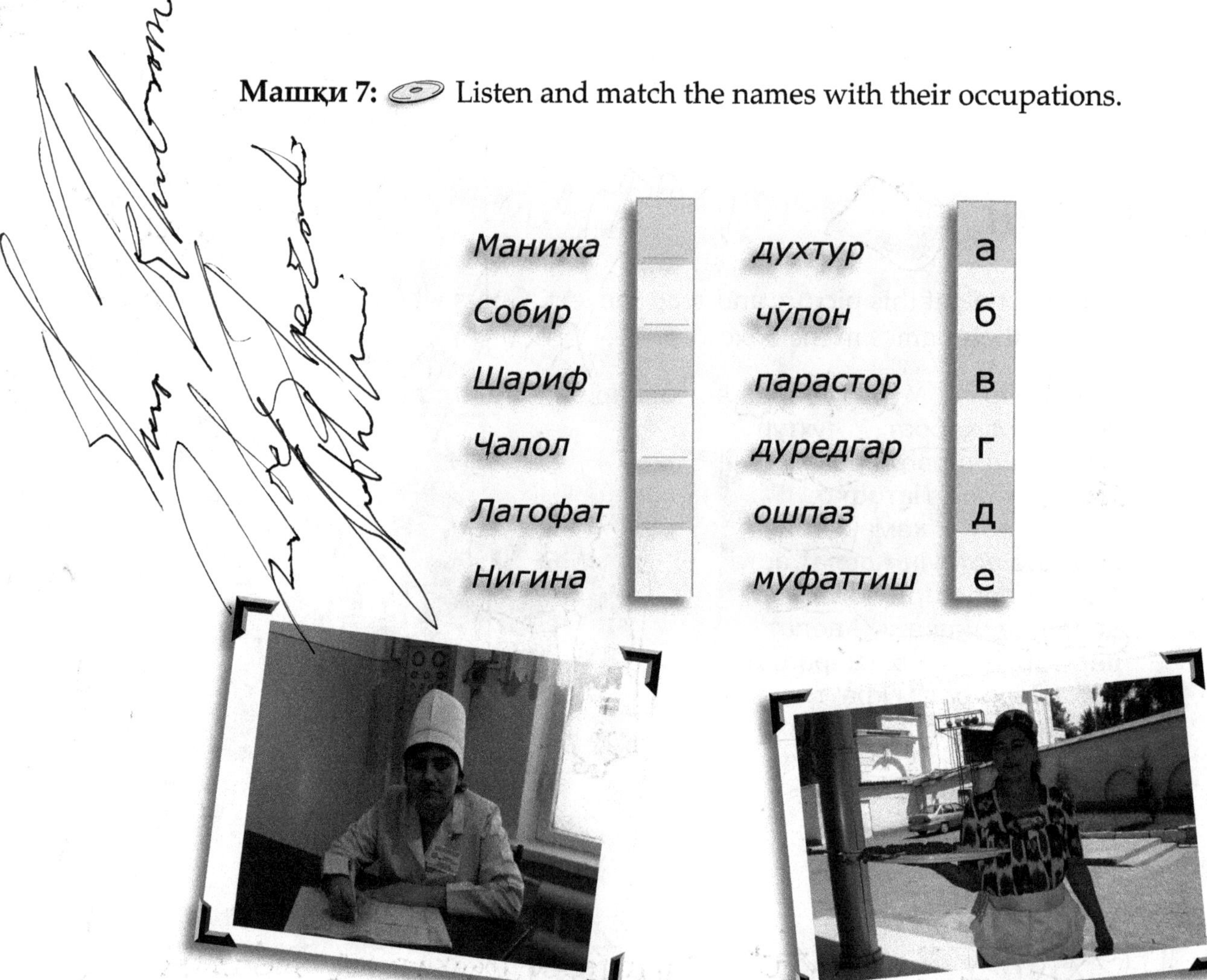

Манижа		*духтур*	а
Собир		*чӯпон*	б
Шариф		*парастор*	в
Ҷалол		*дуредгар*	г
Латофат		*ошпаз*	д
Нигина		*муфаттиш*	е

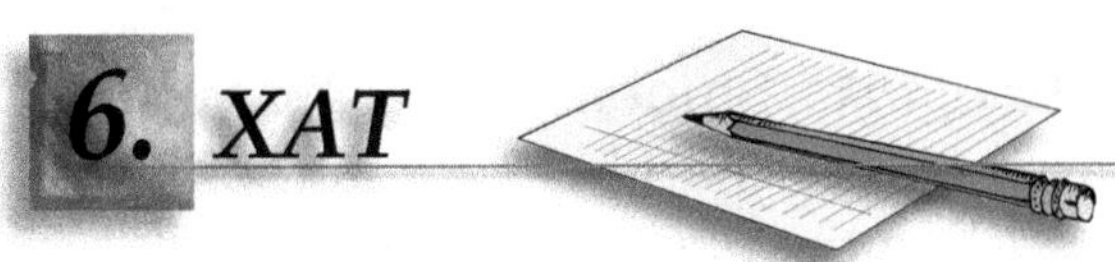

Машқи 8: **For student A:** ***Fill in the blanks***. Student A: Look at the chart and ask your partner questions to fill in the blanks. Then answer your partner's questions based on the chart. Student B: Look at the chart on the next page and follow the instructions there.

Ном	Касб
1. Мурод	1.
2.	2. дуредгар
3. Сурайё	3.
4.	4. рассом
5. Майкл	5.
6.	6. ошпаз
7. Карен	7.
8.	8. духтур
9. Рустам	9.
10.	10. муфаттиш
11. Бежан	11.
12.	12. муаллим

НАМУНА

A: **Касби рақами як чист?**
B: Касби рақами як фурӯшанда аст.

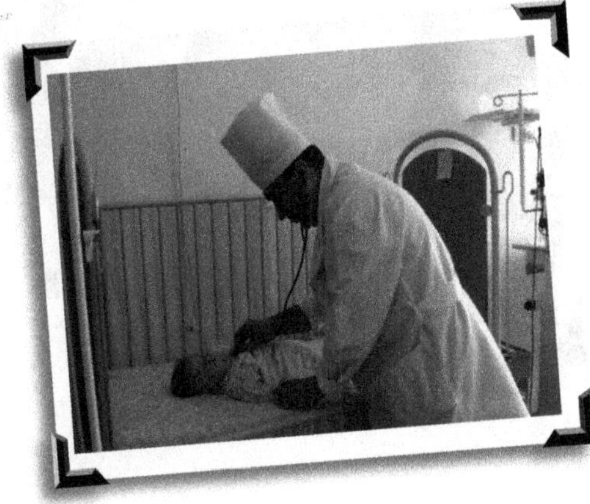

Машқи 8: **For student B:** ***Fill in the blanks*****.** Student B: Answer your partner's questions based on the chart below, and then ask questions in turn to fill in the blanks in the chart.

Ном	Касб
1. ______	1. фурӯшанда
2. Баҳром	2. ______
3. ______	3. котиба
4. Ситора	4. ______
5. ______	5. донишҷӯ
6. Нигина	6. ______
7. ______	7. ҳалабон
8. Мансур	8. ______
9. ______	9. нависанда
10. Доро	10. ______
11. ______	11. сароянда
12 Ҷамшед	______

B: Номи рақами як чист?
A: Номи рақами як Мурод аст.

7. ТАМОШО КУНЕД

Машқи 9: A. Watch the video and fill in the blanks

Ассалом. Ман ____________ Якубова.
Ман ________________ ҳастам.
Падари ман ____________ аст.
Модарам ________ ва ду бародарам бошанд, дар __________ мехонанд.
Номи ман ___________. Падарам _____________ и идораи андоз аст.
Модарам _______________. Бародарам ______________.
Хоҳаронам дар ______________ и миёна мехонанд.
Ман ______________ и соли аввал ҳастам.

B. Now work with a clasmate and ask each other about your family member's professions. Are there any similarities? Whose family has more professions? Tell the class about your findings.

VOCABULARY
ЛУҒАТНОМА

аз	*prep.* from
Аз дидоратон шодам.	*phr.* Pleased to meet you.
Аз Шумо пурсем?	*phr.* And you? (lit., "May I ask you?")
айнак	*n.* eyeglasses
атроф	*prep.* around
ахлотдон	*n.* trashcan
ба	*prep.* towards
байн	*prep.* between
банд	*adj.* busy
бардам	*adj.* healthy, rested
барори кор	*phr.* Have a good day at work, Good luck
бачаҳо хубанд?	*phr.* How are your kids?
ба фикрам	*phr.* in my opinion
бе	*prep.* without
безеб	*adj.* ugly
бемор	*adj.* ill, sick
берун	*prep.* outside
биёбон	*n.* desert
бо	*prep.* with
бой	*adj.* rich
боло	*prep.* above
вай	*pron.* he/she
ганда	*adj.* bad
гурусна (гушна)	*adj.* hungry
дар	*prep.* at, in
дарахт	*n.* tree
дарё	*n.* river
дарун	*prep.* inside
дафтарча	*n.* small notebook
деҳа	*n.* village
доира кашед	*v.* circle (it)!
дуредгар	*n.* carpenter
дуруст	*adj.* correct

духтур	*n.* doctor
дӯст	*n.* friend
зебо	*adj.* pretty
зер	*prep.* under (= **таг**)
ин кас	*n.* this person (polite)
ин ҷо	*pron.* here
исм	*n.* noun, name
камбағал	*adj.* poor
компютер	*n.* computer
куҷо	*pron.* where?
кӯҳ	*n.* mountain
қайчӣ	*n.* scissors
қитъа	*n.* continent
магнитофон	*n.* tape player
мағоза	*n.* store
мамлакат	*n.* nation
ман	*pron.* I, me
миён	*prep.* among, between
милиса	*n.* policeman
мо	*pron.* we, us
муфаттиш	*n.* detective
нависанда	*n.* writer
нағз	*adj.* good (= **хуб**)
назд	*prep.* near
олам	*n.* the world
онҳо	*pron.* they
он ҷо	*pron.* there
ошпаз	*n.* cook
Панохи Худо	*phr.* By the grace of God (lit., "under the protection of the Lord")
парастор	*n.* nurse
пас	*prep.* behind (= **пушт**)
паҳлӯ	*prep.* beside
пеш	*prep.* in front of
пушт	*prep.* behind (= **пас**)
рассом	*n.* painter, artist

рост	*adj.* right
рўзнома	*n.* newspaper
савол	*n.* question
саломат бошед	*interj.* bye (be healthy)
сароянда	*n.* singer
себ	*n.* apple
сер	*adj.* full (of food)
сифат	*n.* adjective, quality
сиҳат	*adj.* healthy, well
сумка	*n.* bag, purse
таг	*prep.* under (= **зер**)
танбал	*adj.* lazy
тараф	*prep.* side
ташаккур	*interj.* thanks, thank you
ташна	*adj.* thirsty
телевизор	*n.* television
то	*prep.* until
тоза	*adj.* clean
то боздид	*phr.* Until we meet again.
то дидан	*phr.* See you.
то пагоҳ	*phr.* Until tomorrow, Until morning.
ту	*pron.* you (sg. informal)
уқёнус	*n.* ocean
ӯ	*pron.* he/she
фурӯшанда	*n.* seller
хайр	*interj.* bye
харидор	*n.* buyer
хаста	*adj.* tired
хат	*n.* line, writing
хафа	*adj.* unhappy
хона	*n.* house
хуб	*adj.* good, fine (= **нағз**)
худат	*prep.* yourself (sg.)
Худоро шукр	*interj.* Thanks to God (everything is fine).
хуш	*adj.* happy, cheerful

Хуш омадед	*phr.* Welcome.
ҳам	*adv.* also
ҳамён	*n.* wallet
ҳамсинф	*n.* classmate
ҳамсоя	*n.* neighbor
ҳамшаҳрӣ	*adj.* from the same city
чап	*adj.* left
чиркин	*adj.* dirty
чӣ хел	*adv.* how?
чӯпон	*n.* shepherd
ҷавоб	*n.* answer
ҷавон	*adj.* young
ҷазира	*n.* island
Шаби хуш	*phr.* Good night.
шаҳр	*n.* city
шод	*adj.* happy
шумо	*pron.* you (pl.)
Шумо	*pron.* you (sg. formal)

Боби чорум
CHAPTER FOUR

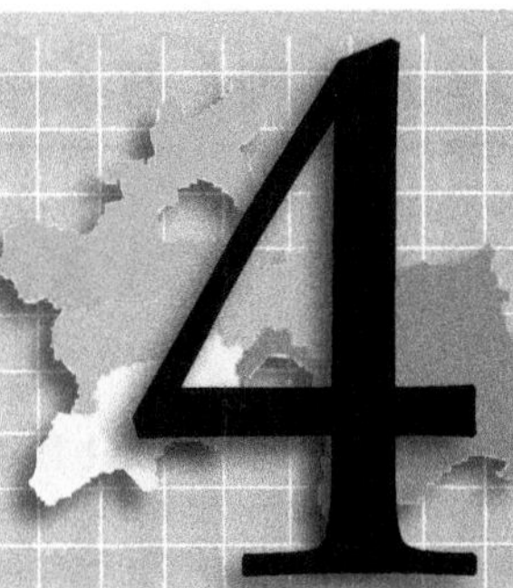

ШИНОСОЙӢ
ACQUAINTANCE

IN THIS CHAPTER

- **Шиносоӣ** Introductions
- **Миллатҳо** Nationalities
- **Муаррафӣ** Introducing Others
- ***Луғатнома*** Vocabulary

А. ШИНОСОЙӢ A. INTRODUCTIONS

1. СЕҲРИ СУХАН!

Машқи 1: Look at these pictures, listen and read the dialogues:

Ардашер: **Ассалом. Бубахшед, номи Шумо чист?**
Наргис: Салом, номи ман Наргис. Номи Шумо чӣ?
Ардашер: Номи ман Ардашер.
Наргис: Аз дидоратон шодам.

Леслӣ: Ассалому алайкум.
Зан: Ваалайкум ассалом. Бубахшед, номатон чист?
Леслӣ: Номам Леслӣ.
Зан: Шумо аз куҷоед?
Леслӣ: Аз Амрико.
Зан: Шумо донишҷӯед?
Леслӣ: Не, ман донишҷӯ нестам, ман муаллимаам.

Салом, номи ман Шаҳриёр
Номи Шумо чист?

Машқи 2: Listen and introduce yourself to your partner, then to your classmates.

Намуна: *Номи ман Лола. Номи хонаводагиам Аюбӣ.*

ном → Лола

номи хонаводагӣ → Аюбӣ

USEFUL EXPRESSIONS

Номи Шумо чист?	What is your name?
Номи хонаводагии Шумо чист?	What is your last name?
Бубахшед	Excuse me
Аз дидоратон шодам.	Nice to meet you.

2. ГУФТУГӮ

Машқи 3: ***Аз дидоратон шодам.*** A. Listen and practice.

Носир: Салом, номи ман Носир Салимзода аст.
Лола: *Ман Лола Аюбӣ.*
Носир: Лола, ман аз дидоратон шодам.
Лола: *Ман ҳам.*
Носир: Бубахшед, номи хонаводагиятонро боз як бор такрор кунед.
Лола: *Аюбӣ.*

B. Using the dialogues given above, write and act out your own introduction dialogues.

Машқи 4: ***Бозӣ: "Номгӯйӣ".*** Make a circle. Learn the names of your classmates and introduce them to each other.

A: Номи ман Шаҳло. Номи хонаводагиам Баҳмандухт.
B: Номи вай Шаҳло. Номи хонаводагиаш Баҳмандухт. Номи ман Зебо. Номи хонаводагиам Ҳумоюнӣ.
C: Номи вай Шаҳло, номи хонаводагиаш Баҳмандухт. Номи вай Зебо, номи хонаводагиаш Ҳумоюнӣ. Номи ман Бежан аст ва номи хонаводагиям Дастғайб аст.

3. *ДАСТУР*

3.1. Personal pronouns

3.1. PARTICLES ҲАМ AND НИЗ

The particles ҳам (general) and низ (literary) have the same meaning, 'also, too.' They are used after the noun or pronoun they refer to.

Ман ҳам (низ) донишҷӯям, 'I am a student too.'
Ӯ ҳам (низ) хаста аст, 'He is tired too.'

In colloquial speech the ҳ of ҳам is usually omitted and the -ам is run together with the noun or pronoun it refers to. After vowels, й is added between the noun and the ам:

Ман ҳам ташнаам (Spoken: **Манам ташна**), 'I am thirsty too.'
Зебо ҳам шод аст (Spoken: **Зебоям шод**), 'Zebo is happy too.'

Машқи 5: There are two ways of expressing possessives in Tajiki. Look at the examples below and see if you can figure out the rule.

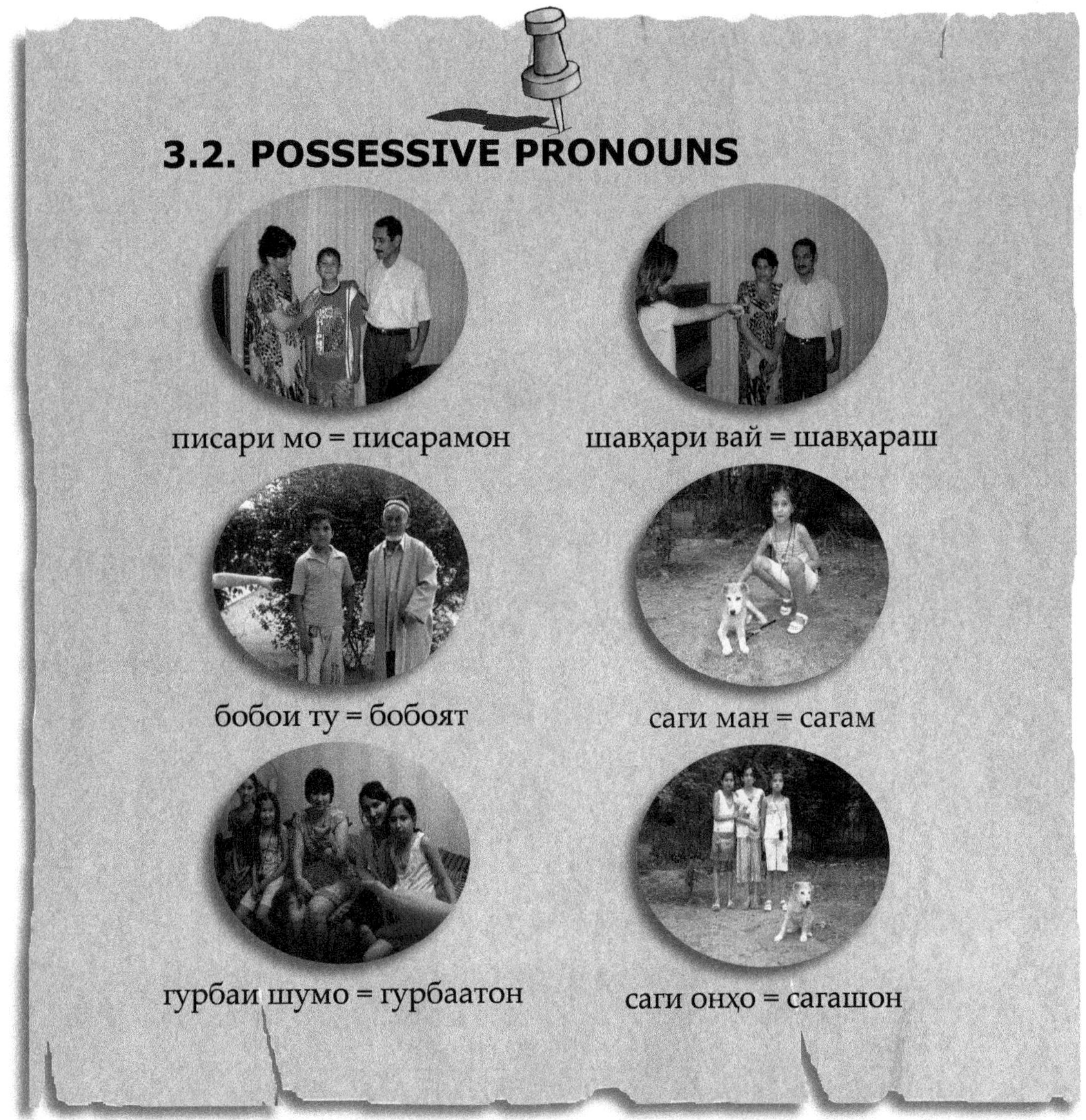

When you have figured out how possession is indicated, fill out the chart below.

PERSON	ENDINGS	
	Singular	Plural
1.	______	______
2.	______	______
3.	______	______

Машқи 6:  Now form the possessives of the given words:

НАМУНА

китоб, ман	китоби ман	китобам
падар, ӯ		
модар, ту		
додар, вай		
бобо, мо		
бибӣ, шумо		
келин, онҳо		

Машқи 7: Practice the following exchanges.

1. **A: Ин ҳамёни туст?**
   B: Не, ҳамёни ман нест.
   A: Ҳамёнат дар куҷост?
   B: Дар кисаам.

2. **A: Калидҳоят дар куҷоянд?**
   B: Онҳо дар ҳамёнам.
   A: Ҳамёнат куҷост?
   B: Дар ҷузвдонам. Оҳ, ҳамёни ман нест. Он дар хонаам.

3.3 SOME QUESTION WORDS

гуфтугӯӣ *(colloquial)*	адабӣ *(literary)*	*English equivalent*
чӣ хел	чӣ тавр, чун	how
чӣ	чӣ	what
кӣ	кӣ	who
канӣ	дар куҷо	where
чаро (чиба, чида)	барои чӣ, чаро	why
кай	кай	when
дар куҷо (да гуҷо)	дар куҷо	where

Чаро is pronounced **чиба** or **чида** in the colloquial language, **куҷо** as **гуҷо**, **дар куҷо** as **да гуҷо**, and **аз куҷо** as a **гуҷо**. In sentences with question words the word order is the same as in a statement. The pronoun он in colloquial language is pronounced as **ун** and its plural form as **уно**. The word **ҷо** is pronounced as **ҷа**. The pronoun **он** in colloquial language is replaced by pronoun **вай**, the plural form of which is pronounced as **ваё** (reduced form of **вайҳо**).

Note that you must use the preposition **дар** with **куҷо**, **ин ҷо**, and **он ҷо**. This is different from English, in which you use where, here, and there without a preposition:

Китоб дар куҷо аст?
'Where is the book?' (not 'At where...')

COMPARE:

QUESTION	ANSWER
Фирӯза дар куҷо аст?	**Фирӯза дар синф аст.**
Ин чӣ аст?/чист?	**Ин қалам аст.**
Шумо чӣ хел(ед)?	**Ман хубам.**
Шумо аз куҷоед?	**Ман аз Кӯлобам.**
Он зан кӣ аст?/кист?	**Он зан муаллими Салим аст.**

Машқи 8: Make and write down questions from the following words and respond to them either affirmatively or negatively. Then switch roles.

НАМУНА

аз кучо/Салим — Салим аз кучо аст ?
Салим аз Ҳисор аст./ Салим аз Рашт аст.
кӣ/онҳо
дар кучо/Шумо
Баҳодур ва Мавзуна /чӣ хел
чӣ/касби Шумо

4. ХОНИШ

Машқи 9: Read these sentences with question words and their answers. Fill in the chart with the Tajiki equivalent of each phrase.

Ин кист?	Ин дӯстам.
Онҳо кистанд?	Онҳо донишҷӯянд.
Номи Шумо чист?	Номи ман Ҷамшед аст.
Шумо аз кучоед?	Ман аз Тоҷикистонам.
Ту чӣ хелӣ?	Ташаккур. Ман хубам.
Ин чист?	Ин соат аст.
Соат дар кучост?	Он дар девор аст.
Китобҳои шумо чӣ хеланд(гунаанд)?	Онҳо хуб ва шавқоваранд.
Китобҳо бо кадом забонанд?	Онҳо бо забонҳои тоҷикӣ ва олмониaнд.

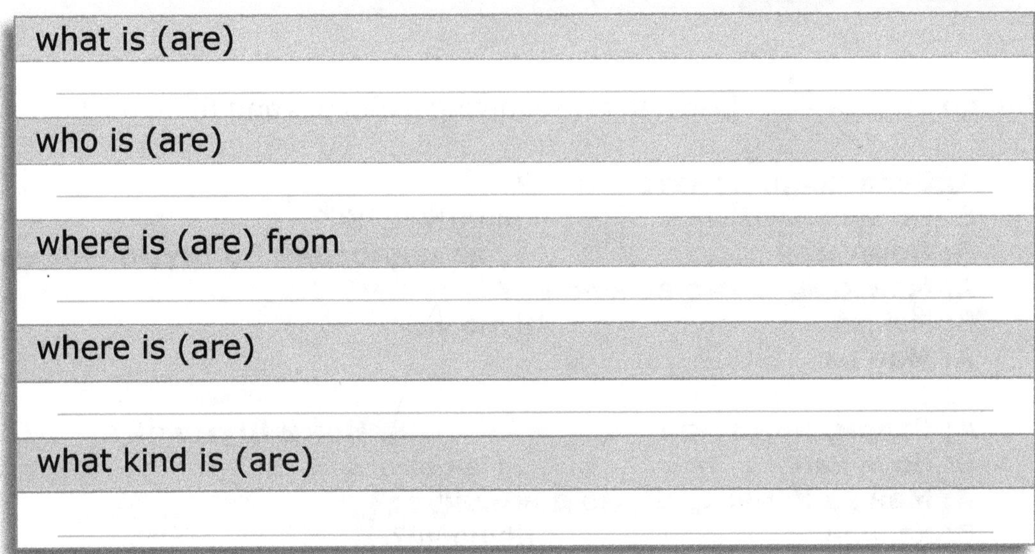

what is (are)
who is (are)
where is (are) from
where is (are)
what kind is (are)

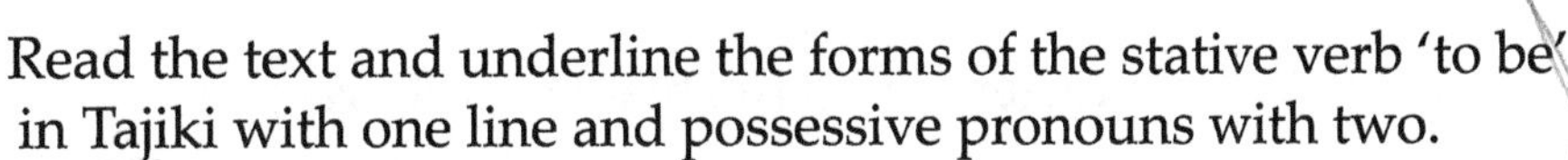

Машқи 10: Read the text and underline the forms of the stative verb 'to be' in Tajiki with one line and possessive pronouns with two.

Номи ман Носир Пӯлодӣ. Ман аз шаҳри Хуҷанд, аз Тоҷикистонам. Инҳо дӯстонам Лора ва Кол. Лора аз шаҳри Кембриҷ. Ӯ аз Ингилистон аст. Номи хонаводагиаш Смис аст. Ӯ муҳандис аст. Кол Витсел аз Амрикост. Хонааш дар иёлати Масачусетс аст. Кол духтур аст. Ин китоби Лора аст. Китобаш бо забони англисӣ аст. Ӯ дар хонааш аст. Хонааш зебо аст. Лора хаста ва хафа аст. Ҳамёнаш ва соаташ нест. Ӯ дар китобхона аст.

5. ГӮШ КУНЕД

Машқи 11: Listen to the following dialogues and fill in the blanks.

1. **А: Бубахшед, номатон чист?**
   В: Номам_______________, номи Шумо чӣ?
   А: Номи ман _______________, аз шиносоии бо Шумо шодам.
   А: Ман ҳам. Шумо аз куҷоед?
   В: Ман аз _______________, Шумо чӣ?
   А: Ман аз _______________.

2. **А: Салом, номи ман _______________. Номи Шумо чӣ?**
   В: Номи ман _______________. Ман аз _______________.
   А: Ман аз Хуҷанд. Шумо донишҷӯед?
   В: Ҳа, ман _______________, Шумо чӣ?
   А: Ман донишҷӯ нестам, ман _______________.

Машқи 12: Listen, fill in the blanks, and practice.

Лола: Оҳ. _______________ дар куҷоянд?
Азиз: Ором шав. Онҳо _______________ нестанд?
Лола: Не, нестанд. Онҳо гум шудаанд.
Азиз: Ба фикрам, онҳо ҳоло ҳам _______________.
Пешхидмат: Бубахшед, инҳо _______________?
Лола: Ҳа, калидҳои ман. Ташаккур!
Азиз: Ана, дидӣ, ҳеҷ гап нест.
Пешхидмат: Ин _______________?
Лола: Умм. Не, ҳамёнам _______________. Азиз, _______________ дар куҷост?
Азиз: Дар кисаам. Э, мебахшед. Истед! Ин _______________ аст!

Машқи 13: Listen to the conversation. Put five things from the classroom, your pockets or your bags onto the table. Find the owner of each item.

А: Карим ин қалами туст?
В: Не, қалами ман нест. Ба фикрам, қалами Лола аст.
А: Лола ин қалами туст?
С: Канӣ, бинам. Ҳа, қалами ман аст.

6. ХАТ

Машқи 14: Write the possessive pronouns to complete these conversations. Then practice them

1. **A: Айнаки ман дар куҷост?**
   B: Он дар сумка ____________ нест?
   A: Не, дар сумка ____________ нест.
   B: Ист. Он дар киса ____________ аст?
   A: Ҳа, бале. Ташаккур.

2. **A: Ин қалами Парвиз аст?**
   B: Не, қалами ӯ нест. Қалам ____________ дар болои китоб ____________ аст.
   A: Бубахшед, ин қалами ман аст?
   B: Не, қалами ту дар рӯи миз ____________ аст.
   A: Ҳа, он дар рӯи миз ____________ аст. Ташаккур.

Машқи 15: *Кор бо гурӯҳ.* Write five questions about your partner and five questions about your partner's best friend. Take turns asking and answering each other's questions.

Your partner	*Your partner's best friend*
Шумо аз куҷоед?	*Дӯсти беҳтарини Шумо кист?*

____

____

____

____

____

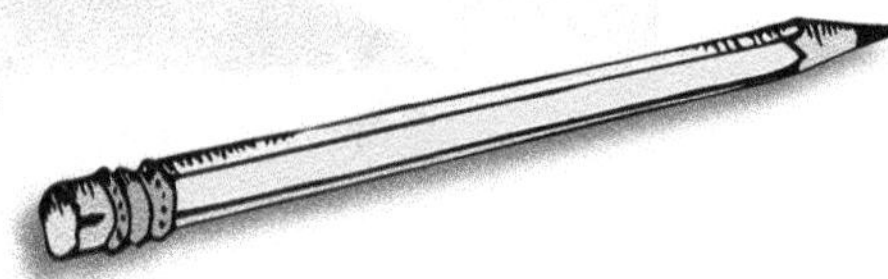

Машқи 16: Complete the conversations with question words. Then practice with a partner.

A: Бубин, вай кист?
B: Ҳа, вай донишҷӯи нав аст.
A: ______________________________
B: Ба фикрам, номаш Ардашери Доропур аст.
A: Ардашери Доропур? ______________________________
B: Ӯ аз Эрон аст.

A: Ҷон, ______________________________
B: Ман аз Амрикоям, аз Чикаго.
A: ______________________________
B: Чикаго хеле зебо аст.

A: Салом Ҷасур. ______________________
B: Ташаккур. Ман хубам. Дӯстам Мишел меҳмони ман аст
A: Мишел? Ман ӯро намешиносам ____________________.
B: Ӯ донишҷӯ аст. Ӯ аз Фаронса аст.
A: ______________________
B: Ҳа, ӯ хеле шӯх аст.

7. ТАМОШО КУНЕД!

Машқи 17: A. Watch the video and guess what the people are talking about. Tell the class what you think.

B. Watch the video one more time and check the correct answers.

1. He is from Pakistan	☐ *true*	☐ *false*
2. He is a student	☐ *true*	☐ *false*
3. He is a sportsman	☐ *true*	☐ *false*

C. Work with a partner. Create a similar dialogue and act it out.

В. МИЛЛАТҲО B. NATIONALITIES

1. СЕҲРИ СУХАН!

Машқи 1: Listen and practice.

Машқи 2: Read the names of the famous people below. Compare the names of their nationalities and their native countries.

Антонио Бандерас	испанӣ	Испания
Марта Стюарт	амрикойӣ	Амрико
Алберт Энштейн	олмонӣ	Олмон
Маҳатма Гандӣ	ҳинду	Ҳиндустон
Никол Кидман	австралиягӣ	Австралия
Исаак Нютон	англис	Англия
Арасту	юнонӣ	Юнон
Чайковский	рус	Россия

2. ГУФТУГӮ

Машқи 3: *Шумо аз куҷоед?* Practice the following dialogue.

A: Салом. Шумо хубед?
B: Салом. Ташаккур. Шумо чӣ хел?
A: Ташаккур. Ман ҳам хубам.
B: Шумо аз куҷоед?
A: Ман аз Тоҷикистон. Ман тоҷикам. Шумо чӣ?
B: Ман аз Амрико. Ман амрикоиям.

Машқи 4: Listen, fill in the blanks, and practice the following dialogue.

Ҷон: Лола, Шумо аз куҷоед?
Лола: Ман ____________________. Шумо чӣ?
Ҷон: Оилаи ман дар Амрико аст, вале мо ________________ ________________.
Лола: Аз Лондон? Ман дар Лондон будам. Он шаҳри хеле зебо аст.
Ҷон: Не, падарам ________________. Ӯ инглис аст. Модарам аз ____________________. Шумо аз кадом шаҳред?
Лола: Ман аз шаҳри Душанбе. Ин шаҳр ________________ ________ аст.
Ҷон: Душанбе шаҳри калон аст?
Лола: Не, ____________________, вале хеле зебо аст.

3. ДАСТУР

Машқи 5: Look at the chart below and try to determine how the names of nationalities are formed in Tajiki:

мамлакат	миллат
Амрико	амрикойӣ
Англия	инглис /англис
Япония	японӣ
Тоҷикистон	тоҷик
Қазоқистон	қазоқ
Туркманистон	туркман
Белгия	белгиягӣ
Ҳолландия	ҳолландӣ
Шотландия	шотландӣ
Бразилия	бразилӣ
Олмон	олмонӣ, немис

Машқи 6: Now, based on what you figured out, write the names of the nationalities for the following countries:

мамлакат	миллат
Португалия	
Ҳиндустон	
Афғонистон	
Ҳабашистон	
Муғулистон	
Канада	
Мексико	
Арманистон	
Бразилия	
Татаристон	

3.1. SUFFIX -ИСТОН

The suffix **-истон** means "land of ..." or "place of many..." It is used to form the names of many countries. If a country's name ends in a vowel the **и** of **-истон** is omitted. In order to find out the nationality of a country formed with the suffix **-истон**, just omit *it*:

Маҷористон > **маҷор,** **Курдистон** > **курд,**
Ӯйғуристон > **ӯйғур,** **Ҳиндустон** > **ҳинду**

3.2. SUFFIX -Й

The suffix **-ӣ** is very active in Tajiki. It forms abstract nouns from adjectives and adjectives from nouns:

хуб 'good > **хубӣ** 'goodness'
китоб 'book' > **китобӣ** 'written'

This suffix and its variants (**-гӣ, -вӣ**) are also used to form the name of a nationality from the country's name.

A) If a country's name ends with the vowel **-a**, add **-гӣ**:

Канада > **кандагӣ,** **Панама** > **панамагӣ,**
Мексика > **мексикагӣ**

B) If a country's name ends in **-ия** and has three or more syllables before **-я**, omit **-ия** and add **-ӣ** to form the nationality of that country:

Япония > **японӣ,** **Нидерландия** > **нидерландӣ,**
Испания > **испанӣ,** **Норвегия** > **норвегӣ**

Exceptions:
Англия > **англис/инглис** **Финландия** > **фин**

B) If a country's name has only one or two syllables before **-я**, add **-гӣ** to form the nationality of that country:
Белгия > **белгиягӣ,** **Латвия** > **латвиягӣ,**
Австрия > **австриягӣ**

D) After consonants add **-ӣ**:
Ветнам > **ветнамӣ** **Лаос** > **лаосӣ**
Чин > **чинӣ**

E) After the vowels **о, у** and **ӯ**, add **-йӣ**:
Амрико > **амрикойӣ** **Осиё** > **осиёйӣ**
Перу > **перуйӣ,** **Чорҷӯ** > **чорҷӯйӣ**

3.3 IZOFAT

Izofat is used to connect a noun to any word that modifies it except numbers, demonstratives, the superlative form of adjectives, and a few other words. It consists of **и** following the noun and is always written joined to the noun. It is never stressed; the stress remains on the last syllable of the noun.

3.3.1 ATTRIBUTIVE IZOFAT

Look at the following examples and compare them with English:

китоби нав	'a new book'
марди хуб	'a good man'
зани зебо	'a beautiful woman'
донишҷӯи хаста	'a tired student'

3.3.2 POSSESSIVE IZOFAT

Look at the following examples and compare them with English:

миллати ман	'my nationality'
дарси мо	'our lesson'
кишвари шумо	'your country'
хонаи мард	'the man's home'
китоби Парвиз	'Parviz's book'
духтари бобо	'the old man's daughter'

Машқи 7:  ***Шумо аз кучоед?*** Where are you from?

A. Survey your classmates and fill in the chart below:

Миллати Шумо чист?
Шумо аз кучоед?

НОМ	МИЛЛАТ	АЗ КУҶО
Майкл	**амрикойӣ**	**аз Техас**

B. Now summarize your survey and report your results to the class:

Майклу Кол амрикойианд.
Майкл аз Техас ва Кол аз Монтана аст...

4. ХОНИШ

Машқи 8: Read and match the questions with their answers, then practice with a partner.

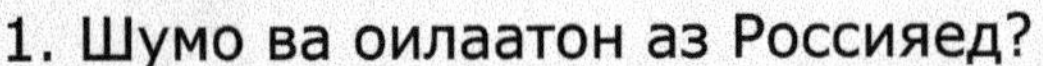

___	1. Шумо ва оилаатон аз Россияед?
___	2. Забони модарии Шумо инглисӣ аст?
___	3. Шумо олмониед?
___	4. Ҷаноби Винфрид аз Белгия аст?
___	5. Модари Шумо аз Амрикост?

a.	Не, ӯ аз Олмон аст.
b.	Не, мо аз Украинаем.
c.	Не, забони модарии ман форсист.
d.	Не, ман юнониям.
e.	Не, ӯ аз Фаронса аст.

5. ГӮШ КУНЕД

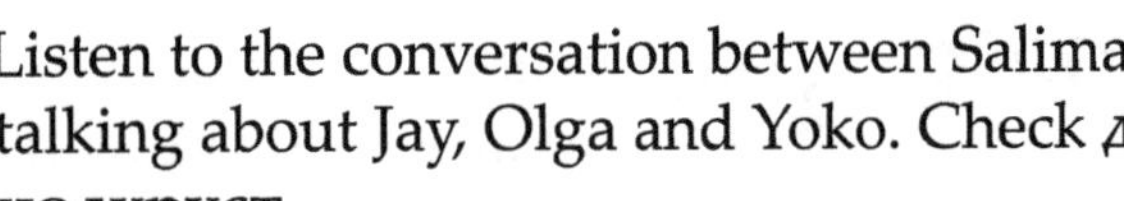

Машқи 9: Listen to the conversation between Salima and Aziz talking about Jay, Olga and Yoko. Check **дуруст** or **нодуруст**.

Н	Д	
		1. Ҷей аз Ингилистон аст.
		2. Олга аз Россия аст.
		3. Ёко аз Япония аст.

Машқи 10:  Complete the conversations, then practice with a partner.

1. **А: Салим, ту ва Баҳром аз Тоҷикистонед?**
   В: Ҳа, мо ____________.
   А: Ту аз Душанбеӣ?
   В: Не, ____________ Хуҷандам.

2. **А: Леслӣ аз Амрико аст?**
   В: Не, ______ аслан ______ Норвегия ______.
   А: Ӯ аз Осло аст?
   В: Ҳа, вале волидайнаш аслан аз Исландияанд.
   А: Забони модарии ӯ исландӣ аст?
   В: Не, ____________ инглисӣ аст.

3. **А: Ӯткир ва Юлдуз аз Қирғизистонанд?**
   В: Не, ____________ Ӯзбакистонанд.
   А: Худатон чӣ? Шумо ____________?
   В: ____________ Олмонам.
   А: Пас, ____________ Шумо олмонист?
   В: Бале, ____________ аст.

6. ХАТ

Машқи 11: *Кор бо шарик.* Write five questions like the following. Ask and answer them with a partner.

НАМУНА **Волидайни Шумо дар Амрикоянд?** Ҳа, онҳо дар Амрикоянд.
Не, онҳо дар Амрико нестанд.

НАМУНА **Шумо ва оилаатон аслан аз Осиёед?** Ҳа.
Не.

Машқи 12: ***Ин одамон аз куҷоянд?*** Where are these people from?

Student A: Guess where these people are from. Ask student B questions.
Student B: Use the map in the appendix to answer student A's questions.

A: Ҳамид Карзай аз Украина аст?
B: Не, ӯ аз Украина нест.
A: Ӯ аз Афғонистон аст?
B: Ҳа, дуруст.

Машқи 13: Find out the name, place of origin, nationality and telephone number of everyone in your class.

A. List them in the table:

НАМУНА

Ном	Шумо аз кучоед?	Рақами телефонатон чанд аст?	Миллати Шумо чист?
Карен	аз Юта	334-4763	белгиягӣ

B. Now according to what you have found, are there two people from the same state, with the same nationality, or with the same phone number? Who are they? Tell the class.

В. Муаррифӣ C. Introducing Others

1. СЕҲРИ СУХАН!

Машқи 1:  A. Listen and match the following introductions and pictures.

1
A: Ассалому алайкум, раис. Ин кас муҳосиб Ташрифзода.
B: Аз дидоратон шодам.
A: Ман ҳам аз дидори Шумо шодам.

2
A: Ин кас устод Ориёнпур. Ин кас аз Эронанд.
B: Аз дидоратон шодам. Номи ман Сӯҳроби Рустампур.
A: Ман ҳам аз дидоратон шодам.

3
A:Номи ин хонум Шаҳло. Ӯ котиба аст.
B:Салом бачаҳо.
A:Салом, аз дидоратон шодем.

4
A:Салом, лутфан шинос шавед. Ин кас Лилӣ. Ин кас аз Амрикоянд ва донишҷӯянд.
B:Салом. Номи ман Далер. Ман аз Исфараам. Аз дидоратон шодам.

B. How would you introduce the person sitting beside you? Find out his or her name and occupation. Write down what you would say to introduce him or her to the class. Then role play introducing each other to your classmate.

ном	касб

2. ГУФТУГӮ

Машқи 2: *Аз дидоратон шодам.* Listen, fill in the blanks, and practice.

Масрур: **Салом Шаҳноз, лутфан ______ шинос шав. Ин кас ҷаноби Смит аз Амрико.**
Шаҳноз: Ассалому алайкум, ҷаноби Смит. Номи ман Шаҳноз.
Ҷаноби Смит: ***______, аз дидоратон шодам.***
Шаҳноз: Ман ҳам ______ шодам. Шинос шавед, ин хонум Бақозода. Ӯ ______ аст.
Ҷаноби Смит: ***Ман Ҷеймс Смит, ______. Аз дидори Шумо низ шодам.***

Машқи 3: *Кор бо шарик.* **Маълумотномаи телефон.**
For student A. Student B: Go to the next page.

A. You are the customer. Student B is a telephone operator. Ask for the telephone numbers of these people.

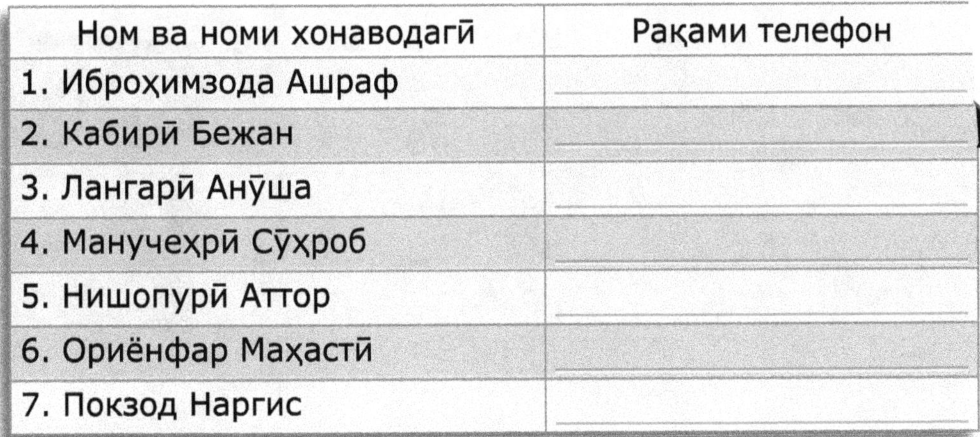

Ном ва номи хонаводагӣ	Рақами телефон
1. Иброҳимзода Ашраф	
2. Кабирӣ Бежан	
3. Лангарӣ Анӯша	
4. Манучеҳрӣ Сӯҳроб	
5. Нишопурӣ Аттор	
6. Ориёнфар Маҳастӣ	
7. Покзод Наргис	

B. Now you are the telephone operator. Student B is a customer. Answer his/her questions and tell the phone number of the people based on the chart below.

Ном ва номи хонаводагӣ	Рақами телефон
1. Рустамдухт Нилуфар	236 - 46 - 79
2. Сурушзод Ҳушёр	337 - 13 - 52
3. Тирмизӣ Ардашер	427 - 18 - 85
4. Умедниё Парвиз	524 - 14 - 78
5. Фурӯзонфар Фаршед	127 - 12 - 63
6. Ҳамадонӣ Гударз	721 - 46 - 11
7. Ҷамшеддухт Фиребо	256 - 90 - 17

НАМУНА

Телефончӣ: Хадамоти маълумоти телефон.
Муштарӣ: Салом. Ба ман рақами телефони ________ лозим аст.
Телефончӣ: Номашонро такрор кунед.
Муштарӣ: ________________
Телефончӣ: Номи хонаводагиашон чист?
Муштарӣ: ________________
Телефончӣ: Ташаккур. Рақами телефон .... аст

Машқи 3: *Кор бо шарик.* **Маълумотномаи телефон.**
For student B.

A. You are the telephone operator. Student A is a customer. Answer his/her questions based on chart below.

Ном ва номи хонаводагӣ	Рақами телефон
1. Иброҳимзода Ашраф	992 - 73 - 23
2. Кабирӣ Бежан	781 - 64 - 13
3. Лангарӣ Анӯша	532 - 46 - 81
4. Манучеҳрӣ Сӯҳроб	390 - 70 - 61
5. Нишопурӣ Аттор	469 - 52 - 24
6. Ориёнфар Маҳастӣ	864 - 32 - 47
7. Покзод Наргис	221 - 17 - 18

B. Now you are the customer. Student A is a telephone operator. Ask for the telephone numbers of these people.

Ном ва номи хонаводагӣ	Рақами телефон
1. Рустамдухт Нилуфар	________
2. Сурушзод Ҳушёр	________
3. Тирмизӣ Ардашер	________
4. Умедниё Парвиз	________
5. Фурӯзонфар Фаршед	________
6. Ҳамадонӣ Гударз	________
7. Ҷамшеддухт Фиребо	________

Телефончӣ: Хадамоти маълумоти телефон.
Муштарӣ: Салом. Ба ман рақами телефони ________ лозим аст.
Телефончӣ: Номашонро такрор кунед.
Муштарӣ: ________________
Телефончӣ: Номи хонаводагиашон чист?
Муштарӣ: ________________
НАМУНА **Телефончӣ: Ташаккур. Рақами телефон .... аст**

3. ДАСТУР

УНВОНҲО - TITLES

Personal names are rarely used in Tajik society, especially when meeting someone in public. In formal or official situations you should address a person with **ҷаноб** or **хонум**. (These titles can be followed by the person's name: **ҷаноби Салимпур**, 'Mr. Salimpur'; **хонуми Аюбӣ**, 'Mrs. Ayubi.') In unofficial situations you should use a title reflecting the other person's age and position as shown in the table below, particularly if you do not know or are not on close terms with the person.

мардона (male)	**занона** (female)	Used with:
ҷаноб - Mr.	**хонум** - Mrs., Miss, Ms.	People in an official situation
бобо - grandfather	**бибӣ** - grandmother	An old person
амак - uncle	**хола** - aunt	An older adult (middle-aged)
устод - master	**устод** - master	A professor
раис - head	**раиса** - head	A boss
ака(ако) - older brother	**апа** - older sister	An adult about your age or somewhat older
додар - younger brother	**хоҳар** - younger sister	A younger adult
писарам - my son	**духтарам** - my daughter	A child
ҷӯра - friend	**дугона** - friend	People of the same age

Машқи 4: *Кор бо гурӯҳ.* Go around the class. Practice greeting your classmates formally and informally, using the titles in the table above in an appropriate fashion.

4. ХОНИШ

Машқи 5: Read the Tajik visa below and answer the following questions in English:

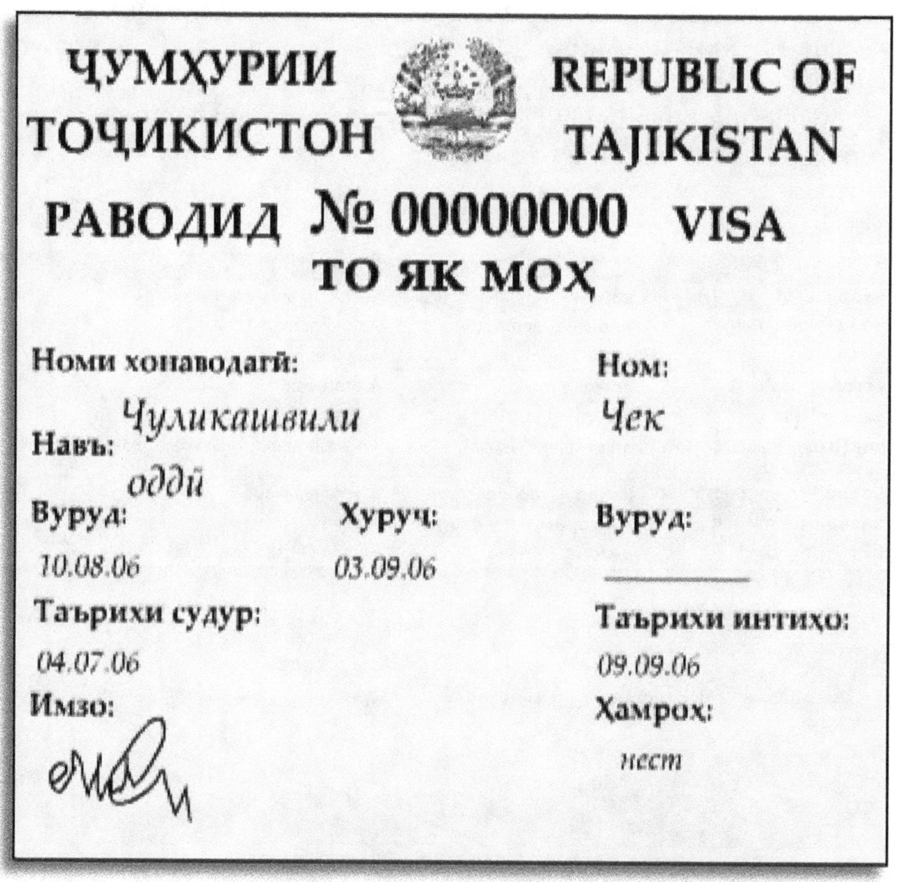

ҶУМҲУРИИ ТОҶИКИСТОН REPUBLIC OF TAJIKISTAN

РАВОДИД № 00000000 VISA

ТО ЯК МОҲ

Номи хонаводагӣ: Ҷуликашвили

Ном: Чек

Навъ: оддӣ

Вуруд: 10.08.06

Хуруҷ: 03.09.06

Вуруд: ________

Таърихи судур: 04.07.06

Таърихи интиҳо: 09.09.06

Имзо:

Ҳамроҳ: нест

1.When does his visa expire?	
2.What is the visa holder's name?	
3.What is his/her surname?	
4.When should he/she leave Tajikistan?	
5.What is the word for "surname" in Tajiki?	
6.What does "имзо" mean?	

5. ГӮШ КУНЕД

Машқи 6: *Номи Шумо чист?* Listen to the conversations and fill in the blanks.

Стюарт: Салом, ҷаноби Шаҳриёр куҷоянд?
Равшан: Он кас нестанд, Шумо кӣ?
Стюарт: Ман ________________ Стюарт.
Равшан: Мебахшед, номатонро ____________ кунед.
Стюарт: С-т-ю-а-р-т. Стюарт.
Равшан: Ташаккур.

Ҷамила: Салом, номи ман Ҷамила. Номи Шумо чист?
Мери: Номи ман Мери, ________________ Бовер.
Ҷамила: Бубахшед, ________________ ________ такрор кунед.
Мери: Б-о-в-е-р. Бовер.
Ҷамила: Ташаккур, аз дидоратон шодам.
Мери: Ман ҳам.

Машқи 7: Listen to the conversations. Complete the sentences by writing in the appropriate titles.

1. **Шароф: Ассалом, Ромиш дар ҳамин ҷо?**
Лола: Не нест. Шумо кӣ?
Шароф: Ман ______________ Шароф.

2. **Муаллим: Донишҷӯён, шинос шавед, ин кас ________ Фурӯзонфар.**
Донишҷӯён: Ассалому алайкум, ____________.
Фурӯзонфар: Ваалайкум салом, донишҷӯёни мӯҳтарам.

3. **Толиб: ______________, Рустам канӣ?**
Зан: Намедонам, ______________.

6. ХАТ

Машқи 8: Fill out the form.

Шӯъбаи корҳои дохилии ноҳияи Шоҳмансур

Варақаи қайд

Ном____________________ **Номи хонаводагӣ**__________________________
Санаи таваллуд___________________ **Ҷойи таваллуд**______________________
Нишонии ҷойи истиқомат____
индекс *шаҳр*

кӯча _____________________ **телефон**___________________
рақами хона____________________ **email** ________________________________
Нишонии истиқомати доимӣ____
индекс *кишвар*

шаҳр _______________**кӯча** ______________________ **рақами хона**________

телефон_________________**факс** ____

Имзо__________________ **Таърихи рӯз**___________________________

санаи таваллуд	*date of birth*
ҷойи таваллуд	*place of birth*
нишонии ҷойи истиқомат	*address*
индекс	*zip code*
шаҳр	*city*
варақаи қайд	*registration form*
таърихи рӯз	*date*
шӯъбаи корҳои дохилӣ	*Department of Internal Affairs (police station)*
кӯча	*street*
рақами хона	*apartment number*

7. ТАМОШО КУНЕД!

Машқи 9: A. Watch the video and fill in the blanks with everyone's names.

1. First girl on the left	
2. Second girl on the left	
3. Young man	

B. Watch the video again and write down everyone's professions.

1. Saodat	
2. Dilshod	

C. Now work in groups of three to create a dialogue based on the video. Act it out, then change roles.

VOCABULARY
ЛУҒАТНОМА

аз	*prep.* from
Аз дидоратон шодам.	*phr.* Nice/pleased to meet you.
Аз дидори Шумо шодам.	*phr.* I am pleased to meet you.
ака (ако)	*n.* older brother; term of address for a man one's age
амак	*n.* uncle; term of address for an older man
англис	*n.* English (person) (= **инглис**)
англисӣ	*adj.* English
апа	*n.* older sister; term of address for a woman one's age
аслан	*adv.* really, in fact
ба	*prep.* towards
бағочхона	*n.* luggage room
бале	*interj.* yes (= **ҳа**)
барои	*prep.* for
барои чӣ	*adv.* why? (= **чаро**)
ба куҷо	*adv.* where to? (= **канӣ**)
Ба Тоҷикистон хуш омадед.	*phr.* Welcome to Tajikistan.
бибӣ	*n.* grandmother; term of address for an old woman
бобо	*n.* grandfather; term of address for an old man
варақаи қайд	*n.* registration form
гузаред	*v.* pass by!
Гум шудаанд.	*phr.* They've gotten lost. (**гум шудан**, to get lost)
дар	*prep.* at, in
дар куҷо	*adv.* where at? (= **канӣ**)
дигар	*adj.* other
Дидӣ?	*phr.* See? (lit., You saw?)

дидор	*n.* meeting
додар	*n.* younger brother; term of address for younger man
дугона	*n.* friend (used between females)
Душанбе	*n.* Dushanbe
иёлат	*n.* state (region)
Иёлоти Мутаҳҳидаи Амрико	*n.* The United States of America
Ингилистон	*n.* England
инглис	*n.* Englishman (= **англис**)
индекс	*n.* zip code
кай	*adv.* when?
калон	*adj.* big, large
канӣ	*adv.* (coll.) where at?, where to? (= **дар куҷо, ба куҷо**)
киса	*n.* pocket
китоб	*n.* book
компютер	*n.* computer
котиб	*n.* male clerk (see **котиба**)
котиба	*n.* female clerk (see **котиб**)
куҷо	*pron.* where? (see **канӣ**)
кушоед!	*v.* open (it)!
Кӯлоб	*n.* Kulob
кӯча	*n.* street
Қӯрғонтеппа	*n.* Qurghonteppa
либос	*n.* clothes
лутфан	*adv.* please (= **марҳамат**)
марҳамат	*interj.* please (= **лутфан**)
Маҷористон	*n.* Hungary
мебахшед	*interj.* sorry
меҳмон	*n.* guest
меҳмонхона	*n.* hotel
муаррафӣ	*n.* (personal) introduction
муҳандис	*n.* engineer

муҳосиб	*n.* accountant
муштарӣ	*n.* customer
нав	*adj.* new
намуна	*n.* example, model
не	*interj.* no
немис	*adj.* German (person) (= **олмонӣ**)
немисӣ	*adj.* German (language) (= **олмонӣ**)
низ	*adv.* (liter.) too (= **ҳам**)
нишонии ҷойи истиқомат	*n.* address
номи хонаводагӣ	*n.* family name (legal term) (= **насаб**)
ноҳия	*n.* district
оила	*n.* family
олмонӣ	*adj.* German (= **немис, немисӣ**)
омадан	*v.* to come
Ором шав.	*phr.* Calm down, don't worry.
раис	*n.* head, boss, chief (male)
раиса	*n.* head, boss, chief (female)
рақами хона	*n.* apartment number
ресторан	*n.* restaurant
рус	*n.* Russian (person)
русӣ	*adj.* Russian (language)
Саломат бошед!	*interj.* You're welcome, all right
санаи таваллуд	*n.* date of birth
сафар	*n.* visit
сумка	*n.* bag (= **ҷузвдон**)
тамошо	*n.* sightseeing
тарабхона	*n.* restaurant (= **ресторан**)
ташаккур	*interj.* thank you
таърихи рӯз	*n.* date
телефончӣ	*n.* (telephone) operator
тоҷик	*n.* Tajik (person)
тоҷикӣ	*adj.* Tajiki (language)

унвон	*n.* title, term of address
устод	*n.* professor, master
фаронсавӣ	*adj.* French (nationality)
форсӣ	*n.* Farsi (Iranian Persian)
фурудгоҳ	*n.* airport
хадамот	*n.* services
хитойӣ	*adj.* Chinese (= **чинӣ**)
хола	*n.* aunt; term of address for an older woman
хонум	*n.* lady; Mrs., Ms.
хоҳар	*n.* younger sister; term of address f a younger woman
хуб	*adj.* okay
Хуҷанд	*n.* Khujand
ҳа	*interj.* yes (= **бале**)
Ҳабашистон	*n.* Abyssinia
ҳадаф	*n.* purpose
ҳам	*adv.* too (= **низ**)
ҳаст	*v.* there is/are
Ҳеҷ гап нест	*interj.* all right
Ҳеҷ қисса нест.	*phr.* There was nothing wrong, it was no big deal (lit., There's no story).
ҳозир	*adv., interj.* one moment
ҳолландӣ	*adj.* Dutch
чанд	*adj.* how much?
чандон	*adv.* so, so much, so many
чаро (чиба, чида)	*adv.* (coll.) why? (= **барои чӣ**)
чиз	*n.* thing
Чикаго	*n.* Chicago
чинӣ	*adj.* Chinese (= **хитоӣ**)
чӣ	*pron.* what?
чӣ тавр, чун	*adv.* (liter.) how? (= **чӣ хел**)
ҷаноби	*n.* mister
ҷойи таваллуд	*n.* place of birth

ҷомадон	*n.* suitcase
ҷӯра	*n.* friend (between males)
шавқовар	*adj.* interesting, fascinating
шаҳр	*n.* city
шиносоӣ	*n.* acquaintance
шод	*adj.* glad
шотландӣ	*adj.* Scottish
шудан (шав)	*v.* to become
шӯх	*adj.* mischievous, joking
шӯъбаи корҳои дохилӣ	*n.* Department of Internal Affairs (police station)

Боби **панҷум**
CHAPTER **FIVE**

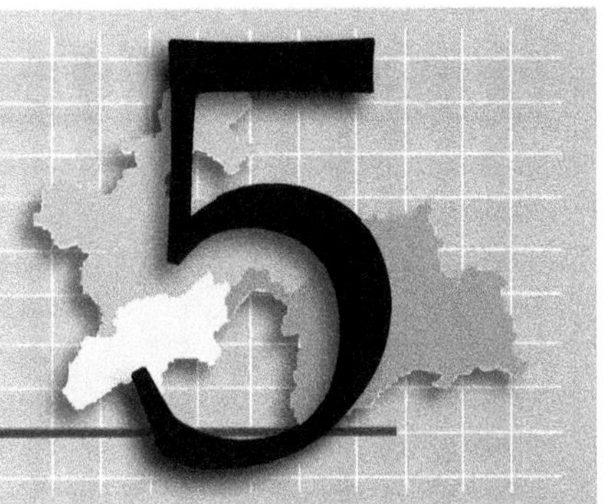

ОБУ ҲАВО
THE WEATHER

IN THIS CHAPTER

- **Ҳаво хуб аст?** Is the Weather Good?
- **Ҳаво чанд дараҷа гарм аст?** How Warm is it?
- **Соат чанд?** What Time is it?
- ***Луғатнома*** Vocabulary

А. ҲАВО ХУБ АСТ? A. IS THE WEATHER GOOD?

1. СЕҲРИ СУХАН!

Машқи 1: Look at these pictures, listen and read the dialogues:

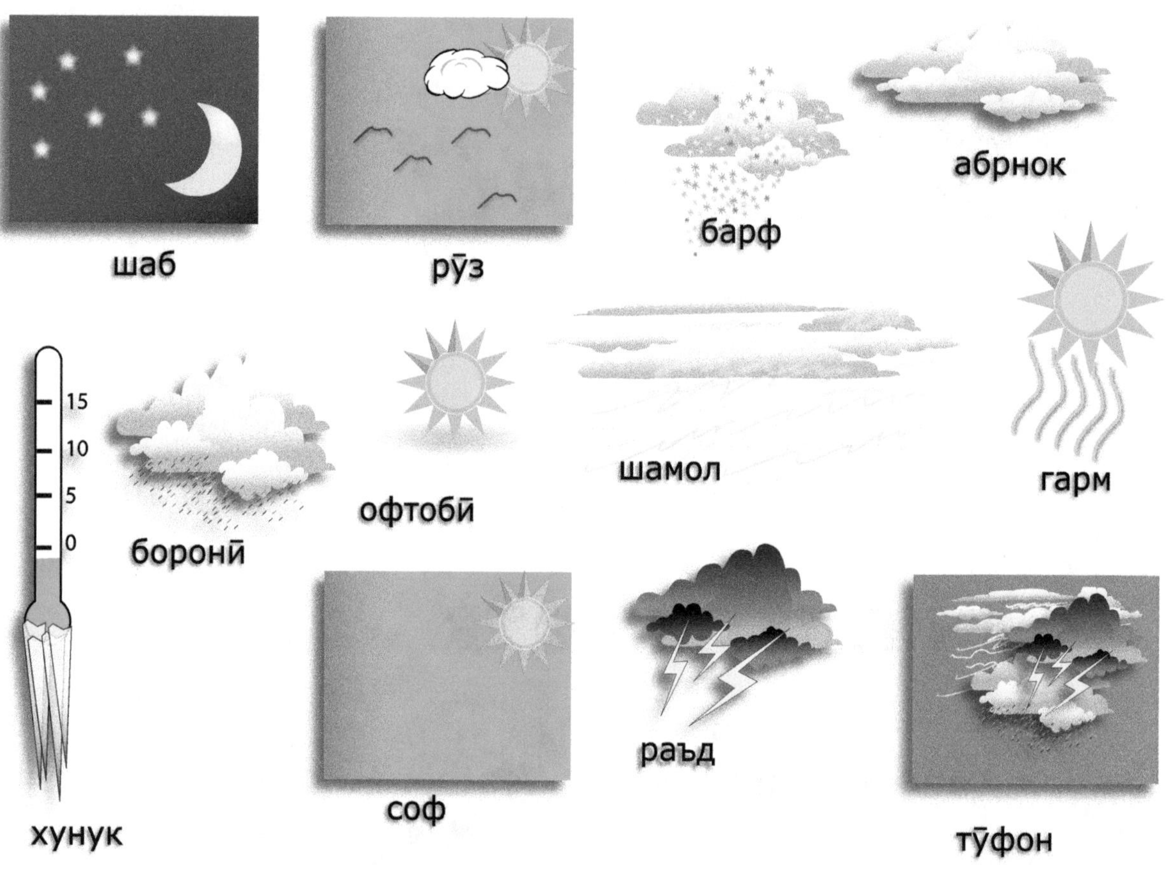

A: Ҳаво чӣ хел аст?
B: Ҳаво гарм аст.

A: Дирӯз ҳаво чӣ хел буд?
B: Дирӯз ҳаво хеле хунук буд.

Машқи 2: ***Кор бо шарик.*** Ask a partner about the weather today and yesterday. Change roles.

2. ГУФТУГӮ

Машқи 3: Listen, fill in the blanks, and practice.

Наргис: Салом Ромиш.
Ромиш: Салом Наргисҷон, __________?
Наргис: Ҳа, каме. Имрӯз ҳаво ______ __________ аст.
Ромиш: Бале. Имрӯз ҳаво хунук аст. Дирӯз ҳаво ____________ буд.
Наргис: Ба ман ҳавои хунук маъқул нест.

Компрон: Ҷаноби Шоҳпур, Шумо хубед?
Ҷаноби Шоҳпур: Раҳмат писарам, ман хубам. __________ __________ аст.
Компрон: Бале, имрӯз ҳаво _______ __________ аст.
Ҷаноби Шоҳпур: ___________ ҳаво ___________ буд.

Гуландом: Уфф, __________ дар Душанбе ҳаво гарм...
Чаман: Ҳа, дугонаҷон, __________ __________ ҳам ҳаво хеле гарм буд.
Гуландом: _______________ ман дар Истанбул будам. ________________ гарм набуд.
Чаман: Аҷойиб, __________ нақл кун, дар Истанбул боз чӣ буд?

3. ДАСТУР

3.1. Personal pronouns

3.1 PAST TENSE OF THE VERB 'TO BE'

3.1.1. AFFIRMATIVE SENTENCES

The past tense of the verb 'to be' in Tajiki is formed by adding the past tense verb endings to the past stem (**буд-**) of the verb **будан**:

Ман донишҷӯ будам	**Мо донишҷӯ будем**
Ту хаста будӣ	**Шумо хаста будед**
Ӯ бемор буд	**Онҳо бемор буданд**

3.1.2. NEGATIVE SENTENCES

The negative form of the verb 'to be' in the past is formed with the prefix **на-**, which receives the stress:

Ман донишҷӯ набудам	**Мо донишҷӯ набудем**
Ту хаста набудӣ	**Шумо хаста набудед**
Ӯ бемор набуд	**Онҳо бемор набуданд**

3.1.3. INTERROGATIVE SENTENCES

The question form of the verb 'to be' in the past is formed by intonation:

Ман гурусна будам?	'Was I hungry?'
Ту хаста будӣ?	'Were you tired?'
Ӯ бемор набуд?	'Wasn't he sick?'
Шумо хаста набудед?	'Weren't you tired?'

3.2. PAST TIME MARKERS

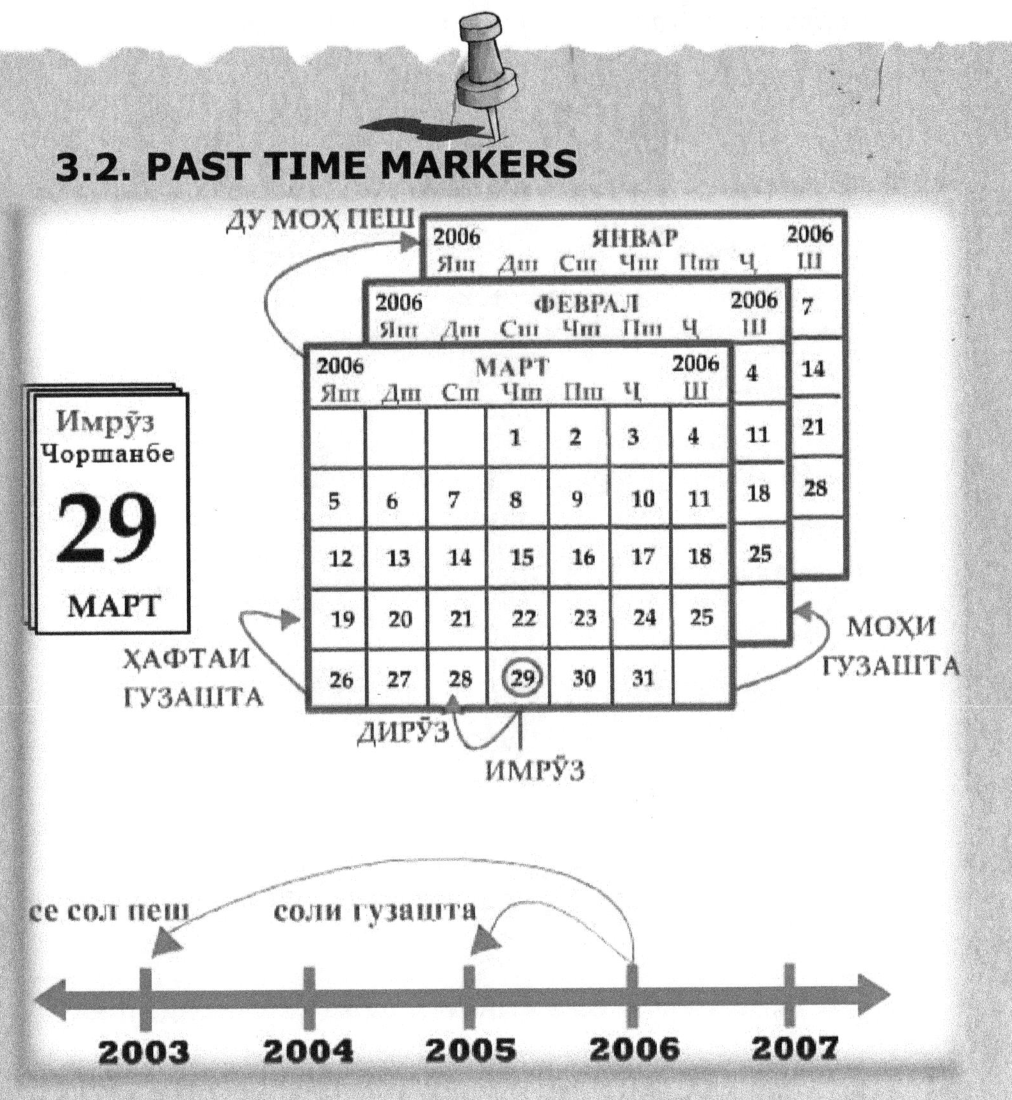

The past time markers come either right before or right after the subject.

Ду рӯз пеш ӯ хеле ғамгин буд, 'Two days ago he was very sad.'
Ӯ ду рӯз пеш хеле хафа буд, 'He was very sad two days ago.'

Basic past time markers and words for units of time include:

дирӯз (дина)	yesterday
имрӯз	today
парерӯз	the day before yesterday
ҳафта	week
моҳ	month
сол	year
рӯз	day
шаб	night
гузашта	last
пеш	ago
моҳи гузашта	last month
ду ҳафта пеш	two weeks ago

Машқи 4: *Кор бо гурӯҳ.* Ask each other about the weather in your cities and fill in the chart.

НАМУНА

А: Ҳафтаи гузашта ҳавои шаҳри Шумо абрнок буд?
В: Не.
В: Ҳафтаи гузашта ҳавои шаҳри Шумо гарм буд?
А: Ҳа

Fill in the first row of the chart below about the weather in your city.

НАМУНА

Шаҳри Шумо	ҳафтаи гузашта	парерӯз	дирӯз	имрӯз
				гарму боронӣ

Report to the class what you found out.

Машқи 5: А. ***Кор бо шарик.*** **Обу ҳавои олам.**

Student A: Look at this page. Ask your partner questions to complete the chart.

Student B: Turn to the next page and follow the instructions there.

ОБУ ҲАВОИ ОЛАМ

	дирӯз	имрӯз
Варшава	гарм/офтобӣ	гарм/абрнок
Вашингтон	хунук/боронӣ	гарм/офтобӣ
Душанбе	хунук/абрнок	хунук/боронӣ
Алмаато		
Маскав		
Париж		

1. Ҳавои Алмаато дирӯз хунук буд?
2. Имрӯз ҳавои Маскав гарм аст?

B. *Кор бо шарик.* Обу ҳавои олам.

Student B: Answer your partner's questions. Then ask your partner questions to complete the chart.

ОБУ ҲАВОИ ОЛАМ

	дирӯз	имрӯз
Варшава		
Вашингтон		
Душанбе		
Алмаато	гарм/абрнок	гарм/соф
Маскав	хунук/боронӣ	хунук/абрнок
Париж	гарм/офтобӣ	гарм/абрнок

1. Ҳавои Варшава дирӯз хунук буд?
2. Имрӯз ҳавои Душанбе чӣ хел аст?

Машқи 6: Work with a partner. Write three true and three false sentences using the words below.

хунук шамол офтобӣ гарм барфолуд боронӣ соф абрнок

1. ________________
2. ________________
3. ________________
4. ________________
5. ________________
6. ________________

Now read your sentences to your partner. Your partner should say **Дуруст** or **Нодуруст** and correct the false sentences.

НАМУНА

А: Имрӯз ҳаво гарм аст.
В: Дуруст.
А: Ҳаво дирӯз соф буд.
В: Нодуруст. Ҳаво дирӯз абрнок буд.

Машқи 7: Read the sentences in both columns. Then match each sentence in column A with the sentence in column B having the opposite meaning.

	A		B
A	Ҳавои ин маҳал хунук аст.		Дар ин шаҳр ҳаво боронӣ нест.
B	Шаҳритус ҷойи гарми Тоҷикистон аст.		Ҳавои ин шаҳр абрнок аст.
C	Дар ин маҳал дирӯз раъду барқ буд.		Ҳавои ин шаҳр барфолуд нест.
D	Дар ин шаҳр ҳаво боронӣ аст.		Дар ин ҷо шамол набуд.
E	Ҳавои ин шаҳр беабр аст.		Шаҳритус ҷойи гарми Тоҷикистон нест.
F	Ин мамлакат гарм аст.		Дар Ню-Орлеанз тӯфон бисёр набуд.
G	Ин шаҳр хунук аст.		Ҳавои ин маҳал хунук нест.
H	Ҳавои ин шаҳр барфолуд аст.		Ин мамлакат хунук аст.
I	Дар Ню-Орлеанз тӯфон бисёр буд.		Дар ин маҳал дирӯз раъду барқ набуд.
J	Дар ин ҷо шамол буд.		Ин шаҳр гарм аст.

5. ГӮШ КУНЕД

Машқи 8:  Listen and fill in the weather information in the chart below:

НОМИ ШАҲР	ДИРӮЗ	ИМРӮЗ
Истанбул		
Ню-Йорк		
Прага		
Остона		
Теҳрон		
Душанбе		

6. ХАТ

Машқи 9:  Look at the chart for the weather in the different cities of Tajikistan and complete the sentences below.

Обу ҳавои Тоҷикистон

	ҳафтаи гузашта	як моҳ пеш
Хоруғ	хунук/абрнок	хунук/беабр
Душанбе	гарм/офтобӣ	гарм/боронӣ
Қӯрғонтеппа	гарм/абрнок	гарм/офтобӣ
Хуҷанд	гарм/ боронӣ	гарм/абрнок

1. **A: Обу ҳавои Хоруғ ҳафтаи гузашта чӣ хел буд?**
   B: Он хунук ва абрнок буд.
   A: Як моҳ пеш чӣ?
   B: Як моҳ пеш он __________-у ______ ______.

2. **A: Ҳавои Душанбе ҳафтаи гузашта хунук буд?**
   B: Не, ҳафтаи гузашта ҳавои Душанбе __________-у ________ буд.
   A: Як моҳ пеш чӣ?
   B: Як моҳ пеш ҳавои Душанбе __________-у __________ буд.

3. **A:Ҳавои Қӯрғонтеппа ҳафтаи гузашта абрнок буд?**
   B: Бале, он ______________ ва _____________.

4. **A: Моҳи гузашта ҳавои Хуҷанд хунук буд?**
   B: Не, он ____________-у ______________.

Б. ҲАВО ЧАНД ДАРАҶА ГАРМ АСТ? B. HOW WARM IS IT?

1. СЕҲРИ СУХАН!

Машқи 1: Listen and practice.

11 ёздаҳ
12 дувоздаҳ
13 сездаҳ
14 чордаҳ
15 понздаҳ
16 шонздаҳ
17 ҳабдаҳ
18 ҳаждаҳ
19 нуздаҳ
20 бист
21 бисту як
22 бисту ду
23 бисту се
24 бисту чор
25 бисту панҷ
26 бисту шаш
27 бисту ҳафт
28 бисту ҳашт
29 бисту нӯҳ
30 сӣ
40 чил (чиҳил)
50 панҷоҳ
60 шаст
70 ҳафтод
80 ҳаштод
90 навад
100 сад
101 яксаду як
199 яксаду наваду нӯҳ
224 дусаду бисту чор
999 нӯҳсаду наваду нӯҳ
1000 ҳазор
1357 як ҳазору сесаду панҷоҳу ҳафт
2006 ду ҳазору шаш
10000 даҳ ҳазор

Машқи 2:  Lola and Daler are making a list of the telephone numbers of their classmates. Listen and complete the chart:

НОМУ НАСАБ	РАҚАМИ ТЕЛЕФОН
Абдуррауф Муродӣ	63-64-78
Ҳумоюни Шаҳриёр	
Мирзои Салимпур	
Сурайё Латифӣ	
Парвинаи Акрамдухт	
Нодираи Хуршед	
Баҳманёри Қиёмпур	
Салими Аюбзод	
Манижаи Давлат	
Маҳина Каримзода	
Музаффар Раҳимӣ	
Латофат Халилӣ	

Машқи 3: *Кор бо шарик.* With another student, ask each other your ages and the years you were born.

А: Тимотӣ, ту чандсолай?
Б: Ман бистусесолаам.

2. ГУФТУГӮ

Машқи 4: *Саёҳати Дилшод.* Listen, fill in the blanks, and practice. With a partner, make your own dialogue and practice it.

Анора: Дилшод, ту чанд рӯз дар Париж ________________?
Дилшод: ________________. Ман дар Рим ҳам будам.
Анора: Дар Рим чанд рӯз будӣ?
Дилшод: Дар он ҷо ________________. Соли гузашта ман дар Рим ________________ будам.
Анора: Ӯҳӯ, чӣ қадар хуб!

3. ДАСТУР

3.1. COMPLEX NUMBERS (11-19)

The numbers from 11 to 19 are complex numbers. They are written as one word and you will need to memorize them.

11	ёздаҳ
12	дувоздаҳ
13	сездаҳ
14	чордаҳ
15	понздаҳ
16	шонздаҳ
17	ҳабдаҳ
18	ҳаждаҳ
19	нуздаҳ

Note: The ҳ in all complex numbers is omitted in colloquial speech, thus **сездаҳ** is pronounced as **сенза, понздаҳ** as **понза**, and **шонздаҳ** as **шонза**.

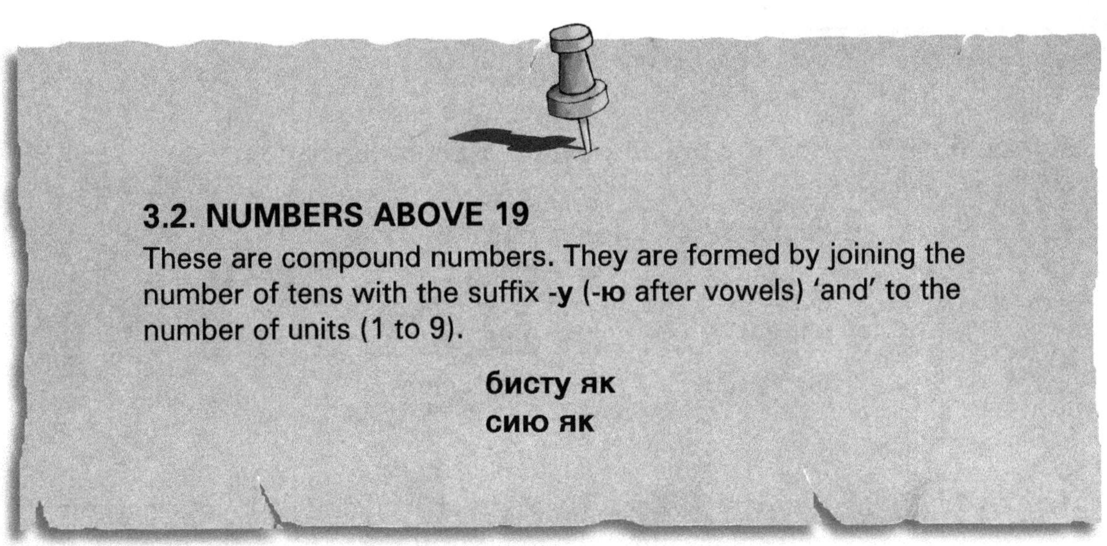

3.2. NUMBERS ABOVE 19

These are compound numbers. They are formed by joining the number of tens with the suffix **-у** (**-ю** after vowels) 'and' to the number of units (1 to 9).

бисту як
сию як

4. *ХОНИШ*

Машқи 5: ***Кор бо шарик.*** Read the following numbers to your friend and check his/her writing. Then switch roles.

Student A	
33	541
98	2589
189	3697
469	9874

Student B	
77	5478
458	2226
1269	1236
234	9874

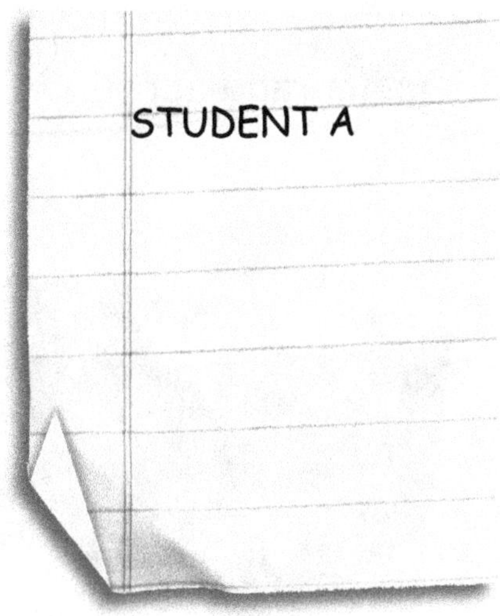

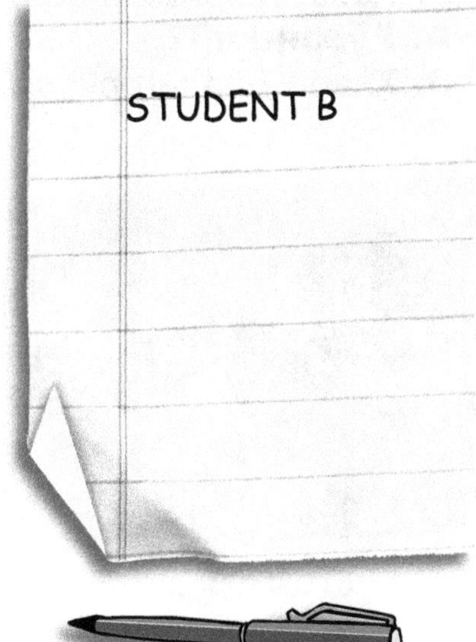

5. ГӮШ КУНЕД

Машқи 6: Listen and practice. Notice the pronunciation.

ёздаҳ	сию чор
дувоздаҳ	бисту ҳафт
чордаҳ	ҳафтоду ду
бисту ҳашт	ҳаштоду ҳашт

Машқи 7: Student A. Looking at the chart below, ask your partner questions about the temperatures to fill in the gaps. Student B. Look at the next page and follow the instructions there.

ШАҲРҲО	ШАБОНА	РӮЗОНА
Остона	-12	-3
Маскав	-8	+2
Париж	+4	+18
Душанбе		
Берлин		
Тошканд		

А: Ҳавои Берлин шабона чанд дараҷа гарм аст?
В: Ҳавои Берлин шабона 11 дараҷа гарм аст.
А: Рӯзона чӣ?
В: Ҳавои Берлин рӯзона 23 дараҷа гарм аст

НАМУНА

Student B. Looking at the chart below, ask your partner questions about the temperatures to fill in the gaps.

ШАҲРҲО	ШАБОНА	РӮЗОНА
Остона	______	______
Маскав	______	______
Париж	______	______
Душанбе	+5	+21
Берлин	+11	+23
Тошканд	+3	+19

B: Ҳавои Остона шабона чанд дараҷа гарм аст?
A: Ҳавои Остона шабона 12 дараҷа хунук аст.
B: Рӯзона чӣ?
A: Ҳавои Берлин рӯзона 3 дараҷа хунук аст.

6. *ХАТ*

Машқи 8: ***Кор бо шарик.*** How old are the people on this picture? Write down your guesses and then compare.

A: Ин зан чандсола аст?
B: Ба гумонам, ӯ сиюпанҷсола аст.
C: Ба фикрам, ӯ чилсола аст.

Машқи 9: Write and practice.

A. Look at the numbers below and fill in the blanks where necessary.

20	бист
21	бисту як
22	бисту ду
23	
24	бисту чор
25	бисту панҷ
26	
27	бисту ҳафт
28	
29	бисту нӯҳ
30	сӣ
34	
40	чил

48	
50	панҷоҳ
53	
60	шаст
65	
70	ҳафтод
76	
80	ҳаштод
87	
90	навад
99	
100	сад
1000	ҳазор

B. Now write the numbers under the corresponding words and vice versa.

нуздаҳ
шасту шаш
чилу нӯҳ
87
71
64
53
565

сездаҳ
ҳаштоду ду
сию ҳашт
34
57
11
26
як ҳазору дусаду бист

бисту панҷ
панҷоҳу ҳашт
дувоздаҳ
100
37
49
82
3547

C. Solve the following math problems and write out your answers in Tajiki.

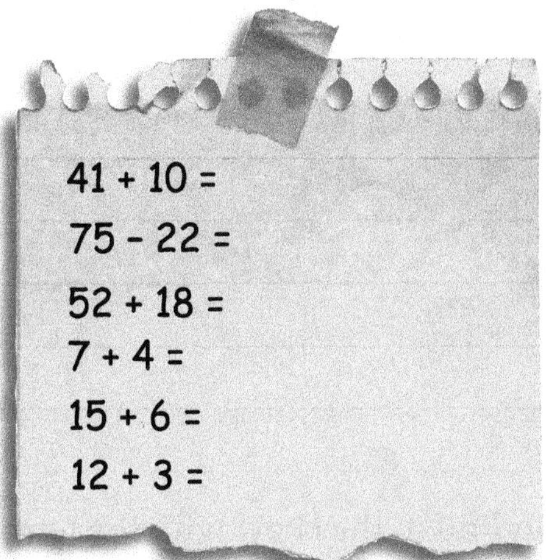

41 + 10 =
75 - 22 =
52 + 18 =
7 + 4 =
15 + 6 =
12 + 3 =

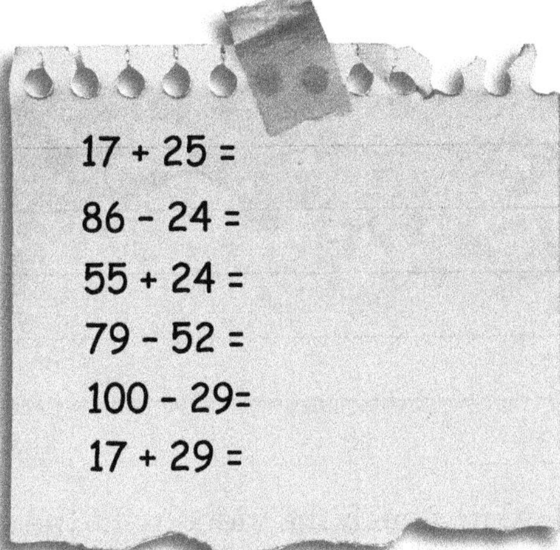

17 + 25 =
86 - 24 =
55 + 24 =
79 - 52 =
100 - 29=
17 + 29 =

7. ТАМОШО КУНЕД

Машқи 10: A. Watch the video with the sound off and write the names of provinces and cities you see.

1.	
2.	
3.	
4.	
5.	
6.	

B. Now watch the video with the sound on and fill in the chart with the temperatures.

	ШАҲР/ВИЛОЯТ	ШАБОНА	РӮЗОНА
1.	Ғарби вилояти Бадахшони кӯҳӣ		
2.	Шарқи вилояти Бадахшони кӯҳӣ		
3.	Хатлон		
4.	Суғд		
5.	Ноҳияҳои тобеи марказ		
6.	Душанбе		

C. Now create a weather report for your city. Read your report to your partner, who should fill in the second row with your information. Then switch roles.

	ШАҲР/ВИЛОЯТ	ШАБОНА	РӮЗОНА
You			
Your partner			

В. СОАТ ЧАНД? C. WHAT TIME IS IT?

1. СЕҲРИ СУХАН!

Машқи 1: Using the examples below, figure out how to tell the time and fill in the blanks.

Соат ҳашт

Соат ________

____

Соат даҳу панҷ дақиқа

Соат яку бисту панҷ дақиқа

Соат ________

Соат ҳашту ним

Соат даҳ-та кам ҳафт

Соат ________
кам ________

Машқи 2: Work with a partner. While one of you reads the time, the other should write what is said without looking at the book. Afterwards check your answers and switch roles.

Student A	Answers
2:20	
3:45	
1:10	
12:05	
4:55	

Student B	Answers
5:25	
7:50	
12:35	
10:40	
3:05	

2. ГУФТУГӮ

Машқи 3: Listen and practice. Then make your own dialogue with a partner practicing how to tell the time.

Далер: **Салом Ҷамшед.**
Ҷамшед: Салом Далерҷон. Мебахшӣ, соат чанд?
Далер: ______________________.
Ҷамшед: Соати ман нодуруст аст. Соати ман __________.
Далер: _______ **атро дуруст кун!**
Ҷамшед: Ҳа, албатта.

3. ДАСТУР

3.1. ORDINAL NUMBERS

Look at the examples below and figure out how ordinal numbers are formed in Tajiki:

як	якум	first
ду	дуюм	second
се	сеюм	third
сӣ	сиюм	thirtieth
панҷ	панҷум	fifth
сад	садум	hundredth
чордаҳ	чордаҳум	fourteenth
бисту ҳафт	бисту ҳафтум	twenty-seventh

Note:

1. Only three numbers in Tajiki end with a vowel: **ду, се,** and **сӣ**. The ordinal forms of these numbers are formed by adding the suffix **-юм.**
   дуюм 'second'
   сеюм 'third'
   сиюм 'thirtieth'
2. In the literary language the ordinal forms of these three numbers can be formed differently:
   дуввум 'second'
   севум 'third'
   сивум 'thirtieth'
3. In Tajiki some Arabic ordinal numbers are also widely used. They are:
   аввал 'first'
   сонӣ 'second'

3.2. DAYS OF THE WEEK

In Tajiki the names for the days of the week from Sunday to Thursday are formed from the numbers one to five and the word **шанбе** 'Saturday' (indicating "first day after Saturday," etc.). Friday, the day of public prayer in Islam, is **ҷумъа**, Arabic for "(day of) gathering." The Tajiki word for Friday is **одина**:

якшанбе	Sunday
душанбе	Monday
сешанбе	Tuesday
чоршанбе	Wednesday
панҷшанбе	Thursday
ҷумъа	Friday
шанбе	Saturday

Note: In Tajiki the days of the week are not capitalized.

4. ХОНИШ

Машқи 4: Hangman game

A. One student reads the clues to the class. The clues spell a word. The class listens and guesses the word.

1. Дар ин калима 5 ҳарф ҳаст.
2. Ҳарфи якум к аст.
3. Ҳарфи охирин б аст.
Калима чист?

4. Ҳарфи и баъди ҳарфи к аст.
Калима чист?
5. Ҳарфи о пеш аз ҳарфи б аст.
Калима чист?

Калима ____________________ аст.

B. Write your own Hangman game. Read it to your class.

5. ГӮШ КУНЕД

Машқи 5: Listen to the CD and write down the times you hear.

____

____

____

____

6. ХАТ

Машқи 6: Student A. Look at the weather forecast for Dushanbe. Ask your partner questions to fill in the blanks. (Source: www.zamon.tj).

Маълумот дар бораи обу ҳаво

Имрӯз чоршанбе, 21-уми сентябр

Душанбе	душанбе 19•09•2005		сешанбе 20•09•2005		чоршанбе 21•09•2005		панҷшанбе 22•09•2005	
	Рӯз	Шаб	Рӯз	Шаб	Рӯз	Шаб	Рӯз	Шаб
Ҳарорати ҳаво °C	31		+32		+32		+32	
Вазъи ҳаво								
Фишор мм. чадвали симоб	695		695		695			
Намнокӣ %	16		14		10		13	
Тулӯъи офтоб соат: дақиқа			**06:10**		**06:11**			
Ғуруби офтоб соат: дақиқа			**18:25**		**18:24**			
Дарозии рӯз соат: дақиқа			**12:15**		**12:12**			
Тулӯъи моҳтоб соат: дақиқа			**19:39**		**20:08**			
Ғуруби моҳтоб соат: дақиқа			**08:34**		**09:46**			

тулӯъи офтоб 'sunrise'
ғуруби офтоб 'sunset'
фишор 'pressure'
моҳтоб 'the moon'
симоб 'mercury, quicksilver'

A: Фишори ҳаво шаби душанбе чанд буд?
B: Фишори ҳаво 693 буд.

Student B. Look at the weather forecast for Dushanbe. Ask your partner questions to fill in the blanks. (Source: www.zamon.tj)

Маълумот дар бораи обу ҳаво

Имрӯз чоршанбе, 21-уми сентябр

Душанбе	душанбе 19•09•2005		сешанбе 20•09•2005		чоршанбе 21•09•2005		панҷшанбе 22•09•2005	
	Рӯз	Шаб	Рӯз	Шаб	Рӯз	Шаб	Рӯз	Шаб
Ҳарорати ҳаво °C		+18		+17		+17		+18
Вазъи ҳаво								
Фишор мм. чадвали симоб		693		693		693		694
Намнокӣ %		45		34		29		27
Тулӯъи офтоб соат: дақиқа	06:10						06:12	
Ғуруби офтоб соат: дақиқа	18:27						18:22	
Дарозии рӯз соат: дақиқа	12:17						12:10	
Тулӯъи моҳтоб соат: дақиқа	19:12						20:42	
Ғуруби моҳтоб соат: дақиқа	07:22						10:57	

тулӯъи офтоб 'sunrise'
ғуруби офтоб 'sunset'
фишор 'pressure'
моҳтоб 'the moon'
симоб 'mercury, quicksilver'

B: Фишори ҳаво рӯзи душанбе чанд буд?
A: Фишори ҳаво 695 буд.

7. ТАМОШО КУНЕД

Машқи 7: A. Watch the video with the sound off and describe the weather on the video.

B. Watch the video with the sound on and fill in the blanks.

A: Салом ____________ хубед?
B: Салом, ҳа, ______ хубам. Имрӯз ҳаво хеле ________ аст.
A: Ҳа, имрӯз ҳаво ______________ аст.
Дирӯз ҳам хеле _____________ буд.
B: Дирӯз ҳаво ____________ ва _____________ буд.
Имрӯз ҳаво ____________ аст.

Барги сабз

Дар байни мардуми тоҷик оид ба рӯзҳои ҳафта фикру ақидаҳои гуногун мавҷуд аст. Баъзеи ин ақидаҳо ба анъанаҳои таърихӣ, баъзеяшон ба дину хурофот марбутанд. Масалан: азбаски рӯзи якшанбе рӯзи истироҳат аст ва мардум одатан дар ин рӯз ба бозорҳо барои харидкунӣ мераванд, аксар вақт ин рӯзро "рӯзи бозор" мегӯянд. Ба ақидаи мардум рӯзҳои душанбе, чоршанбе, ҷумъа ва якшанбе либос шустан хуб аст. Вале рӯзҳои сешанбе, панҷшанбе ва шанбе либос намешӯянд. Рӯзи чоршанбе ба аёдати шахси бемор намераванд. Вале рӯзи чоршанбе ва шанбе мувофиқи анъана волидайни писар ба хонаи духтардор ба хостгорӣ мераванд. Азбаски рӯзи ҷумъа рӯзи намози умум дар масҷид аст, одатан дар ин рӯз шустани сарутан, гирифтани нохунҳо ва шустани бадан хуб аст. Ниҳоят рӯзҳои панҷшанбе ва якшанбе пухтани таоми машҳури тоҷикӣ "оши палав" савоб дониста мешавад.

Одина, ки номи аслии рӯзи ҷумъа аст, ҳоло чун номи одамон боқӣ мондааст: гоҳо кӯдаконеро, ки дар ин рӯз таваллуд мешаванд, Одина ном мегузоранд. Номи Ҷумъа (Ҷумъабой, Ҷумъагул) низ маъмул аст. Дар Бадахшон номҳои Душанбе ва Чоршанбе ҳам вомехӯранд.

VOCABULARY
ЛУҒАТНОМА

абрнок	*adj.* cloudy
аввал	*adj.* first
аёдат	*n.* visit
азбаски	*conj.* because, since
аксар вақт	*adv.* most of the time
ақида	*n.* opinion
албатта	*adv.* certainly, of course
Алмаато	*n.* Almaty (Alma-Ata, former capital of Kazakhstan)
анъана	*n.* tradition
аҷоиб	*adj.* interesting
банда	*n.* slave
барфӣ	*adj.* snowy
баъзе	*adj.* some, several (precedes noun)
беабр	*adj.* cloudless
бисёр	*adj, adv.* much, a lot
бист	*num.* twenty
Борон меборад.	*phr.* It's raining.
боронӣ	*adv.* rainy
вазъ	*n.* condition
гарм	*adj.* hot
гузашта	*adj.* past, last (week, etc.)
гуногун	*adj.* various, different kinds
ғуруби офтоб	*n.* sunset
дақиқа (дақоиқ)	*n.* minute (of time)
дарозӣ	*n.* length
дин	*n.* religion
дирӯз (дина)	*adv., n.* yesterday
Ду ҳафта пеш.	*adv.* Two weeks ago.
дувоздаҳ	*num.* twelve
душанбе	*n.* Monday
ёздаҳ	*num.* eleven
имрӯз	*adv., n.* today

ин қадар	*adv.* so, such, to this extent
Истанбул	*n.* Istanbul
истироҳат	*n.* rest; holiday
калима	*n.* word
камабр	*adj.* partly cloudy
каме	*adv.* a little
мавҷуд	*n.* existence
мамлакат	*n.* nation
марбут	*adj.* related (to)
мардум	*n.* people
марказ	*n.* center
Маскав	*n.* Moscow
масҷид	*n.* mosque
маҳал	*n.* place (= **ҷо**)
машҳур	*adj.* famous
маъқул	*adj.* interesting (**ба ман маъқул аст**, I like...)
маълумот	*n.* information
моҳ	*n.* month; moon
моҳи гузашта	*adv., n.* last month
моҳтоб	*n.* the moon
мувофиқ	*adj.* appropriate
навад	*num.* ninety
нақл кун	*v.* describe!, tell!
намнокӣ	*n.* humidity
намоз	*n.* Muslim prayer offered five times a day
ним	*n.* a half
ниҳоят	*adv.* finally; *n.* end
нохун	*n.* fingernail, nail, claw
нуздаҳ	*num.* nineteen
Ню-Орлеанз	*n.* New Orleans
одатан	*adv.* usually
оид ба	*prep.* about, concerning
Остона	*n.* Astana (capital of Kazakhstan)
офтобӣ	*adv.* sunny

охирин	*adj.* final, the last
оши палав	*n.* pilaf
панҷа	*n.* the five fingers, hand, paw
панҷоҳ	*num.* fifty
панҷшанбе	*n.* Thursday
парерӯз	*adv., n.* the day before yesterday
пеш	*adv.* ago
пойтахт	*n.* capital
понздаҳ	*num.* fifteen
Прага	*n.* Prague
пухтан (паз)	*v.* to cook
раъд	*n.* thunder
рӯз	*n.* day
рӯзона	*adj.* daytime, daily
савоб	*n.* alms-giving, charity
сад	*num.* hundred
сарутан	*n.* clothing
сездаҳ	*num.* thirteen
сентябр	*n.* September
сешанбе	*n.* Tuesday
симоб	*n.* mercury, quicksilver
симобӣ	*adj.* of mercury
сӣ	*num.* thirty
соат	*n.* hour; clock
сол	*n.* year
сонӣ	*adj.* second (after first)
соф	*adj.* clean
таом	*n.* food, a meal
таърихӣ	*adj.* historical
Теҳрон	*n.* Tehran
тулӯъи офтоб	*n.* sunrise
тӯфон	*n.* storm
умум	*n.* the public, the people
фишор	*n.* pressure
хаста	*adj.* tired
хостгорӣ	*n.* matchmaking

хунук	*adj.* cold
хурофот	*n.* superstitious beliefs
ҳабдаҳ	*num.* seventeen
ҳаво	*n.* weather (= **обу ҳаво**)
ҳаждаҳ	*num.* eighteen
ҳазор	*num.* thousand
ҳарорат	*n.* temperature
ҳарф (ҳуруф)	*n.* letter (of alphabet)
ҳафта	*n.* week
ҳафтаина	*adj.* weekly
ҳафтод	*num.* seventy
ҳаштод	*num.* eighty
чандсола	*adj.* how old?
чил (чиҳил)	*num.* forty
чӣ қадар	*adv.* how much?, how many?
чордаҳ	*num.* fourteen
чоршанбе	*n.* Wednesday
ҷасур	*adj.* brave, excellent
ҷаҳон	*n.* world
ҷумъа	*n.* Friday
шаб	*n.* night
шабона	*adj.* at night, nightly
шамол	*n.* wind
шанбе	*n.* Saturday
шаст	*num.* sixty
Шаҳритус	*n.* city in southern Tajikistan (often pronounced **Шаҳртус**)
шонздаҳ	*num.* sixteen
шунидан (шунав)	*v.* to hear, listen
шустан (шӯ, шӯй)	*v.* to wash
якшанбе	*n.* Sunday

Боби шашум
CHAPTER SIX

ХОНАДОН
FAMILY

IN THIS CHAPTER

- **Оилаи тоҷикӣ** The Tajik Family
- **Дар хонадони ҳамсар** At the In-Laws'
- **ӯро тасвир кунед** Describe Him
- ***Л*уғатнома** Vocabulary

А. ОИЛАИ ТОҶИКӢ A. THE TAJIK FAMILY

1. СЕҲРИ СУХАН!

Машқи 1: Listen and practice.

падар

модар

фарзанд

бибӣ

ако

апа

писар

хоҳар
(ука)

бобо

шавҳар

домод

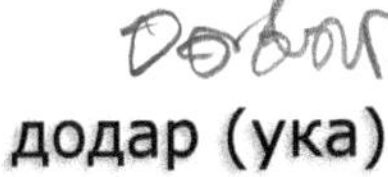

додар (ука)

зан

арӯс
(келин)

Машқи 2: ***Шаҷараи авлодӣ.***

A. Choose several people from the family tree below and write kinship terms which you think can apply to them:

НАМУНА

Бахтиёр: фарзанд, писар, падар, шавҳар

1. Ном		Хешӣ	
2. Ном		Хешӣ	
3. Ном		Хешӣ	

Хешӣ- kinship, relationship

B. Now look again at the family tree above and fill in the blanks:

1. Бахтиёр ______________ Парвина аст.
2. Зулфия ______________ Одил аст.
3. Одил ______________ Зевар аст.
4. Парвина ______________ Нӯъмон аст.
5. Бахтиёр ______________ Фарҳунда аст.
6. Рустам ______________ Нӯъмон аст.
7. Парвина ______________ Зулфия аст.
8. Рустам ______________ Одил аст.
9. Зевар ______________ Одил аст.
10. Бахтиёр ______________ Нӯъмон аст.

C. ***Кор бо шарик.*** Work with a partner. Ask each other questions about the members of the family above.

2. ГУФТУГӮ

Машқи 3: ***Ту чанд бародару хоҳар дорӣ?*** A. Listen and fill in the blanks. Then practice with a partner.

Шаҳло: Сафинаҷон, ту чанд бародару хоҳар дорӣ?
Сафина: Ман як ______________ ва ду __________ дорам.
Шаҳло: Номи онҳо чист?
Сафина: Шаҳриёр, Парвина ва Заррина.
Шаҳло: Бародарат чандсола аст?
Сафина: Бародарам 25-сола аст ва ӯ ________________ дорад.
Шаҳло: Хоҳаронат чӣ?
Сафина: Парвина 18-сола ва Заррина 12-сола.
Шаҳло: Парвина донишҷӯ аст?
Сафина: Ҳа, ӯ донишҷӯи соли ____________ аст.
Шаҳло: Хеле хуб. Шумо расми ____________й доред?
Сафина: Албатта, мо расмҳои гуногун дорем. Аммо ман ҳоло дар даст ягон расм надорам.
Шаҳло: Афсӯс, дугонаҷон.

b. Listen to the rest of the conversation and answer the following questions:

How many people are in Shahlo's family?
How many brothers does she have?
How many sisters does she have?
What do her sisters do?
What her brothers do?

1.
2.
3.
4.
5.

Машқи 4: ***Кор бо шарик.*** Draw your own family tree, then with your partner ask and answer questions about each other's families.

A: Ин кас кӣ?
B: Ин кас падари мананд.
A: Падарат чандсолаанд?
B: Падарам 54-солаанд.
A: Он кас аз куҷоянд?
B: Он кас аслан аз Хуҷанданд, вале ҳоло дар Душанбеанд.

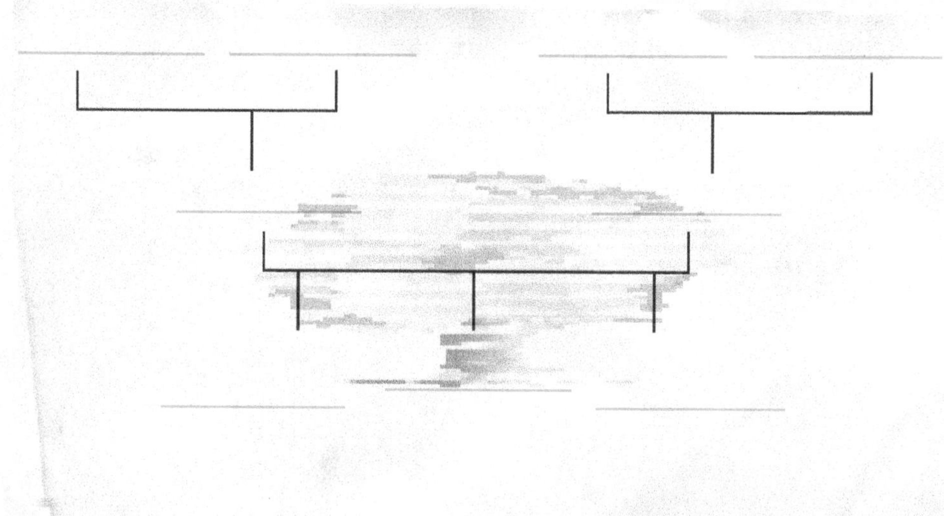

3. ДАСТУР

Феъли доштан

The verb **доштан** means 'to have.' Its present tense is formed as follows:

ман дорам,	'I have'	**мо дорем,** 'we have'
ту дорӣ,	'you have'	**шумо доред,** 'you have'
ӯ дорад,	'he/she/it has'	**онҳо доранд,** 'they have'

4. ХОНИШ

Машқи 5: A. Read about Salim's family and draw his family tree.

Ман падару модар, як бародар ва ду хоҳар, ду бобо, ду бибӣ, се хола, чор тағо, ду амак ва як амма дорам. Мо аз хурдӣ падарамонро "дада" ва модарамонро "оча" мегӯем. Номи бародарам Сиёвуш аст. Номи хоҳаронам Мадина ва Малика аст. Модарам се хоҳар ва чор бародар дорад. Падари модарам падаркалон ва модари модарам модаркалони мананд.
Мо онҳоро "бобо' ва "бибӣ" мегӯем.

Падарам ду бародар ва як хоҳар дорад. Падару модари падарам ҳам падаркалон ва модаркалони мананд. Мо онҳоро ҳам "бобо" ва "бибӣ" мегӯем.

Бародарони падарам амакҳои мананд. Фарзандони онҳо амакбачаҳои мананд. Хоҳари падарам аммаи ман аст. Фарзандони аммаам аммабачаҳои мананд.

Хоҳари модарам холаи ман аст. Фарзандони холаам холабачаҳои мананд. Бародари модарам тағои ман аст. Фарзандони тағоям тағобачаҳои мананд.

Бародари калонии ман оиладор аст. Ҳамсари ӯ - Наҷиба янгаи ман аст. Фарзанди ӯ бародарзодаи ман аст. Хоҳарам Мадина низ оиладор аст. Шавҳари ӯ язнаи ман аст. Фарзандони хоҳарам хоҳарзодаҳои мананд. Мо бародарзода ва хоҳарзодаҳои худро "ҷиян" мегӯем.

мегӯем - *we say, call*

B. Complete the sentences.

1. Сиёвуш ______________________ Салим аст.
2. Малика ______________________ Мадина аст.
3. Бобои Салим ______________________ падараш аст.
4. Бибии Салим ______________________ модараш аст.
5. Бародари модараш ______________________ Салим аст.
6. Хоҳари падараш ______________________ Малика аст.
7. Бародари падараш ______________________ Мадина аст.
8. Фарзанди аммаи Салим ______________________ ӯ аст.
9. Фарзанди холаи Мадина ______________________ ӯ аст.
10. Фарзанди Мадина ______________________ Салим аст.

Машқи 6: ***Оилаи Шоҳрух.*** Shohrukh's family

A. Listen about Shohrukh's family. Write the names in the correct place.

B. Now read the text and check your answers.

Ин сурати оилаи Шоҳрух аст. Шоҳрух барномасоз аст. Шоҳрух зан ва ду фарзанд дорад. Номи зани ӯ Зарнигор аст. Ӯ муаллима аст. Ӯ зани меҳрубону доно аст. Ӯ 46-сола аст. Номи духтараш Заррина аст ва ӯ муҳандис аст. Ӯ 22-сола аст. Заррина арӯси зебост. Шавҳари Заррина дар ин расм нест. Номи писари Шоҳрух Кова аст. Кова 24 - сола аст. Ӯ пизишк аст. Кова муҷаррад аст. Ӯ зан надорад.

C. Ask and answer questions about Shohrukh's family.

Зарнигор кист?

Ӯ зани Шоҳрух аст.

5. ГӮШ КУНЕД

Машқи 7: Listen and write.

A. Listen to the CD and fill in the chart below. How many siblings do they have?

	АКА	ХОҲАР	УКО	АПА
Салима	1	2	1	0
Михаел				
Наташа				
Ноҳида				
Соҷида				
Далер				

B. Listen again and choose the correct answers.

1. **Салима ______ дорад.**

a. хоҳар b. холабача c. бародар d. амакбача

2. **Михаел ______ надорад.**

a. бародар b. хоҳар c. холабача d. зан

3. **Наташа ______ Максим аст.**

a. духтари b. апаи c. хоҳари d. модари

4. **Оилаи дӯсти Соҷида ______ аст.**

a. калон b. хурд c. миёна d. майда

5. **Далер фарзанди ______ аст.**

a. нахустин b. охирин c. миёна d. сеюм

6. ХАТ

Машқи 8: Write these words in the correct place.

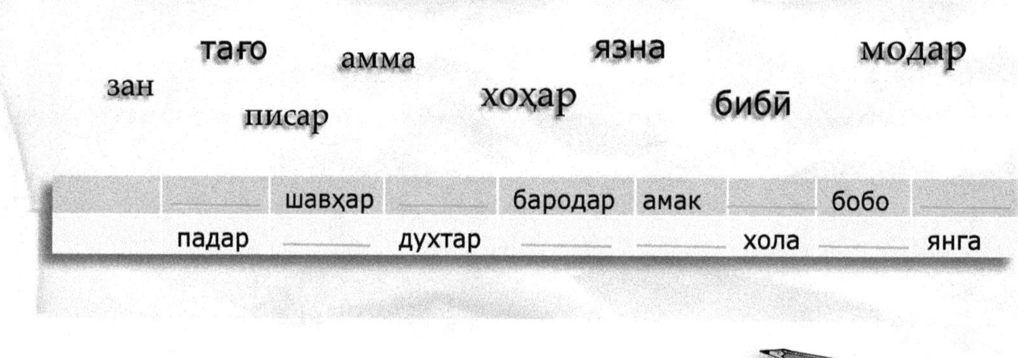

Машқи 9: Play a game. Imagine that your class is one big family and assign each person a role. Draw a family tree of your class, then write a short story about this family. Compare your text with a partner.

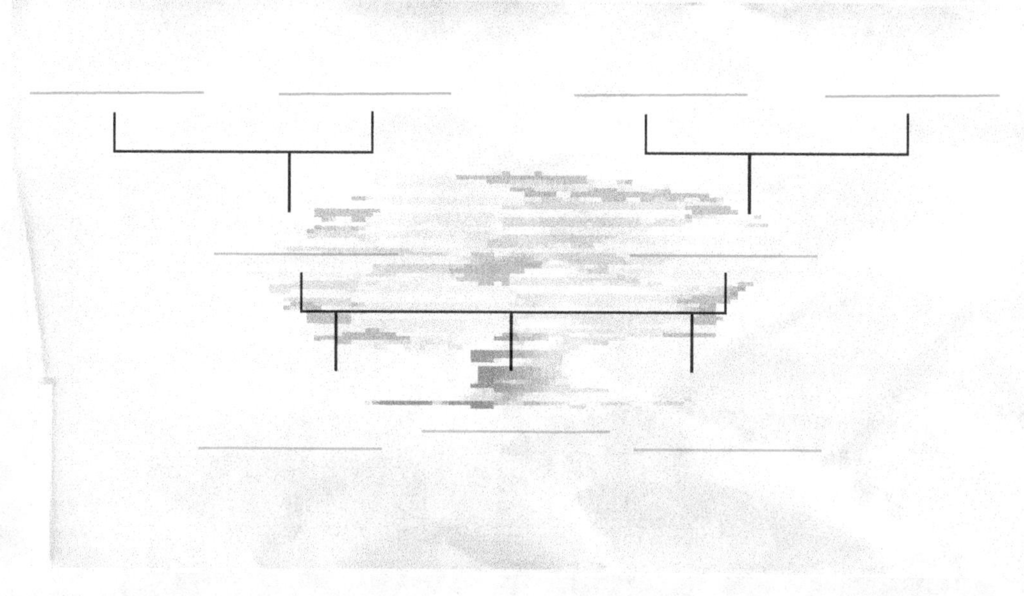

7. ТАМОШО КУНЕД!

Машқи 10:

A. Look at the picture below. Can you guess how these people are related to each other?

B. Number the people from right to left and write down how you think they are related.

НАМУНА

Духтари якум духтари бобо ва бибӣ аст.

1. ______________________
2. ______________________
3. ______________________
4. ______________________
5. ______________________
6. ______________________
7. ______________________
8. ______________________
9. ______________________

C. How are the people arranged? What do you notice about their placement?

D. Watch the video and see if what you thought is true.

E. Watch the video one more time and answer the following questions.

1. How many sons does the man have?

2. How many daughters-in-law (келин) does Нўъмон-бобо have?

3. How about Нўъмон-бобо's grandchildren?

4. What does he do for a living?

Б. ДАР ХОНАДОНИ ҲАМСАР B. At the in-laws'

1. СЕҲРИ СУХАН!

Машқи 1: A. Listen and practice.

падарарӯс, падаршӯй (хусур)	father-in-law
модарарӯс, модаршӯй (хушдоман)	mother-in-law
додарарӯс, додаршӯй (ҳевар)	brother-in-law
хоҳарарӯс, хоҳаршӯй	sister-in-law
боҷа	relationship between the husbands of sisters (brother-in-law by marriage only)
авсун	relationship between the wives of brothers (sister-in-law by marriage only)
арӯс, келин	daughter-in-law
домод	son-in-law
номзад	fiancé, fiancée
янга	sister-in-law (brother's wife)
язна, почо	brother-in-law (sister's husband)
набера	gràndchild

B. Draw your family tree and ask each other about your parents' relatives.

A: Бобои модариат ба падарат кӣ мешаванд?
B: Он кас падарарӯси падарам.

2. ГУФТУГӮ

Машқи 2: *Оилаи ҳамсарат калон аст?* A. Listen, fill in the blanks, and practice.

Фаридун: **Шунидам, ҳафтаи гузашта ба Хуҷанд рафтӣ?**
Шоҳпур: Ҳа, ман бо ҳамсарам ба хонаи ________ ӯ рафтам.
Фаридун: **Оилаи ҳамсарат бузург аст?**
Шоҳпур: Ҳа, волидайни ________ ҳафт фарзанд доранд.
Фаридун: **Ҳамсари ту ________ чандум аст?**
Шоҳпур: Ӯ фарзанди ________ аст.
Фаридун: **Пас, ту додарарӯс ва хоҳарарӯси бисёр дорӣ?**
Шоҳпур: Ҳа, ман ___ додарарӯс ва ___ хоҳарарӯс дорам. Ту чӣ?
Фаридун: **Падарарӯсу модарарӯси ман фақат ду фарзанд доранд: ________ и ман ва бародараш Дилшод. Ман фақат ________ дорам ва хоҳарарӯс надорам.**

B. *Кор бо шарик.* Now ask your partner questions like those in part A.

3. ДАСТУР

3.1. VERBS:

All Tajiki verbs are listed in the dictionary in their infinitive forms. The infinitive always ends in **-ан** and is always stressed on the last syllable. The following are some very common and useful verbs.

рафтан	to go	**гирифтан**	to take
дидан	to see	**додан**	to give
хӯрдан	to eat	**мондан**	to put
харидан	to buy	**фурӯхтан**	to sell
паридан	to fly	**шунидан**	to hear
бурдан	to carry	**хондан**	to read, study
гуфтан	to say, tell	**нӯшидан**	to drink

3.2. THE SIMPLE PAST TENSE

The past stem of the Tajiki verb is formed from the infinitive by dropping the suffix **-ан**. The past stem is the same as the 3rd person singular of the simple past tense.

рафтан 'to go'	**рафт** 'he/she/it went'
дидан 'to see'	**дид** 'he/she/it saw'
хӯрдан 'to eat'	**хӯрд** 'he/she/it ate'
харидан 'to buy'	**харид** 'he/she bought'
паридан 'to fly'	**парид** 'he/she/it flew'

The other forms of the simple past tense are formed by adding the past tense personal endings:

Ман	**рафт**	-ам	I went
Ту	**дид**	-й	you saw
Вай	**хӯрд**	-	he/she ate
Мо	**харид**	-ем	we bought
Шумо	**парид**	-ед	you flew
Онҳо	**шунид**	-анд	they heard

Машқи 3:  Complete these sentences. Conjugate the verbs in the simple past tense and check your answers with a partner.

1. Сарвар (рафтан)	
2. Ману модарам соат (харидан)	
3. Онҳо китоб (хондан)	
4. Шумо (омадан)	
5. Ман (хӯрдан)	
6. Ту (рафтан)	

4. ХОНИШ

Машқи 4: *Даъватнома.*

A. Read the invitation below and answer the questions.

Эй дуст биё, ки ошиқон шод шаванд
Дар мактаби зиндагӣ худ устод шаванд,
Дар партави панду ҳикмату меҳри Шумо
Домоду арӯс хонаобод шаванд.

Мӯҳтарам Юнусов Шермат Юнусович

Ҳузури Шумо дар тӯи арӯсию домодии фарзандонамон

ЗУҲУРШО ва МАДИНА

ки рӯзи 4-июли соли 2003 соати 17.00 дар тарабхонаи "Тоҷикистон" барпо мегардад, боиси сарфарозии мо хоҳад шуд.

Бо эҳтиром,
Хонадони НУРМАХМАТОВҲО ва ЗАРИПОВҲО

Зуҳуршо писари Нурмаҳматов ва домоди Зарипов аст. Ӯ шавҳари Мадина аст.

НАМУНА

1. Зуҳуршо кист?	
2. Мадина кист?	
3. Нурмаҳматов кист?	
4. Зарипов кист?	
5. Тӯй дар куҷо барпо мегардад?	

барпо мегардад - will be, will take place

B. How are wedding ceremonies held in your country? Tell your partner about them.

C. Tell the class about some of the wedding ceremonies of your partner's country.

D. Write an invitation to a wedding party.

5. ГӮШ КУНЕД

Машқи 5: *Сурати оила.* A. Listen and practice.

A: Ин сурати кист?
B: Ин сурати оилаам.
A: Инҳо кистанд?
B: Ин писарам Далер аст. Дар паҳлӯи ӯ келини ман - Дилором.
A: Ин муйсафед кист?
B: Магар намедонӣ? Ин кас шавҳарам Асрорҷон.
A: Ин ҷавон кист.
B: Ӯ домодам, шавҳари духтарам Шаҳло аст.
A: Ӯ чандсола аст?
B: Ӯ аз Шаҳло 4 сол калон аст ва 32-сола аст.

B. Listen to the rest of the conversation and answer the questions:

1. Анора чанд фарзанд дорад?	______
2. Ӯ чанд набера дорад?	______
3. Ӯ чанд келин дорад?	______
4. Ӯ чанд домод дорад?	______
5. Писари ӯ чандсола аст?	______

6. ХАТ

Машқи 6: Complete these conversations, writing the verbs in the simple past tense.

А: Робия китобро дар куҷо	______? (гузоштан)
В: Ӯ китобро дар рӯйи миз	______. (гузоштан)

А: Ту дирӯз ба куҷо	______? (рафтан)
В: Ман ба хонаи бобоям	______. (рафтан)

А: Модари Сӯҳроб чӣ	______? (харидан)
В: Ӯ дафтар, хаткӯркунак ва китоб	______. (харидан)

А: Дирӯз ҳавои деҳаи Хуршед гарм	______? (будан)
В: Не, дирӯз ҳавои деҳаи ман	______. (будан)

Машқи 7: Now draw a picture of your wife/husband's family (if not married, your parents' mother- and father-in-law's families) and describe them.

НАМУНА

Ин кас падарарӯсам. Ин кас модарарӯсам. Ин писар набераи модарам аст.

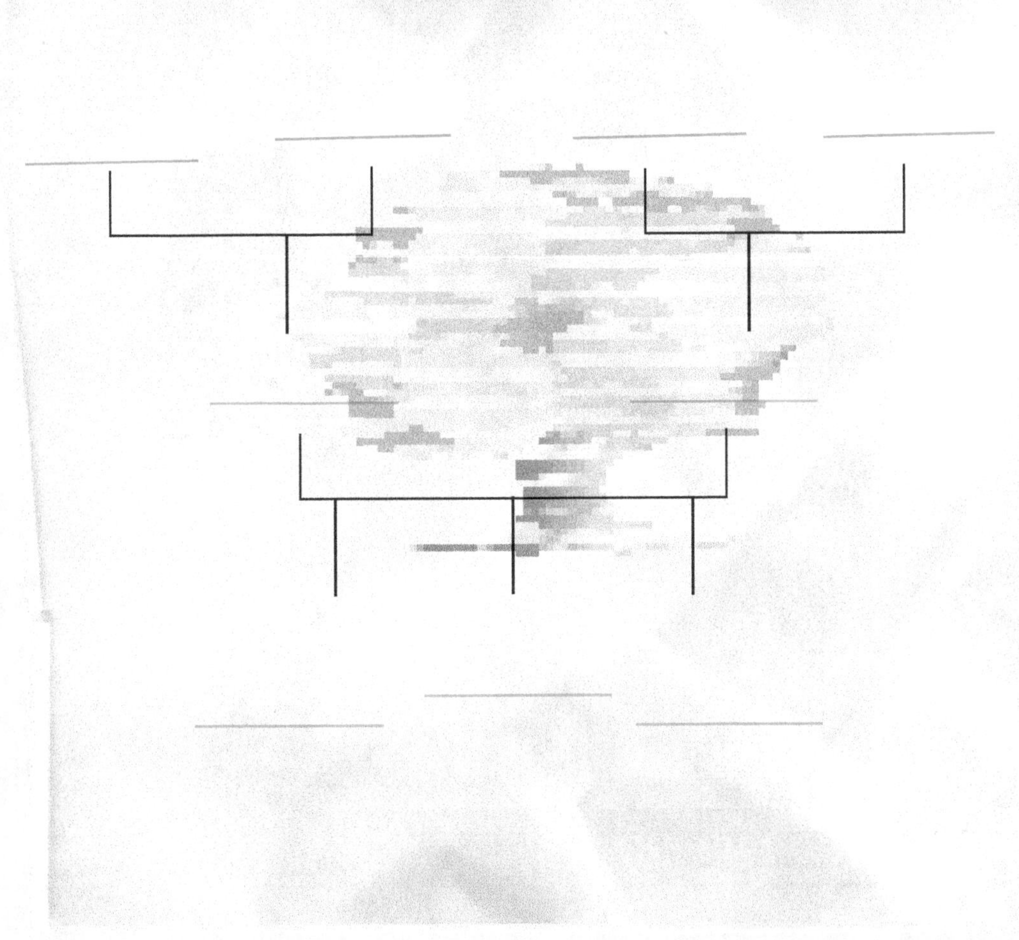

7. ТАМОШО КУНЕД!

Машқи 8:

A. Watch the video where Parvina is talking about her extended family. Write how the people in the pictures are related to her.

B. Watch the video one more time and fill in the blanks.

1. Ман ______________ и ҳамин хонавода.
2. Ин кас ______________ ам.
3. Ин кас ______________ ам.
4. Дар пеши модар, дар паҳлӯи модарарӯсам ______________ ам нишастаанд.
5. Ман соҳиби ________ ________.
6. Ба ин хонавода зиёда аз ________ ________ шуд, ки ҳамчун келин ҳисоб мешавам.
7. Дар паҳлӯи ман ________ ________ нишастаанд. Фирӯза.
8. Ёни ун касба ________ ________, Парвина.
9. Дар ин тараф ________ ________ ам нишастааст. Фозилҷон.
10. Синфи ______________ а тамом кард.
11. Ана, ин тарафамба ______________ и хурдем.
12. Қобилҷон, ______________ и ман.

C. Work with a partner and take the role of one of the people in part A.
Take turns asking each other questions about your relatives.

A: Ин кас ба ту кӣ мешаванд?
B: Ин кас бобоям, падари падарам ва падарарӯси модарам. 

В. ЎРО ТАСВИР КУНЕД C. DESCRIBE HIM.

1. СЕҲРИ СУХАН!

Машқи 1: Listen and practice.

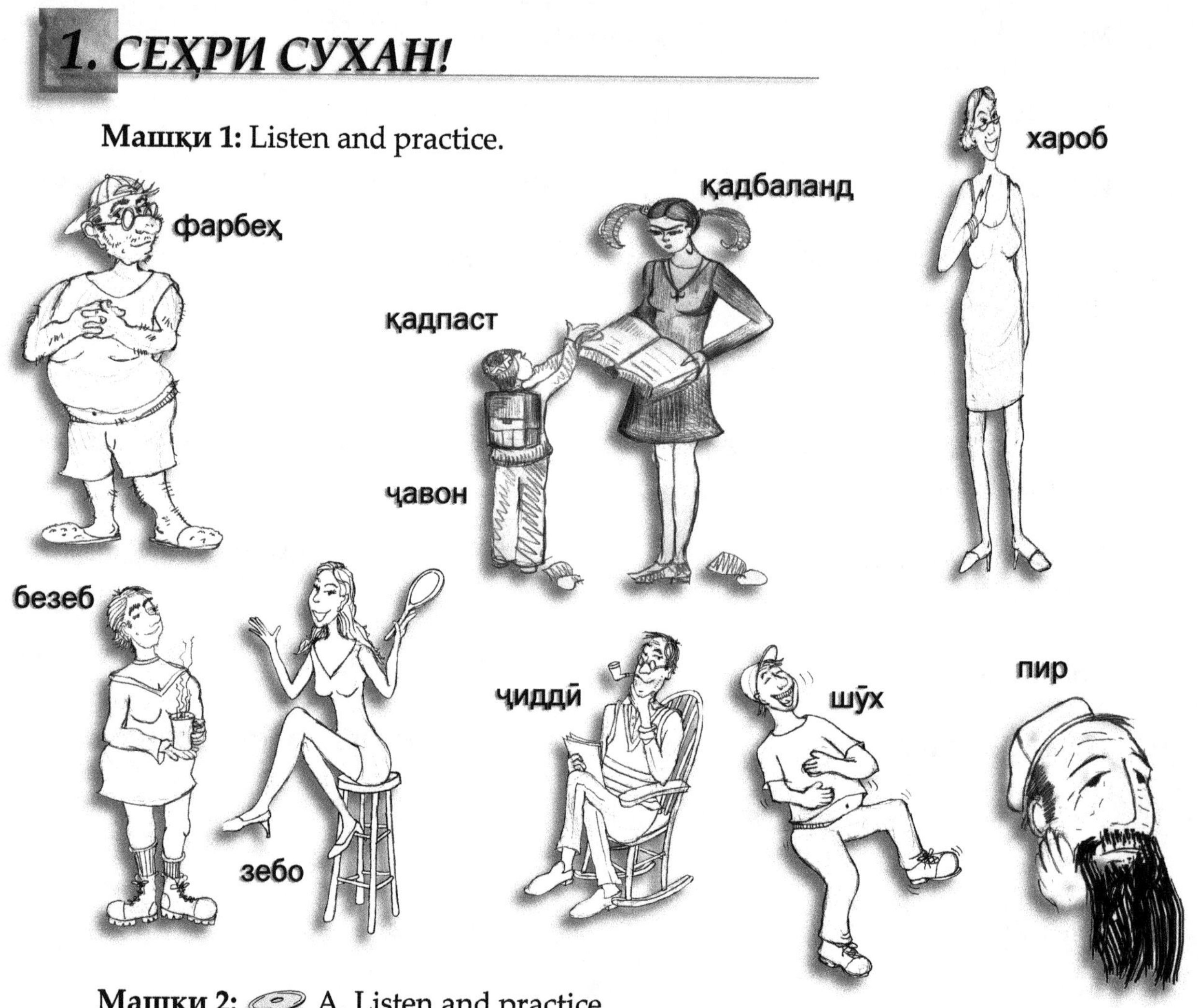

Машқи 2: A. Listen and practice.

Ӯ каме хароб аст.
Ӯ каме фарбеҳ аст.
Онҳо меҳрубонанд.
Ӯ хеле зебо аст.
Вай безеб аст.
Ӯ шармгин аст.
Ӯ хеле дағал аст.
Ӯ бисёр ҷиддӣ аст.
Ӯ доно аст.
Ӯ хеле шӯх аст.
Ӯ қаддароз аст.
Ӯ қадпаст аст.

B. Complete the chart with the words above. Add two more words to each list.

Намуд	Хислат
қадпаст	шӯх

Машқи 3: Listen to the descriptions of four people. Check (✓) the correct words.

ТАВСИФ						
1. Лола	✓	*меҳрубон*	✓	*қадпаст*		қаддароз
2. Ҷон	___	шӯх	___	хароб	___	ҷиддӣ
3. Ардашер	___	шармгин	___	қаддароз	___	доно
4. Заррина	___	каме фарбеҳ	___	безеб	___	шармгин

2. ГУФТУГӮ

Машқи 4: *Бародари Шабнам.* Listen, fill in the blanks, and practice.

Лайло: Ин кист?
Шабнам: Бародарам.
Лайло: Чӣ хел ҷавони ________! Номи ӯ чист?
Шабнам: Дилшод. Ӯ донишҷӯи __________ и давлатӣ аст.
Лайло: Вай чандсола аст?
Шабнам: Ӯ 22-сола аст.
Лайло: __________ чӣ хел аст? Ба фикрам, ӯ инсони хеле хуб аст.
Шабнам: Ҳа, дуруст ________________ аст.

Машқи 5: *Кор бо шарик.* Use the adjectives below to describe a classmate.

Фарангис ҷавон ва қаддароз аст. Мӯяш қаҳваранг аст ← НАМУНА

мӯй	*hair*	қаддароз	*tall*	сиёҳ	*black*
бинӣ	*nose*	қадпаст	*short*	кабуд	*blue*
абрӯ	*eyebrow*	безеб	*ugly*	сабз	*green*
гӯш	*ear*	хароб	*skinny*	қаҳваранг	*brown*
чашм	*eye*	фарбеҳ	*fat*	сафед	*white*
лаб	*lip*	зебо	*pretty*	сурх	*red*
хурд	*small*	вазн	*weight*	сарватманд	*rich*
ҷавон	*young*	нав	*new*	камбағал	*poor*
пир	*old (person)*	калон	*big*	боқувват	*strong*
ҷингиламӯй	*curly-haired*	заиф	*weak*	қад	*height*
хушсимо	*handsome*				

Машқи 6: Look at the family pictures and describe where each person is.

Карим дар тарафи рости Салима аст.
Модар дар назди Наргис ва дар тарафи чапи Хуршед аст.

НАМУНА

3. ДАСТУР

3.1. COMPARATIVES AND SUPERLATIVES OF ADJECTIVES

Look at the words and figure out how the comparative and superlative forms of adjectives are formed in Tajiki:

вазнин	**вазнинтар**	heavier
қимат	**қиматтар**	more expensive
хуб	**хубтарин**	the best
калон	**калонтарин**	the biggest
зебо	**бисёр зебо**	very beautiful
арзон	**хеле арзон**	very cheap

In Tajik comparative adjectives are formed by adding the suffix **-тар** to the adjectives; the suffix **-тарин** is used to form superlatives. The preposition **аз** is used for 'than.'

Машқи 7:  Fill in the blanks with the appropriate comparative suffix if necessary:

1. Нодира духтари хеле зебо ______ аст
2. Карим аз Акмал калон ______ аст.
3. Бозори Шоҳмансур бозори зебо______ и Душанбе аст.
4. Ӯ себро бо нархи хеле арзон ______ харид.
5. Халта хеле сабук ______ аст.
6. Самира назар ба Лайлӣ шӯх ______ аст.

Машқи 8: Form the comparatives and superlatives of the following adjectives. Write down five sentences.

НАМУНА

Қади Фарҳод аз Наргис дарозтар аст. – Farhod is taller than Nargis.

ADJECTIVE	COMPARATIVE	SUPERLATIVE
калон	*калонтар*	*калонтарин*
хурд	*хурдтар*	*хурдтарин*
ҷавон		
пир		
фарбеҳ		
паст		
баланд		
безеб		
зебо		
гарм		
хунук		
қимат		
арзон		
камбағал		
сарватманд		

4. ХОНИШ

Машқи 9: Read and match the adjectives below with their opposites.

қаддароз	a.	**хароб**	1.
беқувват	b.	**пир**	2.
ҷавон	c.	**камбағал**	3.
сарватманд	d.	**хурд**	4.
калон	e.	**боқувват**	5.
зебо	f.	**безеб**	6.
фарбеҳ	g.	**қадпаст**	7.

Машқи 10:  Who is described below? Read about the person described and match the picture with the description.

1. Ӯ хеле ҷавон аст. Ӯ мард нест. Мӯйҳояш сиёҳ ва дарозанд. Ӯ хеле зебо ва шод аст. Ӯ дар саҳна аст. Ӯ кист?

____

2. Ӯ муҷаррад аст. Мӯҳояш сиёҳи кӯтоҳанд. Чашмонаш ҳам сиёҳ. Қадаш миёна аст. Ӯ пешхизмат аст. Ӯ мард аст. Ӯ кист?

____

3. Мӯйҳои ӯ сиёҳанд, вале маълум нест, ки дароз ё кӯтоҳ. Ӯ зан аст.Чашмонаш сиёҳанд. Ӯ хароб нест.Ӯ дар бемористон аст. Ӯ парастор аст. Ӯ кист?

____

4. Ӯ марди камбағал аст. Мӯйҳояш сиёҳанд. Чашмонаш ҳам сиёҳ. Ӯ кор карда истодааст. Ӯ дуредгар аст. Ӯ миёнақад аст. Ӯ кистт?

____

Анӯша

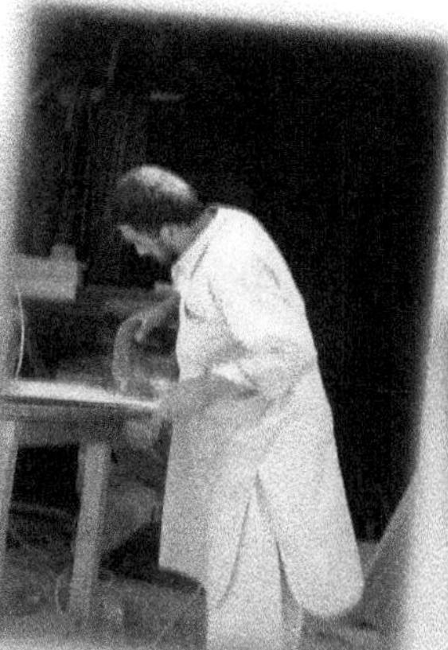

Каюмарс

Манижа

Дориюш

Машқи 11: *Дар ҷустуҷӯи бахт.*

A. Read the following personals and match the people according to their criteria.

A.

Ман 46-солаам. Ман соҳибкорам. Номам Мурод аст. Ман аз Хуҷандам. Мехоҳам бо хонуми меҳрубону зебое шинос шавам. Телефони ман: 34-63-52

B.

Номам Шаҳло. Ман тоҷик, 28-сола. Ман аз шавҳар ҷудо шудаам. Бо марди сарватманду боақл шинос шудан мехоҳам. Телефони ман: 23-41-98

C.

Номам Бунафша аст. Ман 39-солаам ва беваам. Ду духтарча дорам. Ман табибам. Телефони ман: 72-34-43

D.

Номи ман Насим аст. Ман аз Душанбе. Ман сиюҳафтсолаам. Ман ҷарроҳам. Шумо 25-32-солаед? Шумо зебоед? Телефони ман: 21-42-30

____

____

____

____

Vocabulary notes...

- **боақл** – intelligent, smart
- **бо.... шинос шудан мехоҳам** – I would like to meet (get acquainted with) ....
- **меҳрубон** – kind
- **зан** – woman
- **мард** – man
- **ҷудо шудаам** – I am divorced
- **муҷаррадам** – I am not married
- **беваам** – I am a widow

B. Now in the chart provided write a personal ad in which you describe yourself (or someone else) and the person you want to meet. Add your name, age, and telephone number and present it to your classmate.

5. ГӮШ КУНЕД

Машқи 12: A. Listen and fill in the chart with adjectives.

гӯш	чашм	бинӣ	лаб	мӯй
________	________	________	________	________
________	________	________	________	________

B. Based on the chart, describe your partner's body parts.

Машқи 13: Listen, fill in the blanks, and read the conversation.

Духтур: Салом, Ҷасур.
Ҷасур: Ассалом, духтурамак. Шумо чӣ хел?
Духтур: Хубам. Ту чӣ?
Ҷасур: Ман ҳам хубам, вале ман айнаки ____________ надорам.
Духтур: Хуб, канӣ, бинем. Марҳамат, шин. Ба ин ҷадвал нигоҳ кун."Ӯ" дар куҷост?
Ҷасур: Дар тарафи ____________ "Й".
Духтур: Нағз. "У" чӣ?
Ҷасур: "У" дар ____________ "Ӯ" ва "К" аст ва "Ҷ" дар зери "Ӯ" аст.
Духтур: Бисёр хуб. ____________ "С" кадом ҳарф аст?
Ҷасур: ____________.
Духтур: Хеле хуб. Чашмҳои ту бисёр хубанд. То санҷиши соли оянда.
Ҷасур: Бисёр хуб. То дидан.

6. ХАТ

Машқи 14: Fill in the blanks.

1. Ню-Йорк аз Париж ______________.
2. Британиёи Кабир аз Амрико ______________
3. Амрико аз Ҳиндустон ______________.
4. Россия аз Амрико ва ______________.
5. Ирландия аз Мексика ______________ ва ______________.
6. Сингапур аз Берлин ______________, лекин ______________.
7. Тоҷикистон аз Шветсария ______________, вале ______________.
8. Тоҷикистон аз Эрон ______________, вале ______________.

Машқи 15: Write about the people in the pictures below:

1. Қади Парвиз аз Ардашер дарозтар аст.
2. Қади Парвиз аз ҳама дарозтар аст.

3. ______________
4. ______________
5. ______________
6. ______________

Машқи 17: Look at Dilshod's family tree. Complete Dilshod's description of his family by writing in each family member's name and age. Also add some information about their professions and physical characteristics. The first one has been done for you. Use the following kinship terms and do not forget to include the possessive markers:

дада, писар, ака, апа, хоҳар, ука, додар, духтар, бибӣ, бобо, зан, ҳамсар,оча,

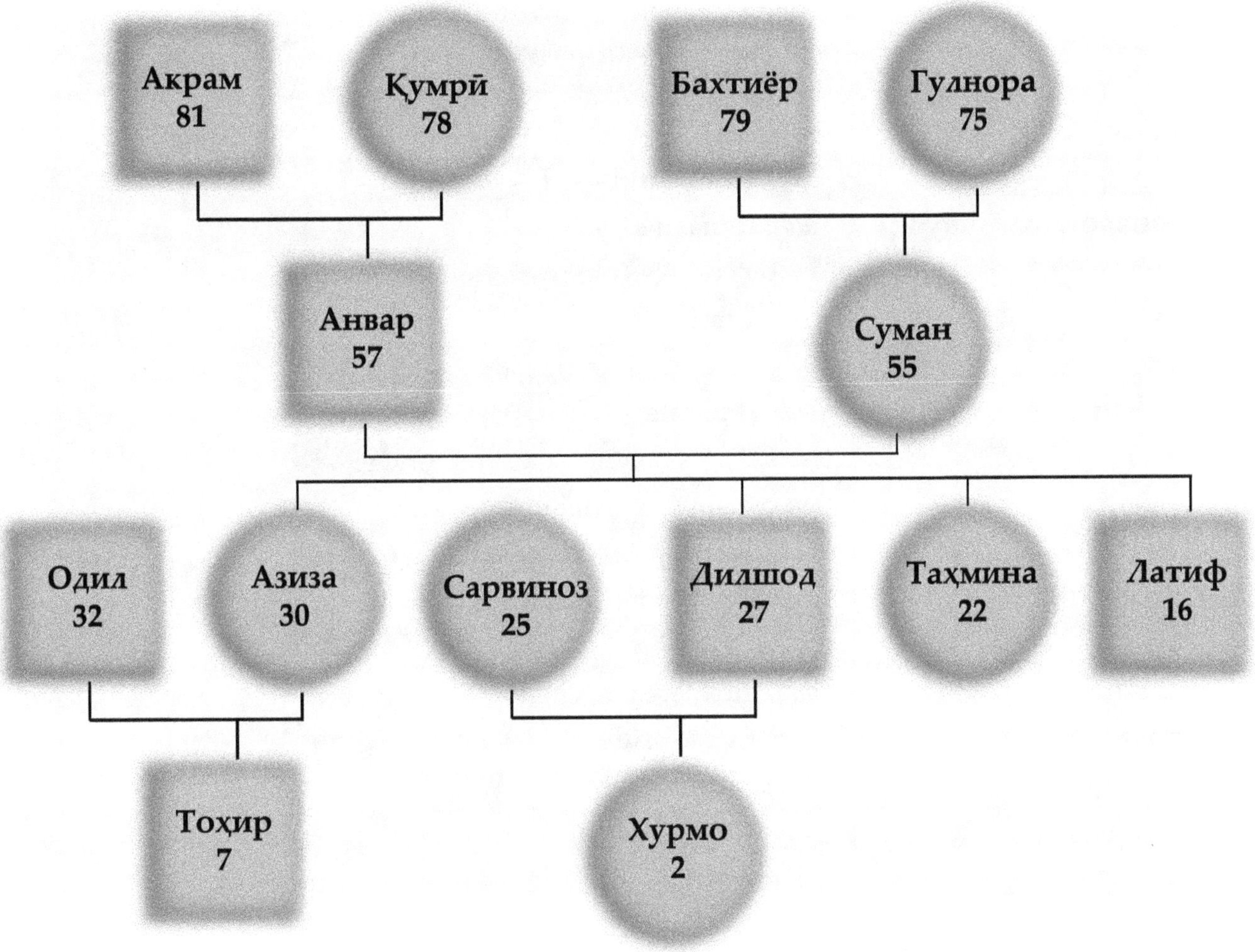

Акрам 81 — Қумрӣ 78 — Бахтиёр 79 — Гулнора 75

Анвар 57 — Суман 55

Одил 32 — Азиза 30 — Сарвиноз 25 — Дилшод 27 — Таҳмина 22 — Латиф 16

Тоҳир 7 — Хурмо 2

Номи падарам Анвар ва модарам Суман аст. Дадаам панҷоҳуҳафтсола аст. Ӯ табиб аст. Модарам панҷоҳупанҷсола аст ва ӯ муҳосиб аст.

VOCABULARY
ЛУҒАТНОМА

абера	*n.* great-grandchild
абрӯ	*n.* eyebrow
авсун	*n.* relationship between the wives of two brothers (sister-in-law by marriage only)
аёдат	*n.* visit
аз хурдӣ	*phr.* from childhood
markup-placeholder	
айвон	*n.* balcony (= **балкон**)
ако	*n.* older brother
акс	*n.* photograph (= **расм, сурат**)
алоҳида	*adj.* separate
амак	*n.* father's brother, paternal uncle
амакбача	*n.* cousin (paternal uncle's child)
амма	*n.* father's sister, paternal aunt
аммабача	*n.* cousin (paternal aunt's child)
апа	*n.* older sister
арзон	*adj.* inexpensive, cheap
арӯс	*n.* fiancée, bride
атроф	*prep.* around
афлесун	*n.* orange (fruit, also **норинҷ**)
ахбор	*n.* news
байн	*adj.* middle (see **миён, миёна**)
балкон	*n.* balcony (= **айвон**)
бар	*n.* width
барқ	*n.* electricity
барномасоз	*n.* programmer
бародар	*n.* brother
барпо гардидан	*v.* to take place
баҳона кардан	*v.* to make an excuse
бева	*n.* widower
бегоҳ	*n.* evening
бегоҳӣ	*adv.* in the evening
бедор шудан	*v.* to wake up (*intr.*)

безеб	*adj.* ugly
берун	*n.* outside
бетартиб	*adj.* messy, disorganized (see **чиркин**)
бибию бобо	*n.* grandparents
бибӣ	*n.* grandmother (= **модаркалон**)
бинӣ	*n.* nose
боақл	*adj.* smart, clever (see **доно**)
бобо	*n.* grandfather (= **падаркалон**)
боду ҳаво	*n.* weather (= **обуҳаво**)
бозӣ	*n.* game
бозӣ кардан	*v.* to play
боқувват	*adj.* strong
боло	*prep.* above
бону	*n.* lady; wife, woman (see **зан**)
боҷа	*n.* relationship between the husbands of two sisters (brother-in-law by marriage only)
бузург	*adj.* big, large (= **калон**)
бунафш	*adj.* violet
бурдан (бар)	*v.* to carry, take, bring
бӯр	*adj.* gray
вазифаи хонагӣ	*n.* homework
вазн	*n.* weight
вазнин	*adj.* heavy, difficult
вай	*pron.* he/she
вақт	*n.* time
вале	*conj.* but
варзиш	*n.* sport
васеъ	*adj.* wide
видеокасета	*n.* videotape
видеомагнитофон	*n.* videocassette player, VCR
волид	*n.* parent
волидайн	*n.* parents
вохӯрдан	*v.* to meet
вуҷуд доштан	*v.* to exist
гап задан	*v.* to speak

гармӣ	*n.* heat
гилем	*n.* rug, carpet (= **қолин**)
гирифтан (гир)	*v.* to take, get
голф	*n.* golf
гузоштан (гузор)	*v.* to put
гулобӣ	*adj.* pink, reddish
гуногун (гӯ, гӯй)	*adj.* various, of different kinds
гурба	*n.* cat (= **пишак**)
гуфтан	*v.* to say, tell
гӯш	*n.* ear
гӯш кардан	*v.* to listen
ғижжак	*n. ghijjak,* Tajik musical instrument
давлатӣ	*adj.* state, national, official
дағал	*adj.* rough, rude
дар даст	*phr.* at hand, on hand
дароз	*adj.* long
дарс додан	*v.* to teach
дарун	*n., prep.* inside
даъват кардан	*v.* to invite (**ба** to)
даъватнома	*n.* invitation (card)
дидан (бин)	*v.* to see
додан (диҳ)	*v.* to give
додар	*n.* younger brother (see **ука**)
додарарӯс	*n.* brother-in-law (= **додаршӯй, ҳевар**)
додарзода	*n.* nephew or niece by a brother (see **ҷиян**)
додаршӯй	*n.* brother-in-law (= **додарарӯс, ҳевар**)
доира	*n.* drum, Tajik musical instrument
доирашакл	*adj.* round (= **мудаввар**)
домод	*n.* groom, son-in-law
доно	*adj.* smart, wise (see **боақл**)
дугоник	*n.* twins
дутор	*n. dutor,* Tajik musical instrument
духтар	*n.* daughter, girl
дӯст	*n.* friend, comrade (= **рафиқ, ҷӯра**)

забон	*n.* language, tongue
завҷа	*n.* wife (see **зан**)
заиф	*adj.* weak
зан	*n.* wife, woman (see **бону, завҷа**)
зард	*adj.* yellow
зебо	*adj.* beautiful
зер	*prep.* under
зиндагӣ	*n.* life (= **ҳаёт**)
зиндагӣ кардан	*v.* to live, reside (see **сокин будан**); to stay (in some place)
издивоҷ кардан	*v.* to marry
издивоҷшуда	*adj.* married (= **мутааҳҳил, оиладор**)
имтиҳон	*n.* exam, test
инсон	*n.* person
истироҳат	*n.* rest
истироҳат кардан	*v.* to have a rest, relax
иҷора	*n.* rent
иҷро кардан	*v.* to fulfill, carry out
кабуд	*adj.* blue
калон	*adj.* big, large (= **бузург**)
калонӣ	*adj.* elder, older (of siblings)
калонсол	*adj.* elder, big (= **кухансол**)
кардан (кун)	*v.* to do, make
кас	*n.* person (= **шахс**)
кат	*n.* bed
келин	*n.* daughter-in-law, bride
компютер	*n.* computer
курсӣ	*n.* chair
кухансол	*adj.* old (= **пир, солхӯрда**); elder, big (= **калонсол**)
кӯдак	*n.* child, kid
кӯтоҳ	*adj.* short
қад	*n.* height
қадбаланд	*adj.* tall (= **қаддароз**)
қаддароз	*adj.* tall (= **қадбаланд**)
қадпаст	*adj.* short (of height)

қарта	*n.* card
қартабозӣ	*n.* card game
қафо	*prep.* behind
қаҳваранг	*adj.* brown
қим(м)ат	*adj.* expensive
қолин	*n.* rug, carpet (= **гилем**)
қудо	*n.* relationship between groom's and bride's parents
лаб	*n.* lip
лифт	*n.* elevator
майда	*adj.* little, small (= **хурд**)
макон	*n.* place
мард	*n.* man
матбах	*n.* kitchen (= **ошхона**)
маҳбуба	*n.* girlfriend, sweetheart
меҳрубон	*adj.* kind
миён	*n., adj.* middle (see **байн, миёна**)
миёна	*adj.* middle (see **байн, миён**)
миз	*n.* desk
модар	*n.* mother
модарарӯс	*n.* mother-in-law
модаркалон	*n.* grandmother (= **бибӣ**)
модаршӯй	*n.* mother-in-law (= **модарарӯс, хушдоман**)
мондан (мон)	*v.* to put
мудаввар	*adj.* round (= **доирашакл**)
муйсафед	*n.* old man
мумкин	*adj.* allowed
мусиқии анъанавӣ	*n.* classical or traditional music
мусиқӣ	*n.* music
мутааҳҳил	*adj.* married (= **издивоҷшуда, оиладор**)
муҷаррад	*n.* bachelor, single
мӯй	*n.* hair
набера	*n.* grandchild
наберадухтар	*n.* granddaughter
набераписар	*n.* grandson

навор	*n.* film
навохтан (навоз)	*v.* to play a musical instrument
назар	*n.* opinion
назд	*prep.* near
нарх	*n.* price
нахустин	*adj.* first
нигоҳ кардан	*v.* to look (**ба** at)
ним	*n.* half
нисфирӯзӣ	*adj.* noontime, midday, early afternoon
номзад	*n.* fiancé, fiancée
нопок	*adj.* unclean; tainted, corrupt (see **чиркин**)
норинҷ	*n.* orange (fruit, also **афлесун**)
нӯшидан	*v.* to drink
оби гарм	*n.* hot water
оила	*n.* family (=**хонавода**)
оилавӣ	*adj.* of the family
оиладор	*adj.* married (= **издивоҷшуда**, **мутааҳҳил**)
ойина	*n.* mirror
охирин	*adj.* last
ошёна	*n.* floor
ошхона	*n.* kitchen (= **матбах**)
пагоҳӣ	*n.* in the morning
падар	*n.* father
падарарӯс	*n.* father-in-law (bride's side)
падаркалон	*n.* grandfather (= **бобо**)
падаршӯй	*n.* father-in-law (= **падарарӯс**, **хусур**)
парда	*n.* curtain
паридан (пар)	*v.* to fly
паст	*adj.* low; *adv.* slightly
паҳлӯ	*prep.* next to
пеш	*n.* front; *adv.*, ago; *prep.* before, ahead (often with **аз**)
пианино	*n.* piano

пир	*adj.* old (= **кухансол, солхӯрда**)
писар (писарбачча)	*n.* son, boy
пишак	*n.* cat (= **гурба**)
покиза	*adj.* clean (= **тоза**)
пухтан	*v.* to cook
пушт	*prep.* back, behind
равшан	*adj.* bright
радио	*n.* radio
рақс	*n.* dance
расм	*n.* photograph (= **акс, сурат**)
рафи китоб	*n.* bookshelf
рафиқ	*n.* friend, comrade (= **дӯст, ҷӯра**)
рафтан (рав)	*v.* to go
регбӣ	*n.* rugby
рок	*n.* rock music
рондан (рон)	*v.* to drive
рост	*adv.* right
рубоб	*n. rubob*, Tajik musical instrument
рустшавакон	*n.* hide and seek (*game*)
рӯзҳои истироҳат	*n.* weekend
сабз	*adj.* green
сабт кардан	*v.* to record
сабук	*adj.* light (not heavy), easy, quick
саг	*n.* dog
сағира	*n.* orphan (= **ятим**)
санаи таваллуд	*n.* date of birth
санҷиш	*n.* examination, test
сарватманд	*adj.* rich (= **бой**)
сафед	*adj.* white
сетор	*n. setor*, Tajik musical instrument
сиёҳ	*adj.* dark
синну сол	*n.* age
сокин будан	*v.* to live, inhabit (see **зиндагӣ кардан**)
солхӯрда	*adj.* old (= **кухансол, пир**)
соҳибкор	*n.* businessman

сурат	*n.* photograph (= **акс, расм**)
суроға	*n.* address
суруд хондан	*v.* to sing
сурх	*adj.* red
табиб	*n.* physician, doctor
таблак	*n.* small drum, Tajik musical instrument
тағо	*n.* mother's brother, maternal uncle
тағобача	*n.* cousin (maternal uncle's child)
талоқ	*n.* divorce (= **ҷудошавӣ**)
талоқшуда	*adj.* divorced (= **ҷудошуда**)
тамошо кардан	*v.* to watch
танг	*adj.* narrow
тараф	*n.* side
тасвир кардан	*v.* to describe
таҳқир кардан	*v.* to offend (= **хафа кардан**)
телевизор	*n.* TV set
телефон	*n.* telephone
теннисбозӣ	*n.* tennis
тиллоранг	*adj.* golden, gold-colored
тоза	*adj.* clean (= **покиза**)
тӯй	*n.* wedding (= **тӯи арӯсӣ**); party
узви оила	*n.* family member
ука	*n.* younger sibling (see **додар, хоҳар**)
устод	*n.* professor, master
утоқ	*n.* room (= **хона, ҳуҷра**)
фақат	*adv.* only
фарбеҳ	*n., adj.* fat
фарзанд	*n.* child
фарқ	*n.* difference
фаррош	*n.* janitor
фотиҳа шудан	*v.* to be/get engaged
фотоаппарат	*n.* camera
фурӯхтан	*v.* to sell (фурӯш)
футбол	*n.* soccer

хабарҳои варзиш	*n.* sports news
халта	*n.* bag
харидан (хар)	*v.* to buy
хароб	*adj.* thin
хафа кардан	*v.* to offend (= **таҳқир кардан**)
хеш (хешованд)	*n.* relatives
хешӣ	*n.* family relationship
хислат	*n.* character, personality
хола	*n.* mother's sister, maternal aunt
холабача	*n.* cousin (maternal aunt's child)
хона	*n.* house, home; room (= **утоқ, ҳуҷра**)
хонавода	*n.* family (= **оила**)
хонаи дуҳуҷрагӣ	*n.* one-bedroom (two-room) house
хондан (хон)	*v.* to read, study
хонум	*n.* Miss, Ms., lady
хор	*n.* thorn
хоҳар	*n.* sister
хоҳарарӯс	*n.* sister-in-law (= **хоҳаршӯй**)
хоҳарзода	*n.* nephew or niece by a sister (see **ҷиян**)
хоҳаршӯй	*n.* sister-in-law (= **хоҳарарӯс**)
хурд	*adj.* little, small (= **майда**)
хусур	*n.* father-in-law (groom's side)
хушдоман	*n.* mother-in-law
хушрӯ	*adj.* handsome, beautiful
хушсимо	*adj.* handsome, beautiful
хӯрдан (хӯр)	*v.* to eat
ҳаёт	*n.* life (= **зиндагӣ**)
ҳайвоноти хонагӣ	*n.* pets
ҳамкор	*n.* co-worker, colleague, partner (= **шарик**)
ҳамсар	*n.* spouse (see **бону, завҷа, зан, шавҳар, шӯй**)
ҳамсинф	*n.* classmate
ҳамсоя	*n.* neighbor

ҳевар	*n.* brother-in-law (= **додарарӯс, додаршӯй**)
ҳисобкунак	*n.* calculator
ҳуҷра	*n.* room (= **утоқ, хона**)
чабера	*n.* great-great-grandchild
чароғ	*n.* lamp
чашм	*n.* eye
чиркин	*adj.* dirty, filthy (see **нопок**); messy (= **бетартиб**)
ҷавон	*adj.* young
ҷавонзан	*n.* young lady
ҷавонтар	*adj.* younger
ҷаз[1]	*n.* fried fat from around the tail of a sheep
ҷаз[2]	*n.* jazz
ҷаноб	*n.* sir, mister, Mr., gentleman
ҷарроҳ	*n.* surgeon
ҷевони либос	*n.* closet
ҷиддӣ	*adj.* serious
ҷингиламӯй	*adj.* curly-haired
ҷиян	*n.* nephew, niece (includes **додарзода** and **хоҳарзода**)
ҷудошавӣ	*n.* divorce (= **талоқ**)
ҷудошуда	*adj.* divorced (= **талоқшуда**)
ҷӯра	*n.* friend, comrade (= **дӯст, рафиқ**)
шавҳар	*n.* husband (= **шӯй**; see **ҳамсар**)
шавҳаркарда	*adj.* married (of a woman)
шарик	*n.* colleague, partner (= **ҳамкор**)
шармгин	*adj.* shy
шахс	*n.* person (= **кас**)
шашмақом	*n. shashmaqom*, classical music of the Tajiks
шинос кардан	*v.* to introduce
шоҳмот	*n.* chess
шудан (шав)	*v.* to become
шунидан (шунав)	*v.* to hear
шӯй	*n.* husband (= **шавҳар**; see **ҳамсар**)

шӯх	*adj.* funny, witty
язна	*n.* brother-in-law (sister's husband, = **почо**)
якчанд	*adj.* quite a few
янга	*n.* brother's wife
ятим	*n.* orphan (= **сағира**)

Боби ҳафтум
CHAPTER SEVEN 7

ДАР БОЗОР
AT THE BAZAAR

IN THIS CHAPTER

- **Мубодилаи арз** Money Exchange
- **Қаторҳои бозор** Market Rows
- **Чанд пул?** How Much?
- ***Луғатнома*** Vocabulary

А. МУБОДИЛАИ АСЪОР A. MONEY EXCHANGE

1. СЕҲРИ СУХАН!

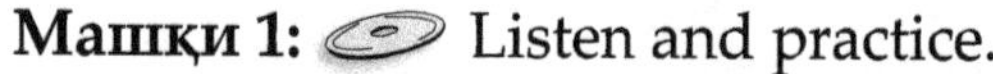
Машқи 1: Listen and practice.

пул

сомонӣ

дирам=0.01сомонӣ

танга

хозин (кассир)

харидор

бонк

мубодилаи арз

Машқи 2:

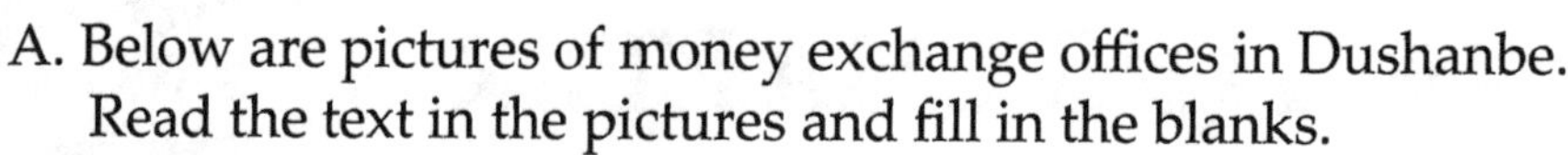
A. Below are pictures of money exchange offices in Dushanbe. Read the text in the pictures and fill in the blanks.

B. Which countries have the following currencies?

Сӯм	
Доллар	
Евро	
Тенге	
Сомонӣ	
Манат	
Фунт	
Сом	
Рубл	

2. ГУФТУГӮ

Машқи 3: *Пулатро иваз кардӣ?* Listen, fill in the blanks, and practice.

Нигора: Собир, дирӯз пулатро иваз кардӣ?

Собир: Ҳа, ман аввал ба дӯкони мубодилаи __________ рафтам. Онҳо пули маро иваз накарданд. Пули тоҷикии онҳо кам буд. Онҳо ба ман суроғаи __________ ро доданд. Баъд ман пуламро дар бонк иваз кардам.

Нигора: Фаҳмо. Ман ба ту ду бор __________ задам, касе ҷавоб надод.

Собир: Ту соати чанд занг задӣ?

Нигора: Соати шаш ва __________ дақиқа.

Собир: Фаҳмо, ман дар ин вақт бо дӯстам Ҷон дар бонк будам.

Нигора: Ту як долларро ба чанд __________ иваз кардӣ?

Собир: Нархи як __________ дар он ҷо __________ буд.

Нигора: Хеле хуб. Ҷон чӣ? Ӯ ҳам пулашро иваз кард?

Собир: Ҷон пули аврупоӣ дошт. Ӯ ҳам пулашро иваз кард. Пули аврупоӣ каме __________ буд.

Нигора: Бисёр хуб, ҳоло __________ мушкиле надоред?

Собир: Не.

Нигора: Хайр, то боздид.

Собир: То дидан.

3. ДАСТУР

COMPOUND VERBS IN THE SIMPLE PAST TENSE

The verbs you learned in earlier chapters were simple verbs. Tajiki also has compound verbs, which are made up of a noun or an adjective and a simple verb. The most common simple verbs that form compound verbs are **кардан** 'to do,' **доштан** 'to have,' **намудан** 'to appear,' **додан** 'to give,' **задан** 'to hit,' and **шудан** 'to become.' The meaning of the verb is determined by the noun or adjective; for example, **сабз** 'green' gives **сабз кардан** 'to grow,' **кор** 'work' gives кор **кардан** 'to work,' **дӯст** 'friend' gives **дӯст доштан** 'to like,' and **занг** 'bell' gives **занг задан** 'to telephone, call, ring (of telephone).' The noun or adjective is written separate from the verb, and receives the stress. The verbal part is conjugated the same way whether as a simple or a compound verb.

4. ХОНИШ

Машқи 4:  Read the bank advertisement and fill in the blanks.

1. Which countries are covered by Amonatbonk?
2.Who is the guaranty for its service?
3.Why is "Western Union" mentioned?
4. How much time does it take to send money from London?
5. How much is the service payment for money transferred from Russia?
6.How many branches does it has nation- wide?

«Амонатбонк»

дар хидмати шумост!

■ Қаламрави мо - аз Ягноби Зарафшон то Бартанги Бадахшон!
■ Робита ва ҳамкорихон мо - аз Маскав то Вашингтон!
■ Кафили амнияти иқтисодии мизоҷони мо - Ҳукумати ҷумҳурӣ ва Вазорати молияи Тоҷикистон
■ «Амонатбонк» - шомили системаи умумиҷаҳонии «Вестерн-Юнион» буда, бо тамоми мамолики дунё робита дорад.
■ Дар ин ҷо шумо метавонед:
■ интиқоли пули хешовандонатонро аз Лондон ё Сингапур баъди 10 дақиқаи ирсол шуданаш он дастрас намоед;
■ бизоати худро дар бозорхои пойтахт фурӯхта, пули онро қаблан ба деҳаи худ фиристед;
■ барои интиқоли пулии пайвандонатон аз Русия ҳамагӣ 2% ҳаққи хизмат супоред;
■ «Амонатбонк» дар 519 агентии худ дар ҳама деҳоти кишвар ба нафақахӯрон пули нафақаашонро дар сари вақт мерасонад.
■ Аз хизмати «Амонатбонк» баҳра баред.

Нишонии он:
Ҷумҳурии Тоҷикистон,
ш.Душанбе,
кӯчаи Лоҳутӣ, 24,
Тел: 21-70-81, 23-14-33.

Машқи 5: Read the conversation with a partner. Then make your own and act it out.

Харидор: **Салом, пули маро иваз кунед.**
Кассир: Шумо чӣ хел пул доред?
Харидор: **Пули ман доллари амрикоӣ.**
Кассир: Нархи як доллар се сомонию даҳ дирам аст.
Харидор: **Ҳамин 100 -долларро иваз кунед.**
Кассир: Марҳамат, се саду даҳ сомонӣ.
Харидор: **Ташаккур.**

5. ГӮШ КУНЕД

Машқи 6: Listen to the CD. Check whether the sentences are true or false.

Н	Д	
__	__	1.Сомонӣ пули миллии Тоҷикистон аст.
__	__	2. Як сомонӣ ба сад дирам баробар аст.
__	__	3. Пули дирам танга аст.
__	__	4. Доллар пули миллии Тоҷикистон аст.
__	__	5. Рубл пули Русия аст.
__	__	6. Сомонӣ пули Тоҷикистон нест.
__	__	7. Номи пули Тоҷикистон тенге аст.
__	__	8. Пули аврупоӣ евро аст.

Машқи 7:  Listen and complete the sentences with the verbs in the list below.

иваз кардан 'to exchange'
нишон додан 'to show'
муроҷиат кардан 'to apply, turn, appeal to'
ҳисоб кардан 'to count'
бовар кардан ' to believe'
тарҷума кардан 'to translate'
ҳурмат кардан 'to respect'
занг задан 'to call'
кор кардан 'to work'
машғул шудан 'to be busy'

1. Манижа ба амакаш ____________
2. Гулрухсор роҳи бонкро ба дӯсташ ____________
3. Пулро дар кӯча ____________
4. Падару модари худро ____________
5. Холаи Саъдӣ панҷ сол дар бонк ____________
6. Ман соли гузашта бо омӯзиши забони фаронсавӣ ____________
7. Ба гапҳои нодуруст ____________
8. Ҳамеша пули худро дар назди хозин ____________
9. Барои мубодилаи пул ба банк ____________
10. Лутфан, калимаи хозинро ба забони англисӣ ____________

6. ХАТ

Машқи 8: Write a report for the Tajik University newspaper about your experiences in Tajikistan telling other people how to exchange money. Be very careful. Your report must be complete. If you leave something out, future visitors will be unprepared for unexpected situations.

Машқи 9: ***Кор бо шарик.*** Write a short script between a cashier and a customer in an exchange office. Act out the play in front of the class.

Харидор: Мана, ин даҳдолларро иваз кунед.
Кассир: Хуб шудаст.

7. ТАМОШО КУНЕД!

Машқи 10: A. Have you ever exchanged money? What unusual situations may happen during the exchange? Discuss these questions with a partner and ask each other about your experiences. (Use your imagination if you haven't ever exchanged money.)

B. Now you will watch a video about exchanging money in Dushanbe. First watch the video with the sound off and guess what happened with Farzona.

C. Watch the video with the sound on, listen to the dialogue between Farzona and the cashier, and fill in the blanks:

Фарзона:	______________________________
Кассир:	______________________________
Фарзона:	**Мебахшед, ҳамин пули бистдоллараро иваз кунед.**
Кассир:	Ҳозир. .... Мебахшед пулам __________ шудааст.
Фарзона:	**Ин пули ман бошад? Ба фикрам, __________ пули ман не.**
Кассир:	Ҳа, пули __________ аст.
Фарзона:	**Ин ҷо ман рақамашро навишта будам. Бинед, ин пули ман не, ин доллари қалбакӣ!**
Кассир:	Мебахшед, __________ пули Шумо.
Фарзона:	**Ҳа, __________ пули ман, __________, ташаккур.**
Кассир:	Саломат бошед.

D. Watch the dialogue again and answer the following questions:

1.	**Фарзона чӣ гуна пулро иваз кардан мехост?**							______
a.	тангаи Қазоқистон	b.	доллари ИМА	c.	сӯми Ӯзбакистон	d.	рубли Россия	

2.	**Барои чӣ кассир пули Фарзонаро иваз накард?**							______
a.	пул надошт	b.	мехост Фарзонаро фиреб диҳад	c.	вай доллари амрикоиро иваз накард	d.	пули Фарзона қалбакӣ буд	

3.	**Чаро Фарзона дафтарчаашро аз кисааш баровард?**							______
a.	барои дидани суроғаи нуқтаи дигари мубодилаи арз	b.	барои навиштани номи кассир	c.	барои гузоштани пул	d.	барои тафтиши рақами пул	

E. Answer the following questions.

1. Фарзона пулро дар куҷо иваз кард?
____
2. Барои чӣ Фарзона пулро ба кассир боз гардонид?
____

Post-listening activities

F. Discuss the following questions in Tajiki:

1. Are you surprised that there are many exchange offices in Dushanbe? Why or why not?
2. Would a Tajik visitor have difficulty finding an exchange office in the US?
3. Why are there so many exchange offices in Dushanbe? Are they for tourists or for local people?
4. Why do local people need a lot of exchange offices?

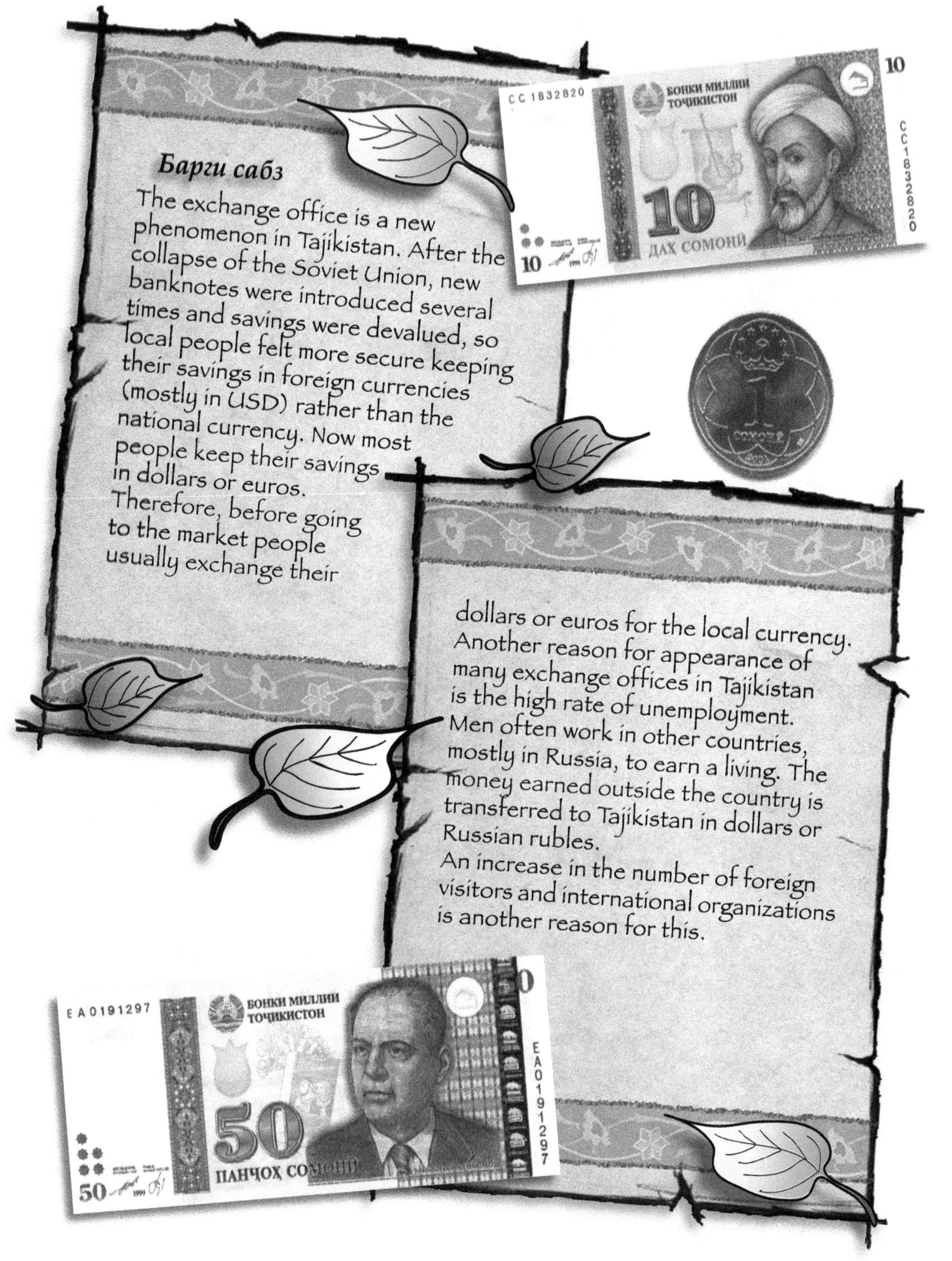

Барги сабз

The exchange office is a new phenomenon in Tajikistan. After the collapse of the Soviet Union, new banknotes were introduced several times and savings were devalued, so local people felt more secure keeping their savings in foreign currencies (mostly in USD) rather than the national currency. Now most people keep their savings in dollars or euros.
Therefore, before going to the market people usually exchange their dollars or euros for the local currency. Another reason for appearance of many exchange offices in Tajikistan is the high rate of unemployment. Men often work in other countries, mostly in Russia, to earn a living. The money earned outside the country is transferred to Tajikistan in dollars or Russian rubles.
An increase in the number of foreign visitors and international organizations is another reason for this.

Б. ҚАТОРҲОИ БОЗОР B. MARKET ROWS

1. СЕҲРИ СУХАН!

Машқи 1: A. Listen and practice.

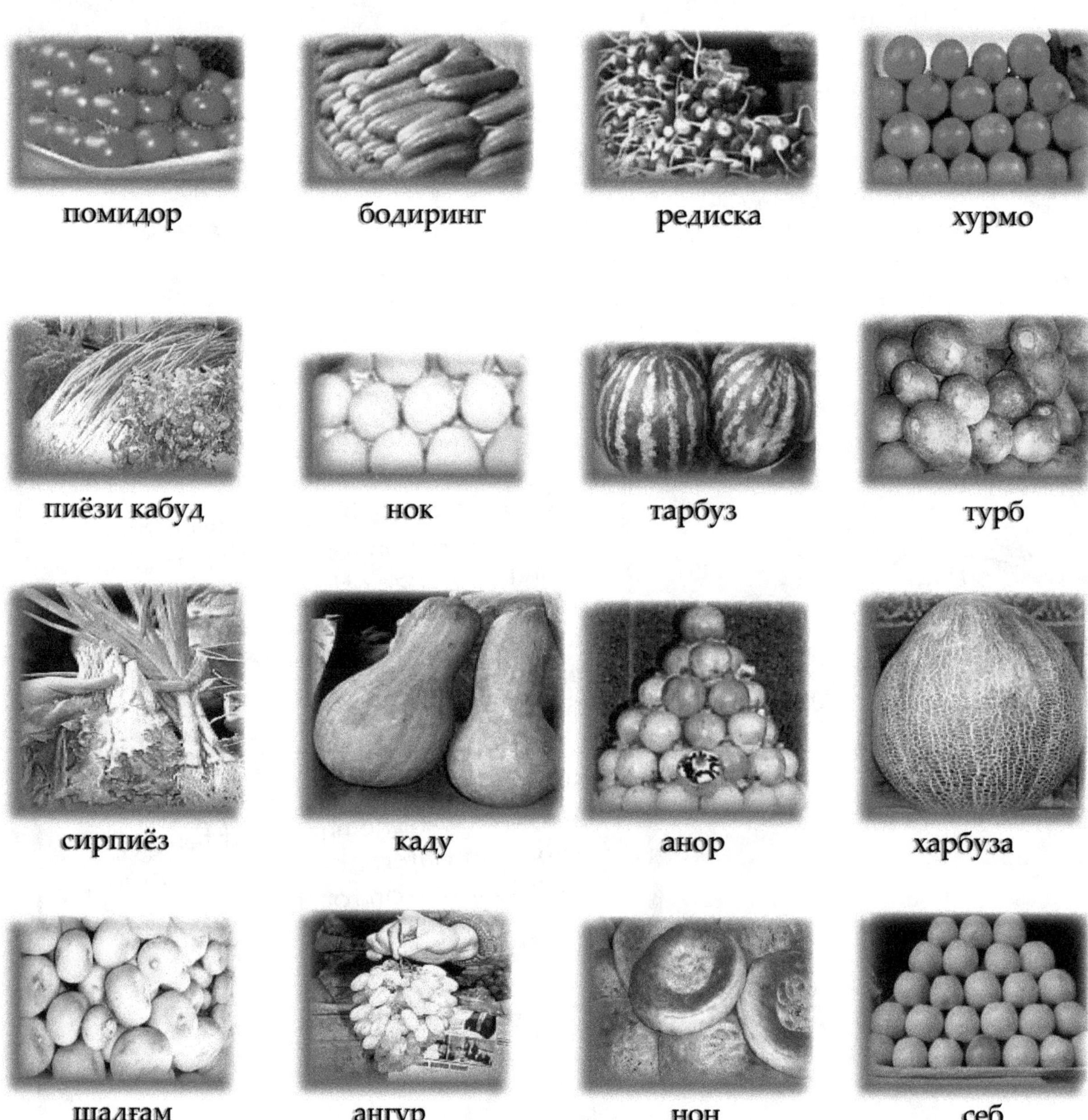

помидор бодиринг редиска хурмо

пиёзи кабуд нок тарбуз турб

сирпиёз каду анор харбуза

шалғам ангур нон себ

B. Bazaars are arranged in rows of stalls. Each row is devoted to one type of food. Read the name of each row in the chart below and guess what is in it. Then put the names of the items above in the appropriate columns.

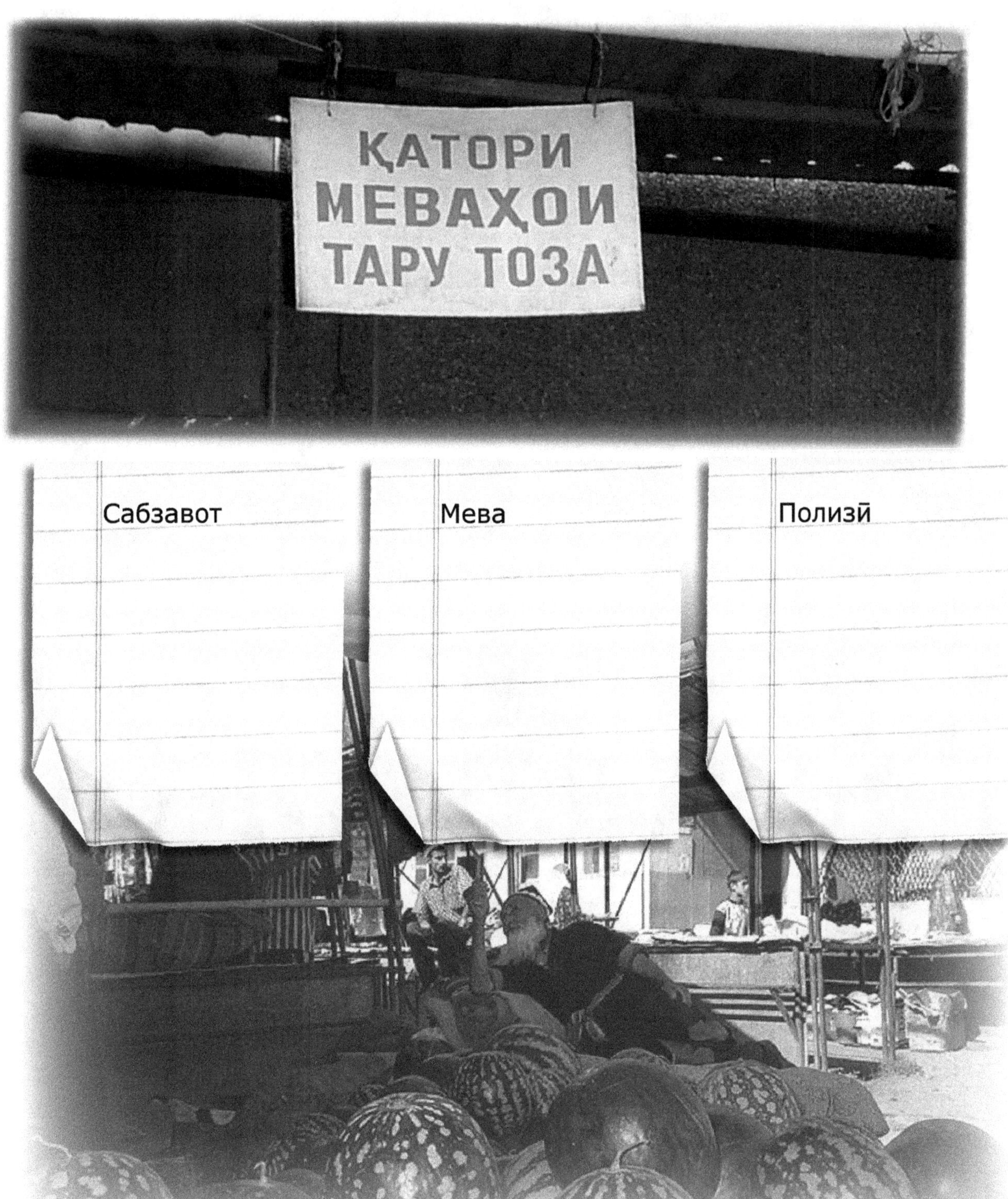

Сабзавот	Мева	Полизӣ

C. Look at pictures below and write the names of the fruits and vegetables you see.

2. ГУФТУГӮ

Машқи 2: *Дар бозор.* Listen to the conversation and fill in the blanks.

Ҷамол: **Салом ҷӯраҷон, дина ту дар куҷо будӣ?**
Суруш: Ман ба бозор рафтам ва каме мева харидам.
Ҷамол: **Хӯш, нархҳо чӣ хел буданд?**
Суруш: Оҳ, напурс. Як ҳафта пеш як кило себ ду сомонӣ буд. Дирӯз ман як кило себро ________________ харидам. Бин, дар як ҳафта як сомонӣ ________________ шуд.
Ҷамол: **Нархи ______________ чӣ?**
Суруш: Якто ____________ се сомонӣ буд, ҳоло панҷ сомонӣ аст. Он ҳам ______________ қиматтар шуд.
Ҷамол: **Наход, чаро нархҳо ______________ қимат шудаанд?**
Суруш: Намедонам, ба фикрам, ҳаво боронӣ буд ва ____________ ба бозор наомаданд.
Ҷамол: **Ман чор рӯз пеш ______________ ангурро ба ду сомонӣ харидам. Ҳоло чанд пул аст?**
Суруш: Нархи ________ ҳамон хел аст. Мебахшӣ, ҷӯраҷон, касе ба хонаам омад, хайр, то сӯҳбати ________________.
Ҷамол: **Хайр, хуш бош.**

Машқи 3: Make your own dialogue and practice with a partner.

3. ДАСТУР

USE OF БУДАН AND ШУДАН.

As you have learned, the predicate endings and **будан** mean *'to be'* and are used to describe the condition of something; they indicate a state. The verb **шудан** *'to become'* is used to indicate a change of state. Thus, **шудан** is often used in sentences with comparative forms of adjectives, but it can be used with any adjective.

Дирӯз ҳаво хунук буд. 'Yesterday the weather was cold.'
Имрӯз боз хунуктар шуд. 'Today it got a little colder.'

Нархи тарбуз як ҳафта пеш арзон буд.
'A week ago melons were cheap.'
Ҳоло тарбуз хеле қимат шуд.
'Now melons are (have become) very expensive.'

4. ХОНИШ

Машқи 4:  Read the text and underline all forms of the verb **будан** and **шудан**.

Шаҳри Душанбе деҳаи хурд буд. Ин деҳа бозори калон дошт. Ҳар рӯзи душанбе одамон ба он ҷо барои харид меомаданд. Аҳолии ин деҳа зиёд набуд. Дар чанд даҳсола ин деҳа шаҳри калону зебо шуд. Кӯчаҳояш калону обод ва аҳолиаш бисёр шуд. Ҳоло аҳолии шаҳри Душанбе тақрибан як миллион аст. Ин шаҳр пойтахти Тоҷикистон аст. Мо соли 2004-ум 80-солагии шаҳри Душанберо ҷашн гирифтем. Шаҳри мо шаҳри офтобист. Ба Душанбе хуш омадед!

5. ТАМОШО КУНЕД!

Машқи 5: A. Watch the video and answer the following questions.

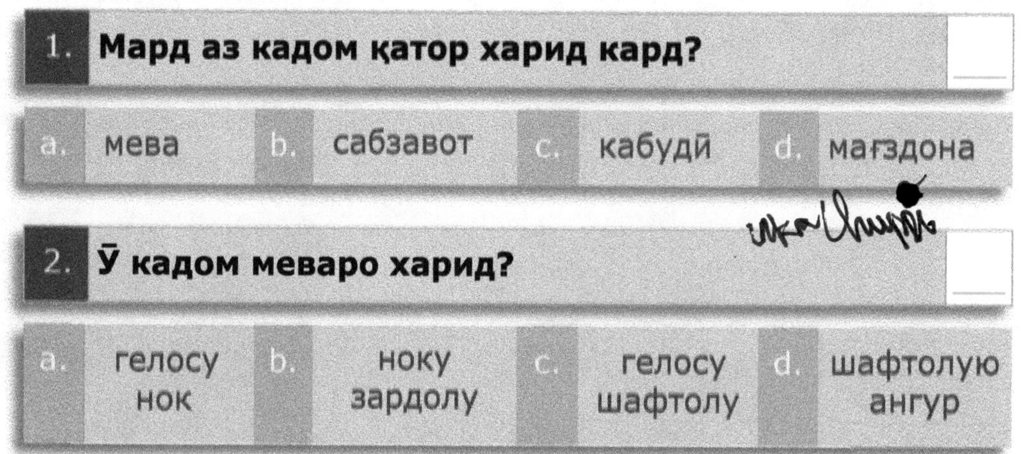

1. Мард аз кадом қатор харид кард? ____

a. мева b. сабзавот c. кабудӣ d. мағздона

2. Ӯ кадом меваро харид? ____

a. гелосу нок b. ноку зардолу c. гелосу шафтолу d. шафтолую ангур

B. Listen again and answer **дуруст** or **нодуруст**.

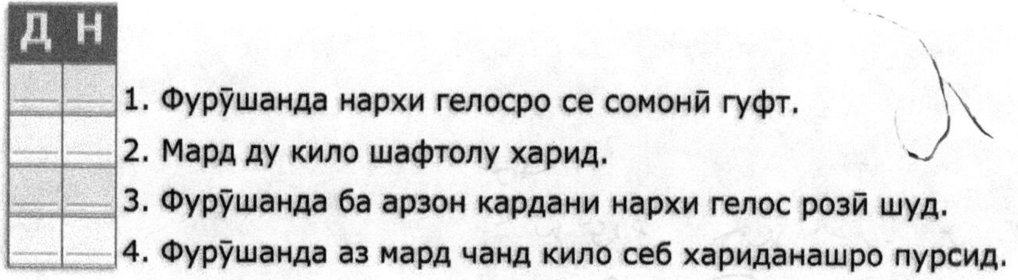

Д	Н	
___	___	1. Фурӯшанда нархи гелосро се сомонӣ гуфт.
___	___	2. Мард ду кило шафтолу харид.
___	___	3. Фурӯшанда ба арзон кардани нархи гелос розӣ шуд.
___	___	4. Фурӯшанда аз мард чанд кило себ хариданашро пурсид.

C.  Now watch the video again and number the sentences in the correct order:

	Мешавад.
	Як кило аз ин, як кило аз ин баркашед.
	Гелос чор сомон.
	Ин шафтолу чанд шуд?
	Чанд мешавад,арзон?
2	Ваалейкум ассалом.
	Инаш якуним, инаш сеюним.
	Ташаккур
4	Ин ду сомон.
	Марҳамат.
	Чор сомон?
1	Ассалому алейкум.
3	Арзон намешавад?
	Гелос чанд пул шуд?

Post-listening activities

D. Discuss with your partner the following questions:

1. Why there are no labels at the bazaar?
2. Do you like bargaining? Why or why not?

6. ХАТ

Машқи 6: Look at the cartoon below and write a short story about it. What is the truck driver thinking about?

Хмм...

Nom Mard, Naseem ast.

Mard as ajeeb. Mard, kyb kartouz

Mard Dushanbe. Kartouz nartyzada.

Mard Hisor furushanda dorad,

зеро Hisor Faron. Зеро, Dushanbe

Naseem nast.

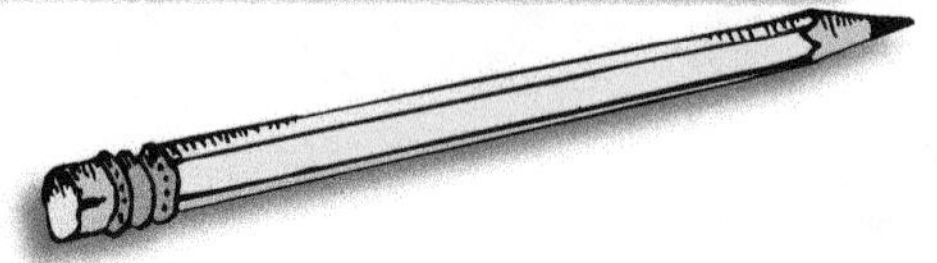

Bargaining Culture

Bargaining is part of Central Asian culture. People normally don't buy anything without bargaining to lower the price. The seller usually exaggerates the price to leave a space for bargaining because the customer will start bargaining from half the initial price. Eventually the buyer and seller will arrive at a reasonable price that will not hurt anybody's pocketbook. So, if you go to a Central Asian market, you will notice that there are no price labels for most of the items because there are no fixed prices and everything can be negotiated. The buyer also can taste anything before buying it.

В. ЧАНД ПУЛ? C. HOW MUCH?

1. СЕҲРИ СУХАН!

Машқи 1: A. Listen and practice.

себи хубонӣ	ангури ҳусайнӣ
харбузаи мирсанҷилӣ	кадуи ошӣ
тарбузи лалмӣ	зардолуи қандак
ангури тойфӣ	ҳандалак

B. How are fruit named in your country? Make a list and go through it with your partner. Switch roles.

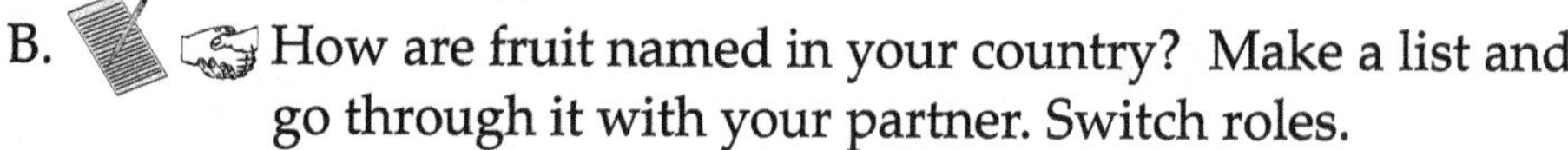

2. ГУФТУГӮ

Машқи 2: *Кадомаш маъқул?* A. Listen, fill in the blanks, and practice the conversation.

А: Зарина, ин себҳоро бин. ________ ва ба фикрам хеле бомаззаанд.
В: ________? ______?
А: Не, ________.
В: ________?
А: Ҳа, хеле зебо-а?
В: Ҳа, ________________ аст, вале ба ман ____________ ________. Ба ман ______ ________ маъқул аст.
А: Ин хел бошад, мана ин себро бин.
В: ________?
А: ____________.
В: Ҳа, ба ман ин себ хеле маъқул аст.

B. Listen to the rest of the conversation. What else do they buy?

Машқи 3: *Кор бо шарик.* Put the items for sale on your desk or table – pictures of fruit in different colors.

Student A: You are the clerk. Answer the customer's questions.
Student B: You are the customer. Ask about the price for each item. Say if you want to buy it.

А: Чӣ хизмат?
В: Ин себҳо чанд пул?
А: Кадомаш?

Now change roles.

Машқи 4: ***Кор бо шарик.*** Compare the fruit. Give your own opinion.

A: Ба ту кадом мева маъқул аст?
B: Ба ман себ маъқул аст, зеро фоидаи он зиёд аст.

3. *ДАСТУР*

3.1. DEMONSTRATIVES *(THIS ONE, THAT ONE)*

There are special demonstratives used when picking out something from a specified group. They are formed by adding the 3rd person singular possessive marker **-аш** to the basic demonstratives; this construction can also be used with adjectives.

Ин себ чанд пул аст?	**Он** себ?	**Кадомаш**?
Инаш?	**Ваяш?**	**Зардаш.**

This construction is not used with plural demonstratives but can be used with plural adjectives, which take the plural possessive suffix **-ашон.**

Ин тарбузҳо чандианд?	**Он** тарбузҳо?	**Кадомашон**?
Инҳо?	**Онҳо**?	Рах-раххояшон?

Машқи 5: Complete the conversations. Then practice with a partner.

1. **А: Бубахшед, ин себҳо чанданд?**
   В: ________? Шумо инҳоро гуфтед?
   А: Не, зардҳояшон.
   В: Ҳаа, нархи ________ 2 сомонӣ аст.
   А: Ду сомонӣ? Бешӯхӣ?
2. А: Ангур чанд шуд?
   В: ________?
   А: Мана инаш, ангури ҳусайнӣ.
   В: ________ 2 сомонӣ, ________ 3.
   А: Шудаш чанд аст?
   В: ________ якуним, ________ дуюним.
   А: Як кило аз ________ ва ду кило аз ________ диҳед.
   В: Марҳамат.

Машқи 6: Add prices to the items. Then ask and answer questions.

Шафтолу чанд аст?	
Кадомаш?	
Шафтолуи сурх.	
3 сомонӣ.	
Ӯҳӯ, хеле қимат-ку!	

USEFUL EXPRESSIONS

Ин арзон аст.	Шудаш чанд аст?
Ин қимат аст.	Арзонтар намешавад?

4. ХОНИШ

Машқи 7: Complete the conversation. Then practice with a partner.

1.	A: Кадом тарбуз калонтар аст?
	B: Инаш калонтар аст, вале ваяш арзонтар аст.
2.	A: Ин ангур аз он ангури тойфӣ ва ҳусайнӣ бомаззатар аст?
	B: Не, ана ин кишмиши сиёҳ аз ҳама бомаззатар аст.
3.	A: Ин зардолуҳоро бин! Кадомаш ба ту бисёртар маъқул аст?
	B: Ба ман инаш бисёртар маъқул аст. Зеро ин зардолуи қандак аст.
4.	A: Ба ту кадом мева бисёртар маъқул аст?
	B: Ба ман гелос аз ҳама бисёртар маъқул аст.
	A: Кадомаш? Гелоси зард ё ҷигарӣ?
	B: Албатта, гелоси ҷигарӣ, чунки он ширинтар аст.

Машқи 8: Read the text below and answer the questions.

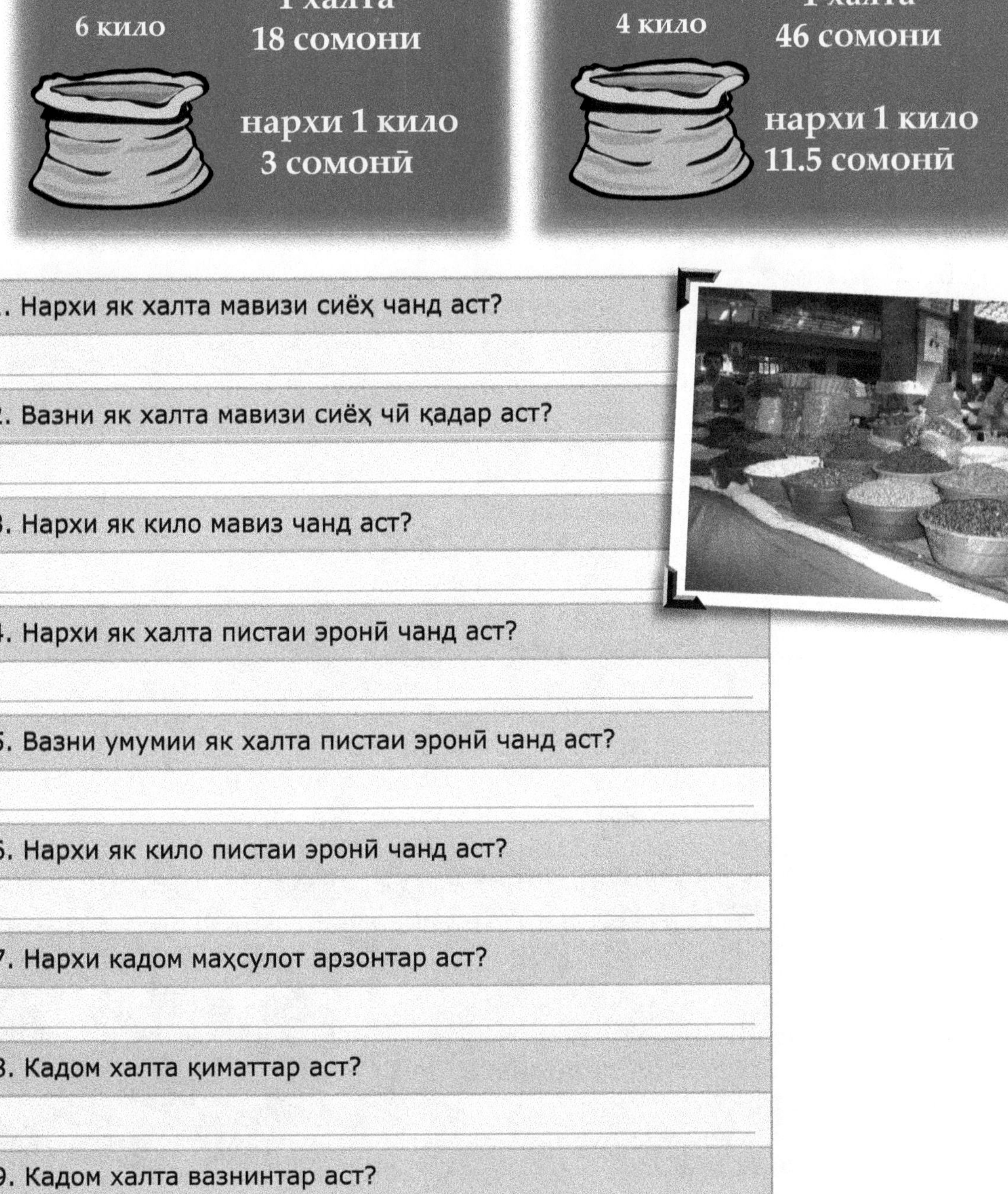

1. Нархи як халта мавизи сиёҳ чанд аст?

2. Вазни як халта мавизи сиёҳ чӣ қадар аст?

3. Нархи як кило мавиз чанд аст?

4. Нархи як халта пистаи эронӣ чанд аст?

5. Вазни умумии як халта пистаи эронӣ чанд аст?

6. Нархи як кило пистаи эронӣ чанд аст?

7. Нархи кадом маҳсулот арзонтар аст?

8. Кадом халта қиматтар аст?

9. Кадом халта вазнинтар аст?

5. ГЎШ КУНЕД

Машқи 8: *"Дар растаи меваҳо!"* Listen to Muzaffar and Rustam shopping. Complete the chart.

мева	нарх	Онҳо хариданд?		Сабаб
		Не	Ҳа	
тарбуз				
себ				
лимӯ				
анор				

Машқи 9: *Кадомаш ба ту маъқул аст?*

A. Listen, fill in the blanks, and practice.

Лола: Бубин, ин ангурҳо чӣ хел зебоянд? Ба ту ________ ________ маъқул аст?
Санавбар: Ба ман ________________.
Лола: ________________? Чаро?
Санавбар: Он бомаззатар аст.
Лола: Ба ман ________________ маъқул аст. Он ________ ________ аст.
Санавбар: Лекин он ________________ аст.
Лола: Дуруст. Бубахшед, нархи ангур чанд аст?
Фурӯшанда: Кадомаш?
Лола: ____________.
Фурӯшанда: Инаш?
Лола: Ҳа, ________.
Фурӯшанда: 5 сомонӣ.
Лола: 5 сомонӣ? Ӯҳӯ, хеле қимат-ку!
Санавбар: Гуфтам-ку!
Фурӯшанда: Барои Шумо 4 сомонӣ.
Лола: Ду кило диҳед.

B. Listen to the rest of the conversation. What does Sanavbar buy? How many kilos?

Машқи 10: Listen and practice.

Ба ту кадомаш маъқул аст?
Ба ман ваяш маъқул аст.
Ба ӯ сурхаш маъқул аст.
Кадомаш бисёртар маъқул аст?
Кадомаш камтар маъқул аст?
Ба ман сурхаш бисёртар маъқул аст.
Ваяш аз сурхаш арзонтар аст.
Инаш аз онаш бомаззатар аст.
Себи сурх аз себи зард калонтар аст.
Ин анор аз вай анор турштар аст.

6. ХАТ

Машқи 11:  How much do these fruit cost in your country? Complete the chart and then compare the prices in your country with the prices in Tajikistan.

3 СОМОНӢ = $1

	Нарх дар кишвари ман	Нарх дар Тоҷикистон
харбуза (1 дона)	________________	2 сомонӣ
ангур (1 кило)	________________	3 сомонӣ
себ (1 кило)	________________	1 сомонӣ
каду (1 дона)	________________	50 дирам

Дар Тоҷикистон бисёр чиз назар ба Амрико арзонтар аст. Масалан, дар Амрико як кило себ 3 доллар аст ва дар Тоҷикистон он фақат 1 сомонӣ - 33 сент аст. Як кило ангур..........

НАМУНА

____
____
____
____
____
____
____

Машқи 12: Conjugate the following verbs in the simple past tense.

харидан	to buy	
фурӯхтан	to sell	
савдо кардан	to bargain	
пурсидан	to ask	
ҷавоб додан	to answer	
иваз кардан	to exchange	
нишон додан	to show	
баркашидан	to weigh	

7. ТАМОШО КУНЕД!

Машқи 13: ***Pre-listening activities*** 

1. What kinds of items would you find being sold at a bazaar? Would you ever go to such a market? Why or why not?
2. What kinds of meat are these? Can you guess how much a kilo of meat costs in Dushanbe?
3. Where do you buy the meat? Do you buy it by the piece or by weight?

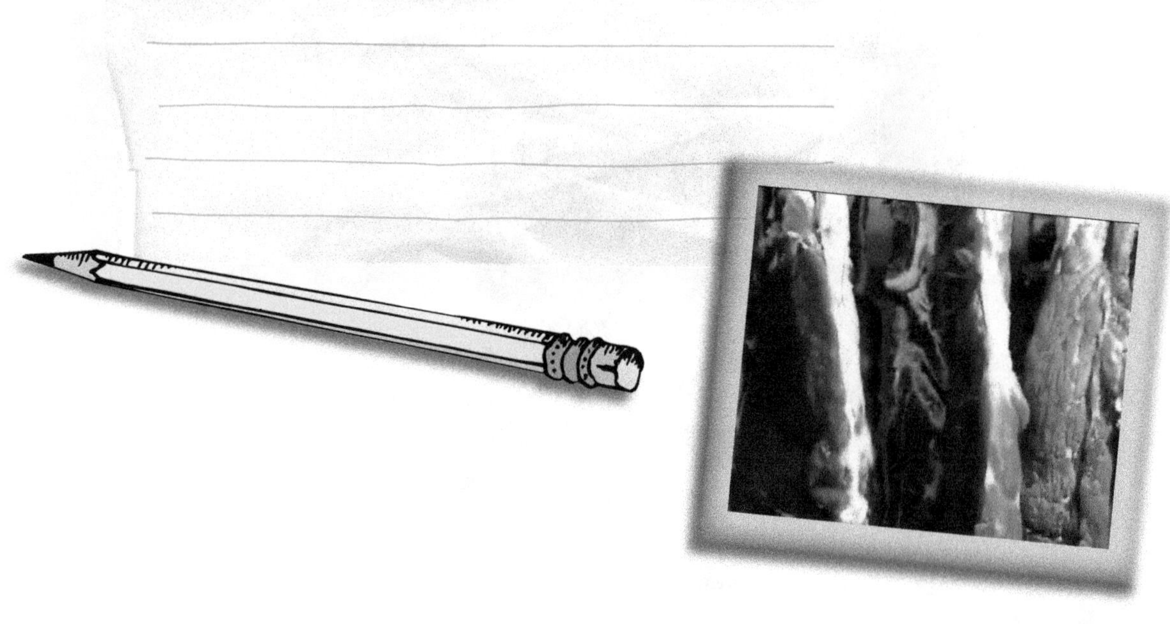

Listening activities

1. Муйсафед ба фурӯшанда чӣ гуна мурочиат кард?

a.	писар	b.	додар	c.	ака	d.	дада

2. Фурӯшанда нархи гӯштро чанд пул гуфт?

a.	чор сомонӣ	b.	ҳафту шашсад	c.	панчуним сомонӣ	d.	шашу ҳаштсад

3. Мӯйсафед ба чанд сомонӣ гӯшт харид?

a.	20 сомонӣ	b.	10 сомонӣ	c.	7 сомонӣ	d.	12 сомонӣ

Post-listening activities

5. Create your own dialogue with the seller and a different customer. Try selling two new things.

Фурӯшанда:	
Харидор:	
Фурӯшанда:	
Харидор:	
Фурӯшанда:	
Харидор:	
Фурӯшанда:	
Харидор:	
Фурӯшанда:	
Харидор:	

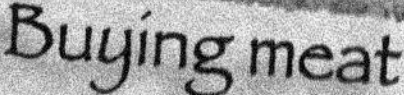

Buying meat

In most Central Asian countries people usually do not buy their meat in the regular stores but in butcher's shops, some of which are located in the bazaars. There are separate butcher's shops in other parts of the city. In the Central Asian and Muslim traditions people prefer to eat freshly-slaughtered meat. It is part of Tajik culinary customs to get meat with the bones left in. There is a saying, "**Гӯшт бе устухон намешавад**" (Meat without bones won't do; real meat has always bones in it). Meat with bones is used in a number of different dishes.

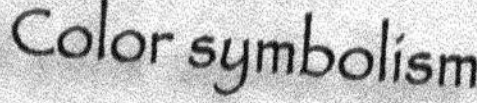

Color symbolism

In Tajik culture, the colors have symbolic meanings. For example:

green **сабз** – eternity; youth
blue **кабуд** – funeral
yellow **зард** – illness
red **сурх** – pride; good health
black **сиёҳ**– tragedy, evil
white **сафед** – cleanliness; luck

VOCABULARY
ЛУҒАТНОМА

Австралия	*n.* Australia
амният	*n.* safety; security
Англия	*n.* England
ангур	*n.* grapes
анор	*n.* pomegranate
арақ	*n.* alcohol/vodka
арзон	*adj.* cheap, inexpensive, low-priced
асал	*n.* honey
асп	*n.* horse
афлесун	*n.* orange (fruit, = **норинҷ**)
аҳолӣ	*n.* inhabitants, population
аҳром	*n.* food pyramid
банан	*n.* banana
банк	*n.* bank (financial) (= **бонк**)
баргардондан	*v.* to return, give back, bring back; restore
баркашидан	*v.* to weigh
баровардан	*v.* to take out (**аз** from)
бахшидан	*v.* to forgive
баҳор	*n.* spring (season)
баҳра бурдан	*v.* to enjoy, take pleasure in, benefit from
бегоҳ	*n.* evening
бенамак	*adj.* salt-free (= **фаҷ**)
биринҷ	*n.* rice
бовар кардан	*v.* to believe
бодиққат	*adv.* attentively, closely; carefully
бодинҷон	*n.* eggplant
бодиринг	*n.* cucumber
бозор	*n.* market, bazaar
бомазза	*adj.* tasty, delicious; good, nice
бонк	*n.* bank (financial) (= **банк**)
буқоқ	*n.* goiter; wen (= **ҷоғар**)
бурида	*n.* slice

витамин	*n.* vitamin
гандум	*n.* wheat
гардон(и)дан	*v.* to turn around, return (*trans.*), hand back (**ба** to)
гелос	*n.* sweet cherry
гов	*n.* cow
гуна	*n.* kind, type
гурусна	*adj.* hungry
гуфтугӯ	*n.* conversation, talk, chat
гӯсфанд	*n.* sheep
гӯшт	*n.* meat
гӯшти барра	*n.* lamb
гӯшти гов	*n.* beef
гӯшти гӯсфанд	*n.* mutton
гӯшти хук	*n.* pork
ғалла	*n.* corn
ғалладона	*n.* grain
ғафс	*adj.* thick
ғизо	*n.* meal
дандон	*n.* tooth, teeth
дег	*n.* pot, cauldron
дирам	*n.* unit of Tajik currency (0.01 **сомонӣ**)
доллар	*n.* dollar
дӯкони ширфурӯшӣ	*n.* dairy store
евро	*n.* euro
зайтун	*n.* olive
замбӯруғ	*n.* mushroom
занг задан	*v.* to call on the telephone (intransitive, requires **ба** to)
зардии тухм	*n.* yolk
зардолу	*n.* apricot
зарф	*n.* vessel; glass
зиёд	*adj.* much; a lot; plenty of
зиёфат	*n.* party
зимистон	*n.* winter
зиндон	*n.* jail

зира	*n.* cumin
зуком	*n.* influenza, grippe, flu
иваз кардан	*v.* to exchange, change, swap (**ба** for)
иқтисод	*n.* economy
илова кардан	*v.* to add
интиқол	*n.* transfer
ирсол	*n.* deposit
истеъмол	*n.* use, usage, application
йод	*n.* iodine
кабудӣ	*n.* greens, fresh herbs
кадом	*pron., adj.* which?
каду	*n.* pumpkin, gourd; squash
кам	*adj.* a little; not enough
Канада	*n.* Canada
карам	*n.* cabbage
картошка	*n.* potato
кашнич	*n.* cilantro
киса	*n.* pocket
кишвар	*n.* country
кишмиш	*n.* raisins (= **мавиз**); type of grape used to make raisins
кокакола	*n.* Coca Cola
кор кардан	*v.* to work
корд	*n.* knife
кӯҳна	*adj.* old (of things)
қадаҳ	*n.* glass (for wine)
Қазоқистон	*n.* Kazakhstan
қаймоқ	*n.* sour cream
қаланфур	*n.* pepper
қаланфури булғорӣ	*n.* green pepper
қалбакӣ	*adj.* false; spurious, forged
қандак	*adj.* small sweet apricot
қандалот	*n.* candy
қассоб	*n.* butcher
қатор	*n.* row; line
қаҳва	*n.* coffee

қимат	*adj.* expensive; costly
Қирғизистон	*n.* Kyrghyzstan
қошуқ	*n.* spoon
қулфинай	*n.* strawberry
лаблабу	*n.* beet
лағмон	*n.* *laghman* (noodle dish)
лимонад	*n.* lemonade
лимӯ	*n.* lemon
лӯбиё	*n.* beans, black-eyed peas, and similar legumes
мавиз	*n.* raisins, sultanas (= **кишмиш**)
мавизи сиёҳ	*n.* black raisins
мағз	*n.* kernel
мағздона	*n.* nuts
мағозаи хӯрокворӣ	*n.* grocery store
май	*n.* wine
макарон	*n.* macaroni; pasta
манат	*n.* *manat* (Turkmen currency)
марҳамат	*interj.* please; here you are; here you go
маст	*adj.* drunk
маҳсулот	*n.* product, produce
машғул шудан	*v.* to be busy (**бо** with)
мева	*n.* fruit
милиса	*n.* militia, police
модда	*n.* nutrient
моҳӣ	*n.* fish
мубодила	*n.* exchange
мубодилаи арз / асъор / пул	*n.* currency exchange, money exchange
мувофиқ омадан	*v.* to coincide, concur, agree (**бо** with)
Муғулистон	*n.* Mongolia
мураббо	*n.* jam, jelly
мурғ	*n.* chicken
мурғобӣ	*n.* duck
мурочиат кардан	*v.* to apply, turn, appeal (**ба** to)
мурч	*n.* black pepper

мушкилӣ	*n.* difficulty
намак	*n.* salt
нарх	*n.* price; worth, value; cost
нафақа	*n.* pension
нафақахӯр	*n.* pensioner
наход	*interj., adv.* really
нахӯд	*n.* pea(s)
нахӯди сабз	*n.* green pea
Нигар!	*interj.* Look here!
нигоҳ доштан	*v.* to keep, preserve, retain; maintain
нигоҳ кардан	*v.* to look at, examine, scrutinize
нишон додан	*v.* to show
нок	*n.* pear
нон	*n.* bread
нонвойхона	*n.* bakery
норинҷ	*n.* orange (fruit, = **афлесун**)
нуқта	*n.* point, place
нӯшокиҳои спиртӣ	*n.* alcoholic drink, liquor
об	*n.* water
оби маъдан	*n.* mineral water
оби ҷав	*n.* beer
ободод	*adj.* cultivated, flourishing
одатан	*adv.* usually; generally; habitually
олболу	*n.* cherry
олу	*n.* plum
омӯзиш	*n.* instruction, training
орд	*n.* flour
ошпаз	*n.* cook (pilaf maker)
палав	*n.* pilaf, pilau
панир	*n.* cheese
пешгирӣ кардан	*v.* to prevent
пешниҳод кардан	*v.* to offer, propose, suggest
пешхизмат	*n.* waiter
пиво	*n.* beer
пиёз	*n.* onion
пиёзи кабуд	*n.* green onion

пиёла	*n.* teacup (Asian traditional)
писта	*n.* pistachios
полизӣ	*n.* melons and gourds
помидор	*n.* tomato
порча	*n.* slice
президент	*n.* president
пудина	*n.* mint (spice)
пул	*n.* money
пул гузоштан	*v.* to deposit money
пурсидан (пурс)	*v.* to ask (**аз** indicates the person asked)
пухтан	*v.* to cook
пӯсида	*adj.* spoilt; rotten
равған	*n.* oil
равғани зард	*n.* butter
раста	*n.* row, line (= **қатор**)
редиска	*n.* radish (= **шалғамча**)
робита	*n.* connection, tie, liaison; means
розӣ шудан	*v.* to agree, consent (**ба** to)
Россия	*n.* Russia (= **Русия**)
рубл	*n.* ruble
сабаб	*n.* reason, purpose, aim
сабзавот	*n.* vegetables
сабзӣ	*n.* carrot
савдо кардан	*v.* to bargain
салат	*n.* salad
самбӯса	*n.* *samsa* (a type of small meat pie)
санҷидан	*v.* to examine, check
сари вақт	*adv.* in time, on time, timely, at the proper/right time
сафедии тухм	*n.* egg-white; protein
саҳар	*n.* morning
себ	*n.* apple
сир(пиёз)	*n.* garlic
сихкабоб	*n.* kebab
сом	*n.* *som* (Kyrghyz currency)

сомонӣ	*n.* *somoni* (Tajik currency)
сум	*n.* general name for all sorts of currency
суроға	*n.* address
сӯҳбат	*n.* conversation
табақча	*n.* plate
тақрибан	*adv.* approximately, nearly
талх	*adj.* bitter
тамом шудан	*v.* to come to an end, end (*intr.*)
танга	*n.* coin
танӯр	*n.* oven
тарбуз	*n.* watermelon
тарҷума кардан	*v.* to translate (**ба** into)
тафтиш	*n.* inspection, examination
тафтиш кардан	*v.* to examine, check (up), test
тахта	*n.* cutting board
ташна	*adj.* thirsty
тенге	*n.* *tenge* (Kazakh currency)
тирамоҳ	*n.* autumn, fall
тобистон	*n.* summer
торт	*n.* cake
тунд	*adj.* sour, tart, spicy
турб	*n.* green turnip
Туркманистон	*n.* Turkmenistan
турш	*adj.* sour
тухм	*n.* egg
тушбера	*n.* a traditional dish
тӯҳфа	*n.* present, gift
Украина	*n.* Ukraine
умумиҷаҳонӣ	*adj.* world; world-wide, universal
умумӣ	*adj.* common, public, general
устухон	*n.* bone
фасл(-и сол)	*n.* season
фатир	*n.* bread made of flour and butter
фиреб додан	*v.* to deceive, cheat, swindle
фоида	*n.* benefit

фунт	*n.* pound
фурӯхтан (фурӯш)	*v.* to sell
фурӯш	*n.* sale
фурӯшанда	*n.* seller, salesman, (store) clerk, shop assistant
хазинадор	*n.* cashier (= **хозин**)
халта	*n.* sack; bag
хамир	*n.* dough
харбуза	*n.* melon
харидан (хар)	*v.* to buy; purchase
харидор	*n.* buyer, customer, client
хидмат	*n.* service
хозин	*n.* cashier (= **хазинадор**)
хокаи қанд	*n.* powdered sugar
хоҳиш кардан	*v.* to desire
хун	*n.* blood
хунук	*adj.* cold
хурмо	*n.* persimmon
хӯрок	*n.* food, meal, dish
хӯроки нисфирӯзӣ	*n.* lunch
ҳазм	*n.* digestion
ҳалво	*n.* halwa (type of sweet)
ҳамеша	*adv.* always
ҳамкорӣ	*n.* collaboration, cooperation
ҳандалак	*n.* canteloupe
Ҳиндустон	*n.* India
ҳисоб кардан	*v.* to count
ҳозир	*adv.* now; hold on; just a minute
Ҳолландия	*n.* Holland
ҳурмат кардан	*v.* to respect
чангак	*n.* fork
чӣ гуна	*adj.* what kind (of)?; *adv.* in what ways?, how?
Чӣ хизмат?	*phr.* How can I help you?
чойи кабуд	*n.* green tea
чормағз	*n.* walnut

чумча	*n.* spoon
ҷавоб додан	*v.* to answer
ҷашн гирифтан	*v.* to celebrate
ҷигар	*n.* liver
ҷигарӣ	*adj.* purple, liver-colored
ҷогар	*n.* goiter; wen (=**буқоқ**)
ҷурғот	*n.* kefir (a beverage of fermented cow's milk)
ҷӯшон(и)дан	*v.* to boil (*tr.*)
шабнишинӣ	*n.* party
шакар	*n.* sugar
шалғам	*n.* turnip
шалғамча	*n.* radish (= **редиска**)
шарбат	*n.* juice
шарбати афлесун	*n.* orange juice
шарбати лимӯ	*n.* lemon juice
шарбати себ	*n.* apple juice
шафтолу	*n.* peach
Швейтсария	*n.* Switzerland
шибит	*n.* dill
шир	*n.* milk
ширбиринҷ	*n.* rice in milk
ширин	*adj.* sweet
ширқаҳва	*n.* coffee with milk
ширчой	*n.* milk tea
шиша	*n.* bottle
шӯрбо	*n.* soup
Эрон	*n.* Iran

APPENDIX 1 Tajiki - English Glossary

абрнок	*adj.* cloudy
абрӯ	*n.* eyebrow
аввал	*adj.* first
Аврупо	*n.* Europe
Австралия	*n.* Australia
Австрия	*n.* Austria
авсун	*n.* relationship between the wives of two brothers (*sister-in-law by marriage only*)
аёдат	*n.* visit
аз	*prep.* from
аз хурдӣ	*phr.* from childhood
азбаски	*conj.* because, since
азнавоиладоршуда	*adj.* remarried
айвон	*n.* balcony, verandah (= **балкон**)
айнак	*n.* eyeglasses
ака (ако)	*n.* older brother; term of address for a man one's age
акнун	*adv.* now
акс	*n.* photograph (= **расм, сурат**)
аксар(и) вақт	*adv.* most of the time
ақида	*n.* opinion
албатта	*adv.* certainly, of course
Алмаато	*n.* Almaty (*Alma-Ata, former capital of Kazakhstan*)
алоҳида	*adj.* separate
Алҷазоир	*n.* Algeria
амак	*n.* father's brother, paternal uncle; term of address for an older man
амакбача	*n.* cousin (*paternal uncle's child*)
Америка	*n.* America; USA (= **Амрико**)
амма	*n.* father's sister, paternal aunt
аммабача	*n.* cousin (*paternal aunt's child*)
амният	*n.* safety; security
Амрико	*n.* America; USA (= **Америка**)
амрикоӣ	*adj.* American
ана, он	*pron.* that one
англис	*n.* English (*person*) (= **инглис**)
англисӣ	*adj.* English
Англия	*n.* England
ангур	*n.* grapes
анор	*n.* pomegranate
анъана	*n.* tradition
апа	*n.* older sister; term of address for a woman one's age
арақ	*n.* alcohol/vodka
арзон	*adj.* cheap, inexpensive, low-priced
Арманистон	*n.* Armenia
арӯс	*n.* fiancée, bride
асал	*n.* honey
аслан	*adv.* really, in fact
асп	*n.* horse
аст	*v.* is
атлас	*n.* atlas silk (*silk from the atlas moth*)
атроф	*prep.* around
Афғонистон	*n.* Afghanistan
афлесун	*n.* orange (*fruit, also* **норинҷ**)
Африқо	*n.* Africa

Африқои Ҷанубӣ	*n.* South Africa
афсӯс	*interj.* unfortunately, alas
ахбор	*n.* news (*pl. of* **хабар**)
ахлотдон	*n.* trashcan
аҳолӣ	*n.* inhabitants, population
аҳром	*n.* pyramid
аҷоиб	*adj.* interesting
ашё	*n.* things, objects
ба	*prep.* towards
ба фикрам	*phr.* in my opinion
бағочхона	*n.* luggage room
Бадахшон	*n.* Badakhshon (*region of Tajikistan*)
баёнот	*n.* expressions
байн	*prep.* between; *adj.* middle (*see* **миён, миёна**)
баланд	*adj.* long
бале	*interj.* yes (= **ҳа**)
балкон	*n.* balcony (= **айвон**)
банан	*n.* banana
Бангола	*n.* Bangladesh
банд	*adj.* busy
банда	*n.* slave
бандча	*n.* bundle
банк	*n.* bank (*financial*) (= **бонк**)
бар	*n.* width
баргардондан	*v.* to return, give back, bring back; restore
бардам	*adj.* healthy, rested
баркашидан (баркаш)	*v.* to weigh (*trans.*)
барқ	*n.* electricity; lightning (*see* **раъду барқ**)
барномасоз	*n.* programmer
баробар	*n.* equal
баровардан (баровар, барор)	*v.* to take out (**аз** from)

бародар	*n.* brother
барои	*prep.* for
барои чӣ	*adv.* why? (= **чаро**)
барпо гардидан	*v.* to take place
барра	*n.* lamb
барф	*n.* snow
барфӣ	*adj.* snowy, of snow
барфреза	*n.* snowflake
бахшидан (бахш)	*v.* to forgive
баҳона кардан	*v.* to make an excuse
баҳор	*n.* spring (*season*)
баҳра бурдан	*v.* to enjoy, take pleasure in, benefit from
баъзе	*adj.* some, several (*precedes noun*)
бе	*prep.* without
беабр	*adj.* cloudless
бева	*n.* widower
бегоҳ	*n.* evening
бегоҳӣ	*adv.* in the evening
бедор шудан	*v.* to wake up (*intr.*)
безеб	*adj.* ugly, unattractive
бемор	*adj.* ill, sick
бенамак	*adj.* salt-free
Берлин	*n.* Berlin
берун	*prep., n.* outside
бетартиб	*adj.* messy, disorganized (*see* **чиркин**)
бибию бобо	*n.* grandparents
бибӣ	*n.* grandmother; term of address for an old woman (= **модаркалон**)
биёбон	*n.* desert
бинӣ	*n.* nose
биринҷ	*n.* rice
бисёр	*adj., adv.* much, a lot
бист	*num.* twenty
бо	*prep.* with

боақл	*adj.* smart, clever (*see* **доно**)
бобо	*n.* grandfather; term of address for an old man (= **падаркалон**)
бовар кардан	*v.* to believe
бодиққат	*adv.* attentively, closely; carefully
бодинҷон	*n.* eggplant
бодиринг	*n.* cucumber
боду ҳаво	*n.* weather (= **обу ҳаво**)
боз як бор	*adv.* once more, again
бозӣ	*n.* game
бозӣ кардан	*v.* to play
бозор	*n.* market, bazaar
бой	*adj.* rich (**аз** in)
Боку	*n.* Baku
боқувват	*adj.* strong
Боливия	*n.* Bolivia
боло	*prep.* above
бомазза	*adj.* tasty, delicious; good, nice
бонк	*n.* bank (*financial*) (= **банк**)
бону	*n.* lady; wife, woman (*see* **зан**)
борон	*n.* rain
боронӣ	*adv.* rainy; *n.* raincoat
борон боридан (бор)	*v.* to rain
боҷа	*n.* relationship between the husbands of two sisters (*brother-in-law by marriage only*)
бубахшед	*interj.* sorry
бузург	*adj.* big, large (= **калон**)
буқоқ	*n.* goiter; wen (= **ҷоғар**)
Булғор	*n.* Bulgaria
бунафш	*adj.* violet
бурдан (бар)	*v.* to carry, take, bring; to win
бурида	*n.* slice
буридан (бур)	*v.* to cut
бӯр[1]	*n.* chalk
бӯр[2]	*adj.* gray
вазифаи хонагӣ	*n.* homework
вазн	*n.* weight
вазнин	*adj.* heavy, difficult, serious
вазъ	*n.* condition
вай	*pron.* he/she
вақт	*n.* time
вале	*conj.* but
варақ	*n.* (sheet of) paper
варақаи қайд	*n.* registration form
варзиш	*n.* sport
Варшава	*n.* Warsaw
васеъ	*adj.* wide
Вашингтон	*n.* Washington
Венгрия	*n.* Hungary (= **Маҷористон**)
видеокасета	*n.* videotape
видеомагнитофон	*n.* videocassette player, VCR
витамин	*n.* vitamin
волид (волидайн)	*n.* parent
вохӯрдан	*v.* to meet
вуҷуд доштан	*v.* to exist
ганда	*adj.* bad
гандум	*n.* wheat
гап	*n.* speech
гап задан (зан)	*v.* to speak
гардон(и)дан (гардон)	*v.* to turn around, return (*trans.*), hand back (**ба** to)
гарм	*adj.* hot
гармӣ	*n.* heat
гелос	*n.* sweet cherry
гиёҳ	*n.* grass, herb
гилем	*n.* rug, carpet (= **қолин**)
гирифтан (гир)	*v.* to take, get

гов	*n.* cow
голф	*n.* golf
гузашта	*adj.* past, last (*week, etc.*)
гузаштан (гузар)	*v.* to pass (**аз** by, across)
гузоштан (гузор)	*v.* to put; allow
гул	*n.* flower
гулдон	*n.* vase
гулобӣ	*adj.* pink, reddish
гум шудан	*v.* to get lost
гуна	*n.* kind, type
гуногун	*adj.* various, of different kinds
гурба	*n.* cat (= **пишак**)
гурусна (гушна)	*adj.* hungry
гуфтан (гӯ, гӯй)	*v.* to say, tell
гуфтугӯ	*n.* conversation, talk, chat
гӯсфанд	*n.* sheep, ewe
гӯш	*n.* ear
гӯш кардан	*v.* to listen
гӯшт	*n.* meat
гӯшти барра	*n.* lamb
гӯшти гов	*n.* beef
гӯшти гӯсфанд	*n.* mutton
гӯшти хук	*n.* pork
ғалла	*n.* grain
ғалладона	*n.* grains
Ғарм	*n.* Gharm
ғафс	*adj.* thick
ғижжак	*n.* *ghijjak*, Tajik musical instrument
ғизо	*n.* nutrition, meal
ғор	*n.* cave
ғуруби офтоб	*n.* sunset
давлатӣ	*adj.* state, national, official
дағал	*adj.* rough, rude
дақиқа (дақоиқ)	*n.* minute (*of time*)
Данғара	*n.* Danghara
дандон	*n.* tooth, teeth
Дания	*n.* Denmark
дар[1]	*n.* door
дар[2]	*prep.* at, in
дарахт	*n.* tree
дарё	*n.* river
дароз	*adj.* long
дарозӣ	*n.* length
даромадан (даро)	*v.* to come in
дарс	*n.* class
дарс додан	*v.* to teach
дарун	*prep.* inside
дар даст	*phr.* at hand, on hand
даст	*n.* hand
дафтар	*n.* notebook
дафтарча	*n.* small notebook
даҳ	*num.* ten
даъват кардан	*v.* to invite (**ба** to)
даъватнома	*n.* invitation (*card*)
девор	*n.* wall
дег	*n.* pot, cauldron
дер кардан	*v.* to be late
деҳа	*n.* village
дигар	*adj.* other
дидан (бин)	*v.* to see
дидор	*n.* meeting
дин	*n.* religion
дирам	*n.* unit of Tajik currency (0.01 **сомонӣ**)
дирӯз (дина)	*adv.*, *n.* yesterday
додан (диҳ/деҳ)	*v.* to give
додар	*n.* younger brother; term of address for younger man (*see* **ука**)
додарарӯс	*n.* brother-in-law (= **додаршӯй, ҳевар**)
додарзода	*n.* nephew or niece by a brother (*see* **ҷиян**)

додаршӯй	*n.* brother-in-law (= **додарарӯс, ҳевар**)
доира	*n.* drum, Tajik musical instrument
доира кашидан (каш)	*v.* to circle
доирашакл	*adj.* round (= **мудаввар**)
доллар	*n.* dollar
домод	*n.* groom, son-in-law
донишҷӯ	*n.* student
доно	*adj.* smart, wise (*see* **боақл**)
ду	*num.* two
дувоздаҳ	*num.* twelve
дугона	*n.* friend (*used between females*)
дугоник	*n.* twins
дуредгар	*n.* carpenter
дуруст	*adj.* correct
дутор	*n. dutor*, Tajik musical instrument
духтар	*n.* daughter, girl
духтур	*n.* doctor
душанбе	*n.* Monday
Душанбе	*n.* Dushanbe (*capital of Tajikistan*)
дӯкони ширфурӯшӣ	*n.* dairy store
дӯст	*n.* friend, comrade (= **рафиқ, ҷӯра**)
евро	*n.* euro
ёд	*n.* memory
ёздаҳ	*num.* eleven
ёқут	*n.* ruby
ёр	*n.* friend
жола	*n.* hail
забон	*n.* language, tongue
завҷа	*n.* wife (*see* **зан**)
Заир	*n.* Zaire
заиф	*adj.* weak
зайтун	*n.* olive
замбӯрӯғ	*n.* mushroom (= **занбӯрӯғ**)
зан	*n.* wife, woman (*see* **бону, завҷа**)
занбӯрӯғ	*n.* mushroom
занг задан	*v.* to call on the telephone (*intr., requires* **ба** to)
зарб	*n.* multiplied by
зард	*adj.* yellow
зардии тухм	*n.* yolk
зардолу	*n.* apricot
зарф	*n.* vessel; glass
зебо	*adj.* pretty, beautiful
зер	*prep.* under (= **таг**)
зиёд	*adj.* much; a lot; plenty of
зиёфат	*n.* party
Зимбабве	*n.* Zimbabwe
зимистон	*n.* winter
зиндагӣ	*n.* life (= **ҳаёт**)
зиндагӣ кардан	*v.* to live, reside (*see* **сокин будан**); to stay (*in some place*)
зиндон	*n.* jail
зира	*n.* cumin, caraway
зоғ	*n.* raven
зодрӯз	*n.* birthday
Зодрӯз муборак!	*phr.* Happy birthday !
зуком	*n.* influenza, grippe, flu
ибора	*n.* phrase
иваз кардан	*v.* to exchange, change, swap (**ба** for)
иёлат	*n.* state (*region*)
Иёлоти Муттаҳидаи Амрико	*n.* The United States of America
издивоҷ кардан	*v.* to marry
издивоҷшуда	*adj.* married (= **мутааҳҳил, оиладор**)

иқтисод	*n.* economy
илова кардан	*v.* to add
имрӯз	*adv., n.* today
имтиҳон	*n.* exam, test
ин	*pron., adj.* this
ин кас	*n.* this person (*polite*)
ин қадар	*adv.* so, such, to this extent
ин ҷо	*pron.* here
Ингилистон	*n.* England
инглис	*n.* Englishman (= **англис**)
индекс	*n.* zip code
Индиана	*n.* Indiana
инсон	*n.* person
интизор шудан	*v.* to wait
интиқол	*n.* transfer
ирсол	*n.* deposit
Исломобод	*n.* Islamabad
исм	*n.* noun, name
Истанбул	*n.* Istanbul
Истаравшан	*n.* Istaravshan
истеъмол	*n.* use, usage, application
истироҳат	*n.* rest; holiday
истироҳат кардан	*v.* to have a rest, relax
истодан (ист)	*v.* to stop, stand
Исфара	*n.* Isfara
иҷора	*n.* rent
иҷро кардан	*v.* to fulfill, carry out
йигит	*n.* young man
йод	*n.* iodine
кабуд	*adj.* blue
кабудӣ	*n.* greens, fresh herbs
кадом	*pron., adj.* which?
каду	*n.* pumpkin, gourd; squash
каён	*n.* ancient Persian kings
кай	*adv.* when?
калид	*n.* key
калима	*n.* word
калон	*adj.* big, large (= **бузург**)
калонӣ	*adj.* elder, older (*of siblings*)
калонсол	*adj.* elder, big (= **куҳансол**)
кам	*adj.* a little; not enough
камабр	*adj.* partly cloudy
камбағал	*adj.* poor
каме	*adv.* a little
камон	*n.* bow (*for arrows*)
Канада	*n.* Canada
канӣ	*adv.* (*coll.*) where at?, where to? (= **дар куҷо, ба куҷо**)
карам	*n.* cabbage
кардан (кун)	*v.* to do, make
картошка	*n.* potato
кас	*n.* person (= **шахс**)
кат	*n.* bed
кашидан (каш)	*v.* to pull, take off, take down; smoke (*tobacco*)
кашнич	*n.* cilantro
Каюмарс	*n.* Kayumars
келин	*n.* daughter-in-law, bride
Киев	*n.* Kiev
кило	*n.* kilogram
киса	*n.* pocket
китоб	*n.* book
китобхона	*n.* library
кишвар	*n.* country
кишмиш	*n.* type of grape used to make raisins; raisins (= **мавиз**)
кӣ	*pron.* who?
кокакола	*n.* Coca Cola

компютер	*n.* computer
Конибодом	*n.* Konibodom
Копенҳаген	*n.* Copenhagen
кор	*n.* job, work, item of business
кор кардан	*v.* to work
корд	*n.* knife
котиб	*n.* male clerk (*see* **котиба**)
котиба	*n.* female clerk (*see* **котиб**)
курсӣ	*n.* chair
куҳансол	*adj.* old (= **пир, солхӯрда**); elder, big (= **калонсол**)
куҷо	*pron.* where? (*see* **канӣ**)
кушодан (кушо)	*v.* to open, unwrap, undo
куштан (куш)	*v.* to kill, turn off (lights, etc.)
кӯдак	*n.* child, kid
Кӯлоб	*n.* Kulob
кӯтоҳ	*adj.* short
кӯҳ	*n.* mountain
кӯҳна	*adj.* old (*of things*)
кӯча	*n.* street
кӯшидан (кӯш)	*v.* to strive, make effort
қад	*n.* height
қадаҳ	*n.* glass (for wine)
қадбаланд	*adj.* tall (= **қаддароз**)
қаддароз	*adj.* tall (= **қадбаланд**)
қадимулайём	*n.* antiquity
қадпаст	*adj.* short (*of height*)
қазоқ	*adj.* Kazakh
Қазоқистон	*n.* Kazakhstan
қаймоқ	*n.* sour cream
қайчӣ	*n.* scissors
қалам	*n.* pencil
қаламтезкунак	*n.* pencil sharpener
қаланфур	*n.* pepper (= **занҷабил**)
қаланфури булғорӣ	*n.* green/sweet pepper
қалбакӣ	*adj.* false; spurious, forged
қандак	*adj.* small sweet apricot
қандалот	*n.* candy
қарта	*n.* card
қартабозӣ	*n.* card game
қассоб	*n.* butcher
қатор	*n.* row; line
қафо	*prep.* behind
қаҳва	*n.* coffee
қаҳваранг	*adj.* brown
қим(м)ат	*adj.* expensive; costly
Қирғизистон	*n.* Kyrghyzstan
қитъа	*n.* continent
қолин	*n.* rug, carpet (= **гилем**)
қошуқ	*n.* spoon
қудо	*n.* relationship between groom's and bride's parents
қулфинай	*n.* strawberry
қуттӣ	*n.* box, chest
Қӯрғонтеппа	*n.* Qurghonteppa (*city of Tajikistan*)
лаб	*n.* lip; *prep.* by, on the edge of
лаблабу	*n.* beet
лағмон	*n.* laghman (*noodle dish*)
лаёқат	*n.* talent
либос	*n.* clothes
лимонад	*n.* lemonade
лимӯ	*n.* lemon
лифт	*n.* lift, elevator
лола	*n.* tulip
Лубнон	*n.* Lebanon
луғат	*n.* dictionary, glossary

лутфан	*adv.* please (= **марҳамат**)
лӯбиё	*n.* beans, black-eyed peas, and similar legumes
Люксембург	*n.* Luxembourg
мавиз	*n.* raisins, sultanas (= **кишмиш**)
мавизи сиёҳ	*n.* black raisins
мавҷуд	*n.* existence
магнитофон	*n.* tape player
мағз	*n.* nut, kernel
мағздона	*n.* nuts
мағоза	*n.* store; shop (= **дӯкон**)
мағозаи хӯрокворӣ	*n.* grocery store, grocer's
Мағриб	*n.* West
май	*n.* wine (= **шароб**)
майда	*adj.* little, small (= **хурд**)
макарон	*n.* macaroni; pasta
макон	*n.* place
мамлакат	*n.* nation
ман	*pron.* I, me
мана, ин	*pron.* this one
манат	n. manat (Turkmen currency)
марбут	*adj.* related
мард	*n.* man
мардум	*n.* people
марказ	*n.* center
марҳамат	*interj.* please (= **лутфан**); here you are; here you go
Маскав	*n.* Moscow
маст	*adj.* drunk
масҷид	*n.* mosque
матбах	*n.* kitchen (= **ошхона**)
маҳ	*n.* moon, month (= **моҳ**)
маҳал	*n.* place (= **ҷо**)
маҳбуба	*n.* girlfriend, sweetheart
маҳсулот	*n.* product, produce, ingredients
Маҷористон	*n.* Hungary (= **Венгрия**)
машғул шудан	*v.* to be busy (**бо** with)
машқ	*n.* exercise
машҳур	*adj.* famous
маъқул	*adj.* interesting
маълумот	*n.* information
маъно	*n.* meaning (= **маънӣ**)
Мебахшед	*interj.* sorry
мева	*n.* fruit
Мексика	*n.* Mexico
метр	*n.* meter
меҳмон	*n.* guest, visitor
меҳмонхона	*n.* hotel; guesthouse
меҳрубон	*adj.* kind
миён	*prep.* among, between; *adj.* middle (*see* **байн, миёна**); *n.* small of the back
миёна	*adj.* middle (see **байн, миён**)
мижа	*n.* eyelash
миз	*n.* table, desk
милиса	*n.* policeman, militia, police
Миср	*n.* Egypt
мо	*pron.* we, us
модар	*n.* mother
модарарӯс	*n.* mother-in-law
модаркалон	*n.* grandmother (= **бибӣ**)
модаршӯй	*n.* mother-in-law (= **модарарӯс, хушдоман**)
модда	*n.* nutrient
мондан (мон)	*v.* to put, place, put down
Монтана	*n.* Montana

моҳ	*n.* month
моҳӣ	*n.* fish
моҳтоб	*n.* the moon
муаллим	*n.* teacher
муаррифӣ	*n.* (personal) introduction
мубодила	*n.* exchange
мубодилаи арз / асъор / пул	*n.* currency exchange, money exchange
мувофиқ	*adj.* appropriate (*see* **мувофиқи**)
мувофиқ омадан	*v.* to coincide, concur, agree (**бо** with)
Муғулистон	*n.* Mongolia
мудаввар	*adj.* round (= **доирашакл**)
муйсафед	*n.* old man
мумкин	*adj.* allowed
мураббо	*n.* jam, jelly
мурғ	*n.* chicken, hen
мурғобӣ	*n.* duck (bird)
мурочиат кардан	*v.* to apply, turn, appeal (**ба** to)
мурч	*n.* black pepper
мусиқии анъанавӣ	*n.* classical or traditional music
мусиқӣ	*n.* music
мутааҳҳил	*adj.* married (= **издивочшуда, оиладор**)
муфаттиш	*n.* detective
муҳандис	*n.* engineer
муҳосиб	*n.* accountant
муҷаррад	*n.* bachelor, single
мушкилӣ	*n.* difficulty
муштарӣ	*n.* customer (*see* **миҷоз**)
мӯй	*n.* hair
Мӯъминобод	*n.* Mu'minobod
набера	*n.* grandchild
наберадухтар	*n.* granddaughter
набераписар	*n.* grandson
нав	*adj.* new
навад	*num.* ninety
нависанда	*n.* writer
навиштан (навис)	*v.* to write
навор	*n.* film
навохтан (навоз)	*v.* to play a musical instrument
нағз	*adj.* good (= **хуб**)
назар	*n.* opinion
назд	*prep.* near
нақл кардан	*v.* to describe, tell
намак	*n.* salt
намнокӣ	*n.* humidity
намоз	*n.* Muslim prayer offered five times a day
намудан (намо)	*v.* to seem, appear
намуна	*n.* example, model
нарх	*n.* price; worth, value; cost
насаб	*n.* last name
нафақа	*n.* pension
нафақахӯр	*n.* pensioner
наход	*interj., adv.* really
нахустин	*adj.* first (*precedes noun*)
нахӯд	*n.* pea(s)
нахӯди сабз	*n.* green pea
не	*interj.* no
немис	*adj.* German (*person*) (= **олмонӣ**)
немисӣ	*adj.* German (*language*) (= **олмонӣ**)
Нигерия	*n.* Nigeria
нигоҳ доштан	*v.* to keep, preserve, retain; maintain
нигоҳ кардан	*v.* to look (**ба** at), examine, scrutinize
Нидерландия	*n.* Netherlands
низ	*adv.* (*literary*) too (= **ҳам**)

ним	*n.* a half (= **нисф**)
нисфирӯзӣ	*adj.* noontime, midday, early afternoon
ниҳоят	*adv.* finally; *n.* end
нишастан (шин)	*v.* to sit down
нишонии ҷойи истиқомат	*n.* address
нишон додан	*v.* to show
нок	*n.* pear (= **муруд**)
ном	*n.* name
номзад	*n.* fiancé, fiancée
номи хонаводагӣ	*n.* family name (*legal term*) (= **насаб**)
нон	*n.* bread
нонвойхона	*n.* bakery
нопок	*adj.* unclean; tainted, corrupt (*see* **чиркин**)
норинҷ	*n.* orange (*fruit*, = **афлесун**)
нохун	*n.* fingernail, nail, claw
ноҳия	*n.* district, region
нуздаҳ	*num.* nineteen
нуқта	*n.* point, place
нур	*n.* light, ray, beam
нӯҳ	*num.* nine
нӯшидан (нӯш)	*v.* to drink
нӯшокиҳои спиртӣ	*n.* alcoholic drink, liquor
Ню-Йорк	*n.* New York
Ню-Орлеанз	*n.* New Orleans
об	*n.* water
оби маъдан	*n.* mineral water
оби ҷав	*n.* beer (= **пиво**)
ободд	*adj.* cultivated, flourishing
обу ҳаво	*n.* weather
одамон	*n.* people
одатан	*adv.* usually; generally; habitually

Озарбойҷон	*n.* Azerbaijan
оид ба	*prep.* about, concerning
оила	*n.* family (= **хонавода**)
оилавӣ	*adj.* of the family
оиладор	*adj.* married (= **издивоҷшуда, мутааҳҳил**)
ойина	*n.* mirror
олам	*n.* the world
олболу	*n.* cherry
Олмон	*n.* Germany
олмонӣ	*adj.* German (= **немис, немисӣ**)
олу	*n.* plum
омадан (о/биё)	*v.* to come
омӯзиш	*n.* instruction, training
он	*pron.* that; he/she/it
онҳо	*pron.* they
он ҷо	*prov.* there
орд	*n.* flour
ором шудан	*v.* to calm down
Осиё	*n.* Asia
Остона	*n.* Astana (*capital of Kazakhstan*)
Оттава	*n.* Ottawa
Офарин!	*interj.* Excellent !
офтобӣ	*adv.* sunny
охирин	*adj.* final, the last (*precedes noun*)
оҳиста	*adj.* slow
ошёна	*n.* storey, floor
оши палав	*n.* pilaf (= **палав**)
ошпаз	*n.* cook (*pilaf maker*)
ошхона	*n.* kitchen (= **матбах**)
пагоҳӣ	*n.* in the morning
падар	*n.* father
падарарӯс	*n.* father-in-law (*bride's side*)
падаркалон	*n.* grandfather (= **бобо**)

падаршӯй	*n.* father-in-law (= **падарарӯс, хусур**)
палав	*n.* palav, pilaf (= **оши палав**)
панир	*n.* cheese
панох̣	*n.* protection
Панох̣и Худо	*phr.* (May you be) under the Lord's n. protectio (*Said in farewell*)
панҷ	*num.* five
панҷа	*n.* the five fingers, hand, paw
Панҷакент	*n.* Panjakent (*major city of Tajikistan*)
панҷох̣	*num.* fifty
панҷшанбе	*n.* Thursday
парастор	*n.* nurse
парда	*n.* curtain
парерӯз	*adv., n.* the day before yesterday
паридан (пар)	*v.* to fly
Париж	*n.* Paris
пас	*prep.* behind (= **пушт**)
паст	*adj.* low; *adv.* slightly
пахта	*n.* cotton
пах̣лӯ	*prep.* beside, next to
пеш	*n.* front; *adv.*, ago; *prep.* before, ahead (*often with* **аз**)
пешгирӣ кардан	*v.* to prevent
пешних̣од кардан	*v.* to offer, propose, suggest
пешхизмат	*n.* waiter, waitress
пианино	*n.* piano
пиво	*n.* beer (= **оби ҷав**)
пиёз	*n.* onion
пиёзи кабуд	*n.* green onion
пиёла	*n.* teacup (*traditional bowl-like cup*)
пир	*adj.* old (= **кух̣ансол, солхӯрда**)
писар	*n.* boy, son
писарбачча	*n.* son, boy
писта	*n.* pistachios
пишак	*n.* cat (= **гурба**)
пойтахт	*n.* capital
покиза	*adj.* clean (= **тоза**)
Покистон	*n.* Pakistan
полизӣ	*n.* melons and gourds
Полша	*n.* Poland
помидор	*n.* tomato
Помир	*n.* Pamir (*mountain range; region of Tajikistan*)
понздах̣	*num.* fifteen
порча	*n.* slice
порчаи шеърӣ	*n.* piece of poetry
почо	*n.* brother-in-law (sister's husband, = **язна**)
Прага	*n.* Prague
президент	*n.* president
пудина	*n.* mint (*spice*)
пул	*n.* money
пул гузоштан	*v.* to deposit money
пурсидан (пурс)	*v.* to ask (**аз** *indicates the person asked*)
пухтан (паз)	*v.* to cook
пушт	*prep.* back, behind (= **пас**)
пӯсида	*adj.* spoilt; rotten
пӯшидан (пӯш)	*v.* to close, cover; to put on, wear, dress
равған	*n.* oil
равғани зард	*n.* butter
равшан	*adj.* bright
радио	*n.* radio
рад кардан	*v.* to refuse, deny
раис	*n.* head, boss, chief (*male*)
раиса	*n.* head, boss, chief (*female*)

рақам	*n.* number
рақами хона	*n.* apartment number
рақс	*n.* dance
расм	*n.* picture, photograph (= **акс, сурат**); custom, convention, rules
рассом	*n.* painter, artist
раста	*n.* row, line (= **қатор**)
рафи китоб	*n.* bookshelf
рафиқ	*n.* friend, comrade (= **дӯст, ҷӯра**)
рафтан (рав)	*v.* to go
раъд	*n.* thunder (= **тундар**)
регбӣ	*n.* rugby
редиска	*n.* radish (= **шалғамча**)
ресторан	*n.* restaurant (= **тарабхона**)
робита	*n.* connection, tie, liaison; means
розӣ шудан	*v.* to agree, consent (**ба** to)
рок	*n.* rock music
рондан (рон)	*v.* to drive
Россия	*n.* Russia (= **Русия**)
рост	*adj.* right
роҳ	*n.* road
рубл	*n.* ruble
рубоб	*n. rubob*, Tajik guitar-like musical instrument
рус	*n.* Russian (*person*)
Русия	*n.* Russia (= **Россия**)
русӣ	*adj.* Russian (*language*)
рустшавакон	*n.* hide and seek (*game*)
рӯз	*n.* day
рӯзнома	*n.* newspaper
рӯзона	*adj.* daytime, daily
рӯзҳои истироҳат	*n.* weekend
сабаб	*n.* reason, purpose, aim
сабз	*adj.* green
сабзавот	*n.* vegetables
сабзӣ	*n.* carrot
сабр кардан	*v.* to wait
сабт кардан	*v.* to record
сабук	*adj.* light (*not heavy*), easy, quick
савдо кардан	*v.* to bargain
савоб	*n.* alms-giving, charity
савол	*n.* question
саг	*n.* dog
сағира	*n.* orphan (= **ятим**)
сад	*num.* hundred
салат	*n.* salad
саломат будан	*v.* to be healthy, welcome
самбӯса	*n. samsa* (*a type of small meat pie*)
санаи таваллуд	*n.* date of birth
санҷидан (санҷ)	*v.* to try, test, examine, check
санҷиш	*n.* examination, test, quiz
сар	*n.* head; beginning; classifier for animals
сарватманд	*adj.* rich (= **бой**)
сари вақт	*adv.* in time, on time, timely, at the proper/ right time
сароянда	*n.* singer
сарутан	*n.* clothing
сафар	*n.* journey, trip, visit
сафед	*adj.* white
сафедии тухм	*n.* egg-white; protein
саҳар	*n.* morning
саҳифа	*n.* page
се	*num.* three
себ	*n.* apple
сездаҳ	*num.* thirteen

сентябр	*n.* September
сер	*adj.* full (*of food*)
сетор	*n. setor*, Tajik stringed musical instrument
сешанбе	*n.* Tuesday
сеюм	*adj.* third
сиёҳ	*adj.* black; dark
симоб	*n.* mercury, quicksilver
симобӣ	*adj.* of mercury
синну сол	*n.* age
синф	*n.* classroom
сир(пиёз)	*n.* garlic
сифат	*n.* adjective; quality
сифр	*num.* zero
сихкабоб	*n.* shishkabob (= **шашлик**)
сиҳат	*adj.* healthy, well
сӣ	*num.* thirty
соат	*n.* hour; clock
сокин будан	*v.* to live, inhabit (see **зиндагӣ кардан**)
сол	*n.* year
солхӯрда	*adj.* old (= **куҳансол, пир**)
сом	*n.* som (*Kyrghyz currency*)
сомонӣ	*n.* somoni (*currency of Tajikistan*)
сонӣ	*adj.* second (= **дуюм**)
соф	*adj.* clean
соҳибкор	*n.* businessman
Суғд	*n.* Sughd (*region of Tajikistan*)
сум	*n.* general name for all sorts of currency
сумка	*n.* bag, purse (= **ҷузвдон**)
сур	n. celebration
сурат	*n.* picture, photograph (= **акс, расм**); face

Сурия	*n.* Syria
суроға	*n.* address (*informal*, = **нишонӣ**)
суруд хондан	*v.* to sing
сурх	*adj.* red
сухан	*n.* speech
сӯҳбат	*n.* conversation
табақ	*n.* large plate, platter
табақча	*n.* small plate
табиб	*n.* physician, doctor
таблак	*n.* small drum, Tajik musical instrument
таг	*prep.* under (= **зер**)
тағо	*n.* mother's brother, maternal uncle
тағобача	*n.* cousin (*maternal uncle's child*)
Тайланд	*n.* Thailand
такрор кардан	*v.* to repeat
тақрибан	*adv.* approximately, nearly
тақсим	*n.* divided by
талоқ	*n.* divorce (= **ҷудошавӣ**)
талоқшуда	*adj.* divorced (= **ҷудошуда**)
талх	*adj.* bitter
тамоку	*n.* tobacco
тамоку кардан / кашидан (каш)	*v.* to smoke
тамом шудан	*v.* to come to an end, end (*intr.*)
тамошо	*n.* sightseeing
тамошо кардан	*v.* to watch
танбал	*adj.* lazy
танг	*adj.* narrow
танга	*n.* coin
танӯр	*n.* oven
таом	*n.* food, a meal
тарабхона	*n.* restaurant (= **ресторан**)

тараф (атроф)	*prep.* beside; *n.* side, direction
тарбуз	*n.* watermelon
тарҳ	*n.* minus
тарҷума кардан	*v.* to translate (**ба** into)
тасвир кардан	*v.* to describe
тафтиш	*n.* inspection, examination, check
тафтиш кардан	*v.* to examine, check (up), test
тахта	*n.* board, cutting board
тахтаи синфӣ	*n.* classroom blackboard
таҳқир кардан	*v.* to offend (= **хафа кардан**)
ташаккур	*interj.* thank you
ташна	*adj.* thirsty
таъмин	*n.* supply
таърихи рӯз	*n.* date
таърихӣ	*adj.* historical
телевизор	*n.* television (*TV set*)
телефон	*n.* telephone
телефончӣ	*n.* (telephone) operator
тенге	*n.* tenge (*Kazakh currency*)
теннисбозӣ	*n.* tennis
Техас	*n.* Texas
Теҳрон	*n.* Tehran
тиллоранг	*adj.* golden, gold-colored
тирамоҳ	*n.* autumn, fall
тиреза	*n.* window
то	*prep.* until; so as to, in order to
тобистон	*n.* summer
тоза	*adj.* clean (= **покиза**)
торт	*n.* cake
тоҷик	*n.* Tajik (*person*)
Тоҷикистон	*n.* Tajikistan
тоҷикӣ	*adj. Tajiki (language)*
Тоҷикобод	*n.* Tajikabad (*city*)
ту	*pron.* you (*sg. informal*)
тулӯъи офтоб	*n.* sunrise
тунд	*adj.* sour, tart, spicy
тундар	*n.* thunder (= **раъд**)
турб	*n.* green turnip
Туркия	*n.* Turkey
Туркманистон	*n.* Turkmenistan
турш	*adj.* sour
тухм	*n.* egg
тушбера	*n.* a traditional dish
тӯй	*n.* wedding (= **тӯйи арӯсӣ**); party
тӯйи арӯсӣ	*n.* wedding (= **тӯй**)
тӯфон	*n.* storm
тӯҳфа	*n.* present, gift
узви оила	*n.* family member
ука	*n.* younger sibling (*see* **додар, хоҳар**)
Украина	*n.* Ukraine
уқёнус	*n.* ocean
умум	*n.* the public, the people
умумиҷаҳонӣ	*adj.* world; world-wide, universal
умумӣ	*adj.* common, public, general
унвон	*n.* title, term of address, rank
устод	*n.* professor, master
устухон	*n.* bone
утоқ	*n.* room (= **хона, ҳуҷра**)
ӯ	*pron.* he/she
ӯзбак	*adj.* Uzbek
Ӯзбакистон	*n.* Uzbekistan
фақат	*adv.* only
фалсафа	*n.* philosophy

фарбеҳ	*n., adj.* fat
фарзанд	*n.* child
фарқ	*n.* difference
фаромӯш кардан	*v.* to forget
Фаронса	*n.* France
фаронсавӣ	*adj.* French (*nationality*)
фаррош	*n.* janitor
фасл(-и сол)	*n.* season
фатир	*n.* oil-based bread made of flour and butter
фаҳмидан (фаҳм)	*v.* to understand
фаҳмо	*adj.* clear
фач	*adj.* salt free (= **бенамак**)
фиреб додан	*v.* to deceive, cheat, swindle
фишор	*n.* pressure
Флорида	*n.* Florida
фоида	*n.* benefit, profit
форсӣ	*n.* Farsi (*Iranian Persian*)
фотиҳа шудан	*v.* to be/get engaged
фотоаппарат	*n.* camera
фунт	*n.* pound
фурудгоҳ	*n.* airport
фурӯхтан (фурӯш)	*v.* to sell
фурӯш	*n.* sale
фурӯшанда	*n.* seller, salesman, (store) clerk, shop assistant
футбол	*n.* soccer
хабарҳои варзиш	*n.* sports news
хадамот	*n.* services
хазинадор	*n.* cashier (= **хозин**)
хайр	*interj.* bye
халта	*n.* sack, bag
хамир	*n.* dough
харбуза	*n.* melon
харидан (хар)	*v.* to buy, purchase
харидор	*n.* buyer, customer, client
харита	*n.* map
хароб	*adj.* thin
хаста	*adj.* tired
хат	*n.* line, writing
хаткӯркунак	*n.* rubber eraser
Хатлон	*n.* Khatlon
хафа	*adj.* unhappy
хафа кардан	*v.* to offend (= **таҳқир кардан**)
хестан (хез)	*v.* to stand up, get up
хеш (хешованд)	*n.* relatives
хешӣ	*n.* family relationship
хидмат	*n.* service
хислат	*n.* character, personality
Хитой	*n.* China (= **Чин**)
хитойӣ	*adj.* Chinese (= **чинӣ**)
хозин	*n.* cashier (= **хазинадор**)
хокаи қанд	*n.* powdered sugar
хола	*n.* mother's sister, maternal aunt; term of address for an older woman
холабача	*n.* cousin (*maternal aunt's child*)
хома	*n.* pen (*for writing*)
хона	*n.* house, home; room (= **утоқ, ҳуҷра**)
хонавода	*n.* family (= **оила**)
хонаи дуҳуҷрагӣ	*n.* one-bedroom (two-room) house
хондан (хон)	*v.* to read, study
хонум	*n.* lady; Mrs., Ms.
хор	*n.* thorn
Хоруғ	*n.* Khorugh
хостгорӣ	*n.* matchmaking
хоҳар	*n.* younger sister; term of address for a younger woman

хохарарӯс	*n.* sister-in-law (= **хохаршӯй**)
хохарзода	*n.* nephew or niece by a sister (*see* **ҷиян**)
хохаршӯй	*n.* sister-in-law (= **хохарарӯс**)
хохиш	*n.* wish
хохиш кардан	*v.* to desire
хуб	*adj.* good, okay, fine (= **нағз**)
худ	*n., pron.* self
Худоро шукр!	*phr.* Thanks to the Lord (everything is fine).
хун	*n.* blood
хунук	*adj.* cold
хурд	*adj.* little, small (= **майда**)
хурмо	*n.* persimmon
хурофот	*n.* superstitious beliefs
хусур	*n.* father-in-law (*groom's side*)
Хуҷанд	*n.* Khujand (*major city of Tajikistan*)
хуш	*adj.* happy, cheerful, good, nice
хушдоман	*n.* mother-in-law
хушрӯ	*adj.* handsome, beautiful
хушсимо	*adj.* handsome, beautiful
хӯрдан (хӯр)	*v.* to eat
хӯрок	*n.* food, meal, dish
хӯроки нисфирӯзӣ	*n.* lunch
ҳа	*interj.* yes (= **бале**)
Ҳабашистон	*n.* Abyssinia
ҳабдаҳ	*num.* seventeen
ҳаво	*n.* weather (= **обу ҳаво**)
ҳадаф	*n.* purpose
ҳаёт	*n.* life (= **зиндагӣ**)
ҳаждаҳ	*num.* eighteen
ҳазм	*n.* digestion
ҳазор	*num.* thousand
ҳайвоноти хонагӣ	*n.* pets
ҳалво	*n. halwa* (*type of sweet*)
ҳам	*adv.* also, too (= **низ**)
ҳамдигар	*pron.* each other (= **якдигар**)
ҳамеша	*adv.* always
ҳамён	*n.* wallet
ҳамин	*pron.* this (same) one
ҳамкор	*n.* co-worker, colleague, partner (= **шарик**)
ҳамкорӣ	*n.* collaboration, cooperation
ҳамон	*pron.* that (same) one
ҳамроҳ	*n.* fellow traveler, companion
ҳамсар	*n.* spouse (*see* **бону, завҷа, зан, шавҳар, шӯй**)
ҳамсинф	*n.* classmate
ҳамсоя	*n.* neighbor
ҳамшаҳрӣ	*adj.* from the same city
ҳандалак	*n.* canteloupe
ҳарорат	*n.* temperature
ҳарф (ҳуруф)	*n.* letter (*of alphabet*)
ҳаст	*v.* there is/are
ҳафт	*num.* seven
ҳафта	*n.* week
ҳафтаина	*adj.* weekly
ҳафтод	*num.* seventy
ҳашт	*num.* eight
ҳаштод	*num.* eighty
ҳаяҷон	*n.* excitement
ҳевар	*n.* brother-in-law (= **додарарӯс, додаршӯй**)
Ҳиндустон	*n.* India
ҳисобгар	*n.* calculator
ҳисоб кардан	*v.* to count

ҳисобкунак	*n.* calculator
Ҳисор	*n.* Hisor
ҳиҷо	*n.* syllable
ҳозир	*adv., interj.* now; one moment, hold on, just a minute
Ҳолландия	*n.* Holland
ҳолландӣ	*adj.* Dutch
ҳурмат кардан	*v.* to respect
ҳуҷра	*n.* room (= **утоқ, хона**); apartment
ҳуш	*adj.* conscious
чабера	*n.* great-great-grandchild
чангак	*n.* fork
чанд	*adj.* how much?
чандин	*adv.* this much, so much; several
чандон	*adv.* so, so much, so many
чандсола	*adj.* how old?
чап	*adj.* left (*direction*)
чаро (чиба, чида)	*adv.* (*coll.*) why? (= **барои чӣ**)
чароғ	*n.* lamp
чарх	*n.* wheel
чашм	*n.* eye
чиз	*n.* thing
Чикаго	*n.* Chicago
Чилӣ	*n.* Chile
чил (чиҳил)	*num.* forty
Чин	*n.* China (= **Хитой**)
чинӣ	*adj.* Chinese (= **хитоӣ**)
чиркин	*adj.* dirty, filthy (see **нопок**); messy (= **бетартиб**)
чӣ	*pron.* what?
чӣ гуна	*adj.* what kind (of)?; *adv.* in what ways?, how?
чӣ қадар	*adv.* how much?, how many?
чӣ тавр	*adv.* (*literary*) how? (= **чун, чӣ хел**)
чӣ хел	*adv.* how?
чой	*n.* tea
чойи кабуд	*n.* green tea
чор	*num.* four
чордаҳ	*num.* fourteen
чормағз	*n.* walnut
чоршанбе	*n.* Wednesday
чумча	*n.* spoon
чун	*adv.* (*literary*) how? (= **чӣ тавр, чӣ хел**)
чӯпон	*n.* shepherd
ҷавоб	*n.* answer
ҷавоб додан	*v.* to answer
ҷавон	*adj.* young
ҷавонзан	*n.* young lady
ҷадвал	*n.* ruler, yardstick; table, chart
ҷаз[1]	*n.* fried fat from around the tail of a sheep
ҷаз[2]	*n.* jazz
ҷазира (ҷазоир)	*n.* island
ҷамъ	*n.* plus, total
ҷаноб	*n.* sir, mister, Mr., gentleman
ҷаноби	*n.* Mr.
ҷарроҳ	*n.* surgeon
ҷасур	*adj.* brave, excellent
ҷаҳон	*n.* world
ҷаҳоннамо	*n.* TV broadcast
ҷашн гирифтан	*v.* to celebrate
ҷевон	*n.* shelf
ҷевони либос	*n.* closet
ҷигар	*n.* liver
ҷигарӣ	*adj.* purple, liver-colored
ҷиддӣ	*adj.* serious
ҷингиламӯй	*adj.* curly-haired

ҷиян	*n.* nephew, niece (*includes* **додарзода** *and* **хоҳарзода**)
ҷогар	*n.* goiter; wen (= **буқоқ**)
ҷойи таваллуд	*n.* place of birth
ҷомадон	*n.* suitcase
ҷудошавӣ	*n.* divorce (= **талоқ**)
ҷудошуда	*adj.* divorced (= **талоқшуда**)
ҷузвдон	*n.* bag
ҷумла	*n.* sentence
ҷумъа	*n.* Friday
ҷурғот	*n. kefir* (*a beverage of fermented cow's milk*), yogurt
ҷӯра	*n.* friend (*between males*), comrade (= **дӯст, рафиқ**)
ҷӯшидан (ҷӯш)	*v.* to boil (*intr.*)
ҷӯшон(и)дан (ҷӯшон)	*v.* to boil (tr.)
шаб	*n.* night
шабнишинӣ	*n.* party
шабона	*adj.* at night, nightly
шавқовар	*adj.* interesting, fascinating
шавҳар	*n.* husband (= **шӯй**; *see* **ҳамсар**)
шавҳаркарда	*adj.* married (*of a woman*)
шакар	*n.* sugar
шалғам	*n.* turnip
шалғамча	*n.* radish (= **редиска**)
шамол	*n.* wind, breeze (= **бод**)
шанбе	*n.* Saturday
шарбат	*n.* juice (= **афшура**)
шарбати афлесун	*n.* orange juice
шарбати лимӯ	*n.* lemon juice
шарбати себ	*n.* apple juice
шарик	*n.* colleague, partner (= **ҳамкор**)
шармгин	*adj.* shy
шаст	*num.* sixty
шафтолу	*n.* peach
шахс (ашхос)	*n.* person (= **кас**)
шаҳр	*n.* city
Шаҳритус	*n.* city in southern Tajikistan (*often* **Шаҳртус**)
шаш	*num.* six
шашмақом	*n. shashmaqom*, classical music of the Tajiks
Швейтсария	*n.* Switzerland
Шветсия	*n.* Sweden
шеър	*n.* poem
шибит	*n.* dill
шимол	*n.* north
шинос кардан	*v.* to introduce
шиносойӣ	*n.* acquaintance
шир	*n.* milk
ширбиринҷ	*n.* rice in milk
ширин	*adj.* sweet
ширқаҳва	*n.* coffee with milk
ширчой	*n.* milk with tea
шиша	*n.* bottle
шод	*adj.* happy, glad
шом	*n.* evening
шонздаҳ	*num.* sixteen
шотландӣ	*adj.* Scottish
шоҳмот	*n.* chess
шудан (шав)	*v.* to become
шумо	*pron.* you (*pl.*)
Шумо	*pron.* you (*sg. formal*)
шунидан (шунав)	*v.* to hear, listen
шустан (шӯ, шӯй)	*v.* to wash
шӯй	*n.* husband (= **шавҳар**; *see* **ҳамсар**)
шӯрбо	*n. shurbo* (*Tajik soup*)
шӯх	*adj.* funny, witty, mischievous, joking

шӯъбаи корҳои дохилӣ	*n.* Department of Internal Affairs (*police station*)
Эрон	*n.* Iran
Юнон	*n.* Greece
Юсуф	*n.* Joseph
Яғноб	*n.* Yaghnob
язна	*n.* brother-in-law (*sister's husband*)
як	*num.* one
якдигар	*pron.* each other (= **ҳамдигар**)
якчанд	*adj.* quite a few
якшанбе	*n.* Sunday
янга	*n.* brother's wife
Япония	*n.* Japan
ятим	*n.* orphan (= **сағира**)
ях	*n.* ice
яхдон	*n.* icebox
яхмос	*n.* ice cream

APPENDIX 2 English - Tajiki Glossary

a little	*adj*: кам; *adv*: андак, каме
about	*prep* around: *атроф; concerning: дар бораи, оид ба; *adv*: тақрибан
above	*prep*: *боло
Abyssinia	*n*: Ҳабашистон
accountant	*n*: муҳосиб
acquaintance	*n*: шиносоӣ
add	*vt*: илова кардан
addition	*n*: илова
address	*n*: суроға, нишонӣ; bureaucratic: нишонии ҷои истиқомат
adjective	*n*: сифат
Afghanistan	*n*: Афғонистон
Africa	*n*: Африқо
airport	*n*: фурудгоҳ
alcohol	*n*: арақ
Algeria	*n*: Алҷазоир
allowed	*adj*: мумкин
Almaty	*n*: Алмаато
also	*adv*: ҳам; in this way: ҳамчунин; in that way: ҳамчунон
always	*adv*: ҳамеша
America	*n*: Амрико, Америка (used for both the continents and the United States)
American	*adj*: амрикоӣ
among	*prep*: *миён
answer	*n*: ҷавоб; *vt*: ҷавоб додан (ба indicates the person answered)
antiquity	*n*: қадимулайём
apartment	*n*: ҳуҷра, квартира
apple	*n*: себ
apply	*vi*: to department, etc.: ариза додан; be applicable: татбиқ шудан; *vt* put into practice: татбиқ кардан
appropriate	*adj*: мувофиқ
approximately	*adv*: тақрибан, тахминан
apricot	*n* generally: зардолу; a small sweet variety: қандак; dried: зардолуқоқ
Armenia	*n*: Арманистон
around	*prep*: *атроф
Asia	*n*: Осиё
ask	*vt*: пурсидан (пурс) (аз indicates the person asked)
Astana	*n*: Остона
at	*prep*: дар
aunt	*n* paternal aunt: амма; maternal aunt: хола
Australia	*n*: Австралия
Austria	*n*: Австрия
autumn	*n*: тирамоҳ; *adj*: тирамоҳӣ
Azerbaijan	*n*: Озарбойҷон
bachelor	*n*: муҷаррад
back	*n*: пушт; **small of the back**: миён
bad	*adj*: бад, ганда
bag	*n*: халта, сумка; pack: ҷузвдон, борхалта; tote bag: халтача
bakery	*n*: нонвойхона
Baku	*n*: Боку
balcony	*n*: айвон, балкон
banana	*n*: банан
Bangladesh	*n*: Банғола

bank	*n* of river: соҳил, канор(а); financial: банк/бонк
bargain	*vi*: савдо кардан
beans	*n*: лӯбиё
because	*conj*: азбаски, зеро (ки), чаро ки, чунки
become	*vi*: шудан (шав)
bed	*n*: кат
beef	*n*: гӯшти гов
beer	*n*: оби ҷав, пиво
beet	*n*: лаблабу
behind	*prep*: *пас, *пушт, *қафо
believe	*vt*: бовар кардан
benefit	*n* value: манфиат, фоида; beneficial quality: баҳрабардорӣ; *vi*: баҳра бурдан (аз **from**)
beside	*prep*: *паҳлӯ, *тараф (атроф)
between	*prep*: *байн, *миён
big	*adj*: калон, бузург; in age: калонсол; of elder generation: куҳансол
birthday	*n*: зодрӯз; day of birth: рӯзи таваллуд; date of birth: санаи таваллуд
bitter	*adj*: талх
black	*adj*: сиёҳ; **black and white** *adj*: ало
blackboard	*n*: тахтаи синфӣ
blood	*n*: хун
blue	*adj*: кабуд
board	*n*: тахта
boil	*vi*: ҷӯшидан (ҷӯш); *vt*: ҷӯшон(и)дан (ҷӯшон)
boiling	*n*: ҷӯшиш; *adj*: ҷӯшон
bold	*adj*: бошуҷоат
bone	*n*: устухон
book	*n*: китоб
bookshelf	*n*: рафи китоб
bottle	*n*: шиша
bow	*n* motion: таъзим; for arrows: камон
box	*n*: қуттӣ
boy	*n*: писар, писарбачча
brave	*adj*: далер, ҷасур, боҷуръат, бошуҷоат
bread	*n*: нон; small bread: кулча; big, thin bread: чаппоти; oil-based bread made of flour and butter: фатир
bride	*n*: арӯс, келин
bright	*adj*: равшан
bring	*vt*: бурдан (бар), овардан (овар, ор, биёр)
brother	*n* generally: бародар; older brother: ака/ако; younger brother: додар
brother-in-law	*n* wife's brother: додарарӯс, ҳевар; husband's brother: додаршӯй; sister's husband: язна (southern), поччо (northern); relationship between husbands of two sisters: боҷа
brown	*adj*: қаҳваранг
Bulgaria	*n*: Булғор
bundle	*n*: бандча
businessman	*n*: соҳибкор
busy	*adj*: банд, машғул; **be busy** *vi*: машғул шудан (бо **with**)
but	*conj*: аммо, вале, лекин
butcher	*n*: қассоб
butter	*n*: равғани зард
buy	*vt*: харидан (хар)
buyer	*n*: харидор
by	*prep*: *лаб; see **beside**
bye	*interj*: хайр
cabbage	*n*: карам
cake	*n*: торт

calculator	*n*: ҳисобгар, ҳисобкунак
call	*vt* by shouting: фарёд кардан; on telephone: занг задан (intransitive in Tajiki, requires ба **to**); give a name: номидан (ном)
calm	*adj*: ором
calm down	*vi*: ором шудан; *vt*: ором кардан
camera	*n*: фотоаппарат
candy	*n*: қандалот
canteloupe	*n*: ҳандалак
capital	*n* political center: пойтахт; wealth: сармоя
caraway	*n*: зира
carefully	*adv*: бодиққат
carpenter	*n*: дуредгар
carrot	*n*: сабзӣ
carry	*vt*: бурдан (бар)
cashier	*n*: хазинадор, хозин
cat	*n*: гурба, пишак
cave	*n*: ғор
celebrate	*vt*: гузаронидан (гузарон), пешвоз гирифтан, ҷашн гирифтан
celebration	*n*: сур
center	*n*: марказ
certainly	*adv*: албатта
chair	*n*: курсӣ
chalk	*n*: бӯр
chalkboard	*n*: тахтаи синфӣ
character	*n* distinctive quality: хусусият, сифат; personality: хислат, шахсият; in book: характер, қаҳрамон
cheap	*adj*: арзон
cheese	*n*: панир
cherry	*n*: олболу; sweet: гелос
chess	*n*: шоҳмот; **play chess**: шоҳмотбозӣ кардан
chicken	*n* generally: чӯҷа; hen: мурғ
child	*n* offspring: фарзанд; in age: кӯдак; *adj*: бачагона
Chile	*n*: Чили
China	*n*: Хитой, Чин
Chinese	*adj*: хитойӣ, чинӣ
cilantro	*n*: кашнич
circle	*vt*: доира кашидан
city	*n* large: шаҳр; small: шаҳрак
class	*n*: дарс
classmate	*n*: ҳамсинф
classroom	*n*: синф
clean	*adj*: тоза, пок, покиза, соф
clear	*adj* transparent: тоза, соф; of weather: соф, равшан; comprehensible: фаҳмо; distinct: аниқ; evident: маълум
close	*adj*: наздик
close	*vt*: пӯшидан (пӯш)
closet	*n*: ҷевони либос
clothes	*n*: либос
clothing	*n*: сарутан
cloud	*n*: абр
cloudless	*adj*: беабр
cloudy	*adj*: абрнок; **partly cloudy**: камабр
Coca Cola	*n*: кокакола
coffee	*n*: қаҳва
coin	*n*: танга
coincide	*vi*: мувофиқ омадан (бо **with**)
cold	*adj*: хунук; *n*: сармо; **take cold**: шамол хӯрдан
collaboration	*n*: ҳамкорӣ
colleague	*n*: ҳамкор, шарик
come	*vi*: омадан (о/биё)

common	*adj* general: умумӣ; customary: маъмул
computer	*n*: компютер; *adj*: компютерӣ
condition	*n* situation: шарт, аҳвол, вазъ, ҳол; term: нукта; **on condition that**: ба шарте ки
connection	*n*: робита
conscious	*adj*: ҳушёр
continent	*n*: қитъа
conversation	*n*: гуфтугӯ, сӯҳбат
cook	*n*: ошпаз; *vt*: пухтан (паз); *vi*: пухта шудан
Copenhagen	*n*: Копенҳаген
correct	*adj*: дуруст; *vt*: ислоҳ кардан
cotton	*n*: пахта; *adj*: пахтагӣ
count	*n*: ҳисоб; *vt*: ҳисоб кардан
country	*n*: кишвар
cousin	*n* paternal uncle's child: амакбача; paternal aunt's child: аммабача; maternal uncle's child: тағобача; maternal aunt's child: холабача
cover	*n*: сарпӯш; *vt*: пӯшидан (пӯш)
cow	*n* general: гов; female: модагов
co-worker	*n*: ҳамкор
cucumber	*n*: бодиринг
cultivated	*adj*: обод
cumin	*n*: зира
curly-haired	*adj*: ҷингиламӯй
currency exchange	*n*: мубодилаи арз / асъор / пул
curtain	*n*: парда
customer	*n*: харидор, муштарӣ, (mostly used in Dushanbe) миҷоз
daily	*adj*: рӯзона
dairy store	*n*: дӯкони ширфурӯшӣ
dance	*n*: рақс; *vi*: рақс кардан, рақсидан (рақс)
Danghara	*n*: Данғара
date	*n*: таърихи рӯз
daughter	*n*: духтар
daughter-in-law	*n*: келин
day	*n* time of daylight: рӯз; 24-hour period: шабонарӯз; *adj*: рӯзона
day after tomorrow	*adv, n*: пасфардо
day before yesterday	*adv, n*: парерӯз
deceive	*vt*: гумроҳ кардан, фиреб додан
delicious	*adj*: болаззат, бомазза
Denmark	*n*: Дания
deposit	*n*: ирсол; *vt* money: пул гузоштан; item: тарк кардан
describe	*vt*: тасвир кардан, нақл кардан
desert	*n*: биёбон, саҳро
desire	*n*: орзу; *vt*: хоҳиш кардан
detective	*n*: муфаттиш
dictionary	*n*: луғат
difference	*n*: фарқ
difficulty	*n*: мушкилӣ
digestion	*n*: ҳазм
dill	*n*: шибит
dirty	*adj*: чиркин
district	*n*: ноҳия
divide	*vt*: тақсим кардан, ҷудо кардан (ба **into**); **divided by**: тақсими
divorce	*n*: талоқ, ҷудошавӣ
divorced	*adj*: талоқшуда, ҷудошуда
do	*vt*: кардан (кун)
doctor	*n*: духтур, табиб
dog	*n*: саг; female: модасаг; *adj*: сагона

dollar	*n*: доллар
door	*n* general: дар; outside door of house: даргоҳ
dough	*n*: хамир
drink	*n* soft drink: нӯшоба; alcoholic: нӯшокиҳои спиртӣ; *vt*: нӯшидан (нӯш)
drive	*vt*: рондан (рон)
drum	*n* large: доира; small: таблак
drunk	*adj*: маст
duck	*n*: мурғобӣ
Dushanbe	*n*: Душанбе
Dutch	*adj*: ҳолландӣ
each other	*pron*: ҳамдигар, якдигар
ear	*n*: гӯш
eat	*vt*: хӯрдан (хӯр)
economy	*n*: иқтисод
eggplant	*n*: бодинҷон
egg-white	*n*: сафедии тухм
Egypt	*n*: Миср
eight	*num*: ҳашт
eighteen	*num*: ҳаждаҳ
eighty	*num*: ҳаштод
elder	*adj*: калонсол, куҳансол; of siblings: калонӣ
electricity	*n*: барқ
eleven	*num*: ёздаҳ
engineer	*n*: муҳандис
England	*n*: Англия, Ингилистон
English	*adj* person: англис; things: англисӣ
Englishman	*n*: инглис, англис
enjoy	*vt* take pleasure in: дӯст доштан; receive benefit: баҳра бурдан (аз indicates source of benefit)
equal	*n*: баробар; *vt* in math: баробари (будан)
euro	*n*: евро
Europe	*n*: Аврупо
evening	*n*: бегоҳ, шом; **in the evening**: бегоҳӣ
exam	*n*: имтиҳон
examination	*n* medical: санҷиш, муойина; inspection, check: тафтиш; in school: имтиҳон
examine	*vt* survey: нигоҳ кардан (ба indicates object); medical: санҷидан (санҷ); inspect: тафтиш кардан
example	*n*: намуна, мисол; **for example**: масалан
excellent	*adj*: ҷасур; *interj*: офарин!
exchange	*n*: мубодила; *vt*: иваз кардан (ба **for**)
excitement	*n*: ҳаяҷон
exercise	*n*: машқ
exist	*vi*: вуҷуд доштан
existence	*n*: мавҷуд
expensive	*adj*: қим(м)ат(баҳо)
expressions	*n*: баёнот
eye	*n*: чашм
eyebrow	*n*: абрӯ; **with arched eyebrows**: абрӯкамон
eyeglasses	*n*: айнак
eyelash	*n*: мижа
false	*adj*: қалбакӣ
family	*n*: оила, хонавода; *adj*: оилавӣ; **family member** узви оила
famous	*adj*: машҳур
Farsi	*n*: форсӣ
fat	*n*: чарбу, фарбеҳ; *adj*: фарбеҳ
father	*n*: падар
father-in-law	*n* husband's side: падаршӯй, хусур; wife's side: падарарӯс
fellow traveler	*n*: ҳамроҳ

fiancé	*n*: номзад; **fiancée**: номзад, арӯс
fifteen	*num*: понздаҳ
fifty	*num*: панҷоҳ
film	*n* movie: навор
final	*adj*: охирин (precedes noun)
finally	*adv*: ниҳоят, тамоман
fingernail	*n*: нохун
first	*adj*: нахустин (precedes noun), аввал
fish	*n*: моҳӣ; small: моҳича
five	*num*: панҷ
flour	*n*: орд
flower	*n*: гул; *vi*: гул кардан
fly	*n*: пашша; *vi*: паридан (пар); *vt*: парондан (парон)
food	*n*: хӯрок, та(ъ)ом
for	*prep*: барои
forget	*vt*: фаромӯш кардан
forgive	*vt*: бахшидан (бахш)
fork	*n*: чангак
forty	*num*: чил (чиҳил)
four	*num*: чор
fourteen	*num*: чордаҳ
fourth	*n*: чоряк, рубъ (rare)
France	*n*: Фаронса
French	*adj*: фаронсавӣ
Friday	*n*: ҷумъа
friend	*n*: дӯст, ёр, рафиқ; between men: ҷӯра; between women: дугона
from	*prep*: аз
front	*n*: пеш
fruit	*n*: мева
fulfill	*vt*: иҷро кардан
full	*adj* generally: пур; of food: сер (аз **of**)
funny	*adj*: шӯх
game	*n* sport: бозӣ; match: мусобиқа; **solo games**: бозиҳои якка; **team games**: бозиҳои гурӯҳӣ; **card game**: қартабозӣ
garlic	*n*: сир(пиёз)
German	*n*: немис; *adj*: немисӣ, олмонӣ
Germany	*n*: Олмон
girl	*n*: духтар
girlfriend	*n*: маҳбуба
give	*vt*: додан (диҳ/деҳ)
glass	*n*: зарф
glossary	*n*: луғат
go	*vi*: рафтан (рав)
goiter	*n*: буқоқ, ҷогар
gold	*n*: тилло
golden	*adj* material: тиллоӣ; color: тиллоранг
golf	*n*: голф
good	*adj*: нағз, хуб; of food: хуштаъм
grain	*n*: ғалла
grains	*n*: ғалладона
grandchild	*n*: набера
granddaughter	*n*: набераду хтар
grandfather	*n*: бобо, падаркалон
grandmother	*n*: бибӣ, модаркалон
grandparents	*n*: бибию бобо
grandson	*n*: набераписар
grape	*n* generally: ангур; for raisins: кишмиш
grass	*n*: алаф, гиёҳ
gray	*adj*: бӯр, хокистарранг
great-grandchild	*n*: абера
great-great-grandchild	*n*: чабера
Greece	*n*: Юнон
green	*adj*: сабз
green onion	*n*: пиёзи кабуд
green pea	*n*: нахӯди сабз
green tea	*n*: чойи кабуд

green turnip	*n*: турб
green/sweet pepper	*n*: қаланфури булғорӣ
greens	*n*: кабудӣ
grocery store	*n*: мағозаи хӯрокворӣ
groom	*n*: домод
guest	*n*: меҳмон
hail	*n*: жола
hair	*n*: мӯй; on head: мӯйи сар
halwa	*n*: ҳалво
hand	*n*: даст; **at/on hand**: дар даст
handsome	*adj*: хушрӯ, хушсимо
happy	*adj*: шод, хуш
he	*pron*: вай, ӯ, он
head	*n* of body: сар; of group: раис (female раиса)
healthy	*adj*: бардам, сиҳат; **be healthy**: саломат будан
hear	*vt*: шунидан (шунав)
heat	*n* generally: гармӣ; hot weather: гармо; *vt* generally: гарм кардан; oil for frying: доғ кардан; *vi*: гарм шудан
heavy	*adj*: вазнин
height	*n*: қад
here	*pron*: ин ҷо
hide-and-seek	*n*: рустшавакон
historical	*adj*: таърихӣ
Holland	*n*: Ҳолландия
home	*n*: хона, (*literary*) кӯй
homework	*n*: вазифаи хонагӣ
honey	*n*: асал
horse	*n*: асп; **go horseback riding**: аспсаворӣ кардан; **on horseback**: савора
hot	*adj*: гарм
hotel	*n*: меҳмонхона
hour	*n*: соат
house	*n*: хона; private house with yard: ҳавлӣ; *adj*: хонагӣ
how	*inter.adv*: чӣ хел, чӣ гуна; (*literary*) чӣ тавр, чун
how much	*inter.adj*: чанд
how much/many	*inter.adv*: чӣ қадар
how old	*inter.adj*: чандсола
humidity	*n*: нам, намнокӣ, рутубат
hundred	*num*: сад
Hungary	*n*: Венгрия, Маҷористон
hungry	*adj*: гурусна (гушна)
husband	*n*: шавҳар, шӯй
I	*pron*: ман
ice	*n*: ях
ice cream	*n*: яхмос
icebox	*n*: яхдон
ill	*adj*: бемор, касал
in	*prep*: дар
India	*n*: Ҳиндустон
information	*n*: маълумот, иттилоот; **receive information**: хабар гирифтан (ро **about, from**)
inhabitants	*n*: аҳолӣ
inside	*prep*: *дарун
inspection	*n*: тафтиш, муойина
instruction	*n* directions: дастур, фармон; training: омӯзиш, таълим
interesting	*adj*: маъқул; of people: аҷоиб; of things: шавқовар
introduce	*vt*: шинос кардан
introduction	*n*: муаррифӣ, шиносойӣ
invitation	*n*: даъват; card: даъватнома
invite	*vt*: даъват кардан (ба **to**)
iodine	*n*: йод

Iran	*n*: Эрон
is	*vi*: аст
Isfara	*n*: Исфара
Islamabad	*n*: Исломобод
island	*n*: ҷазира (ҷазоир)
Istanbul	*n*: Истанбул
Istaravshan	*n*: Истаравшан
it	*pron*: он
jail	*n*: зиндон
jam	*n* jelly: мураббо
Japan	*n*: Япония
jelly	*n*: мураббо
job	*n*: кор
Joseph	*n*: Юсуф
journey	*n*: сафар
juice	*n*: шарбат, афшура; **orange juice**: шарбати афлесун; **lemon juice**: шарбати лимӯ; **apple juice**: шарбати себ
Kazakh	*adj*: қазоқ
Kazakhstan	*n*: Қазоқистон
keep	*vt*: нигоҳ доштан
key	*n*: калид
Khatlon	*n*: Хатлон
Khorugh	*n*: Хоруғ
Khujand	*n*: Хуҷанд
Kiev	*n*: Киев
kill	*vt*: куштан (куш)
kilogram	*n*: кило
kind	*adj* gracious: мехрубон; generous: дилкушод; *n* type: гуна; category: қабил
kitchen	*n*: ошхона, матбах
knife	*n*: корд; small: кордча
Konibodom	*n*: Конибодом
Kulob	*n*: Кӯлоб
Kyrghyzstan	*n*: Қирғизистон
lady	*n*: хонум, бону
lamb	*n* animal: барра; meat: гӯшти барра

lamp	*n*: чароғ
language	*n*: забон
last	*adj* preceding: гузашта; final: охирин (precedes noun)
lazy	*adj*: танбал
Lebanon	*n*: Лубнон
left	*adj* direction: чап
lemon	*n*: лимӯ
lemonade	*n*: лимонад
length	*n*: дарозӣ
letter	*n* mail: нома, мактуб; of alphabet: ҳарф (ҳуруф)
library	*n*: китобхона
life	*n*: зиндагӣ, ҳаёт
light	*adj* of weight: сабук; of brightness or color: равшан; *n*: нур; *vt*: афрӯхтан (афрӯз)
lightning	*n*: барқ
line	*n* generally: хат, раста; transportation: қатор
lip	*n*: лаб
listen	*vi*: гӯш кардан (ба **to**); шунидан (шунав) (ро **to**)
little	*adj*: хурд, майда
live	*vi*: зиндагӣ кардан, сокин будан
liver	*n*: ҷигар
long	*adj*: дароз; **so long as**: ба шарте ки
look	*vi*: нигоҳ кардан (ба **at**)
look for	*vt*: кофтан (коб)
Look here!	*interj*: нигар
low	*adj*: паст
luggage room	*n*: бағочхона
lunch	*n*: хӯроки нисфирӯзӣ
Luxembourg	*n*: Люксембург
macaroni	*n*: макарон
man	*n*: мард; young man: йигит

map	*n*: харита
market	*n*: бозор
married	*adj*: оиладор, мутааҳҳил, издивоҷшуда; of a woman: шавҳаркарда
marry	*vt*: издивоҷ кардан
matchmaking	*n*: хостгорӣ
me	*pron*: ман (accusative маро)
meal	*n*: хӯрок, ғизо, та(ъ)ом
mealtime	*adj*: хӯрокхӯрӣ
meaning	*n*: маънӣ, маъно
meat	*n*: гӯшт
meet	*vt*: вохӯрдан, пешвоз гирифтан
meeting	*n*: дидор, маҷлис, мулоқот
melon	*n*: харбуза, полизӣ
memory	*n*: ёд, хотир
mercury	*n*: симоб; *adj*: симобӣ
messy	*adj* disordered: бетартиб, титу парешон; dirty: чиркин
meter	*n* distance: метр
Mexico	*n*: Мексика
middle	*adj*: байн, миён, миёна
milk	*n*: шир; *adj*: ширӣ
mineral water	*n*: оби маъдан
mint	*n* spice: пудина
minus	*n* math: тарҳи
minute	*n*: дақиқа (дақоиқ)
mirror	*n*: ойина
mister	*n*: ҷаноби
Monday	*n*: душанбе
money	*n*: пул; currency: сум
Mongolia	*n*: Муғулистон
month	*n*: маҳ/ моҳ
moon	*n*: Моҳтоб
morning	*n*: саҳар, пагоҳ; *adj*: саҳарӣ, пагоҳӣ; **in the morning**: пагоҳӣ
Moscow	*n*: Москав
mosque	*n*: масҷид
most of the time	*adv*: аксар вақт
mother	*n*: модар
mother-in-law	*n* husband's side: модаршӯй; wife's side: модарарӯс, хушдоман
mountain	*n*: кӯҳ
Mr.	*n*: ҷаноб
Mrs., Ms.	*n*: хонум
Mu'minobod	*n*: Мӯъминобод
much	*adj*: бисёр (before noun), зиёд; *adv*: бисёр
mushroom	*n*: занбӯруғ
music	*n* general: мусиқӣ; tune: оҳанг; classical/ traditional: мусиқии анъанавӣ; Tajiki classical music: шашмақом
mutton	*n*: гӯшти гӯсфанд
name	*n* personal: ном; family: насаб, номи хонаводагӣ (official term)
narrow	*adj*: танг
nation	*n* country: мамлакат; people: халқ
near	*prep*: *назд
neighbor	*n*: ҳамсоя
nephew	*n*: ҷиян; by a brother: додарзода; by a sister: хоҳарзода
Netherlands	*n*: Нидерландия
new	*adj*: нав
New Orleans	*n*: Нию-Орлеанз
New York	*n*: Ню-Йорк
news	*n*: хабар (ахбор); **sports news**: хабарҳои варзиш; **get news**: хабар гирифтан (ро **about, from**)
newspaper	*n*: рӯзнома

niece	*n* generally: чиян; by a brother: додарзода; by a sister: хоҳарзода
Nigeria	*n*: Нигерия
night	*n*: шаб; *adj*: шабона; **at night** *adv*: шабона
nine	*num*: нӯҳ
nineteen	*num*: нуздаҳ
ninety	*num*: навад
no	*interj*: не
noon	*n*: нисфирӯз; *adj*: нисфирӯзӣ, пешинӣ
north	*n*: шимол
nose	*n*: бинӣ
notebook	*n*: дафтар; small: дафтарча
noun	*n*: исм
now	*adv*: ҳоло, ҳозир, акнун, алҳол; **just now**: навакак, ҳозиракак; **until now**: то ҳол
number	*n*: рақам
nurse	*n*: парастор
nut	*n*: мағз
nutrient	*n*: модда
nutrition	*n*: ғизо
nuts	*n*: мағздона
ocean	*n*: уқёнус
of course	*adv*: албатта
offend	*vt*: таҳқир кардан, ранҷондан (ранҷон), хафа кардан; **be offended**: таҳқир шудан, ранҷидан (ранҷ) (аз **by**)
offer	*vt*: пешниҳод кардан
oil	*n*: равған; **vegetable oil**: равғани растанӣ
old	*adj* of people: пир, куҳансол, солхӯрда; of things: кӯҳна
old man	*n*: муйсафед, пирамард
old woman	*n*: пиразан
older	*adj* of siblings: калонӣ
olive	*n*: зайтун
one	*num*: як
onion	*n*: пиёз
only	*adv*: фақат
open	*vt*: кушодан (кушо); *adj*: кушода; **open area**: саҳн
operator	*n* telephone: телефончӣ
opinion	*n*: ақида, назар; **in my opinion**: ба фикрам
orange	*n* fruit: норинҷ, афлесун; color: ранги норинҷӣ; *adj*: норинҷӣ
orphan	*n*: сағира, ятим
other	*adj*: дигар
outside	*prep*, *n*: *берун
oven	*n*: танӯр
page	*n*: саҳифа
painter	*n*: рассом
Pakistan	*n*: Покистон
Pamir	*n*: Помир
Panjakent	*n*: Панҷакент
paper	*n* substance: коғаз; sheet: варақ; newspaper: рӯзнома; article: мақола; *adj*: коғазӣ
parent	*n*: волид (волидайн)
Paris	*n*: Париж
party	*n* social gathering: шабнишинӣ; celebration, feast: тӯй, зиёфат; group: гурӯҳ; political: ҳизб

pass	*n* of ball: зарба; through mountains: гузаргоҳ, роҳ; *vt* a place: гузаштан (гузар) (аз indicates place passed); time: гузарондан (гузарон); a class: супоридан (супор); a thing: додан, дароз кардан; a law: қабул кардан
past	*n*: гузашта
pea(s)	*n*: нахӯд, лӯбиё; **pea soup**: нахӯдшӯрбо
peach	*n*: шафтолу
pear	*n* large: нок; small: муруд
pen	*n* for writing: хома; for animals: оғил
pencil	*n*: қалам
pencil sharpener	*n*: қаламтезкунак
pension	*n*: нафақа
pensioner	*n*: нафақахӯр
people	*n* in general: одамон; the public: мардум; a nation: халқ; **the people**: умум
pepper	*n*: қаланфур; green: қаланфури булғорӣ; black: мурч
persimmon	*n*: хурмо
person	*n* generally: кас; individual: нафар, шахс (ашхос); human: инсон
pets	*n*: ҳайвоноти хонагӣ
philosophy	*n*: фалсафа
photograph	*n*: сурат, акс, расм
phrase	*n*: ибора
physician	*n*: табиб, ҳаким
piano	*n*: пианино
picture	*n*: сурат, расм; **be pictured**: тасвир шудан
pilaf	*n*: (оши) палав/палов
pink	*adj*: гулобӣ
pistachios	*n*: писта
place	*n* generally: ҷой, макон; region: маҳал; point: нуқта; proper place: маврид; *vt* generally: мондан (мон), гузоштан (гузор); in pocket, drawer, etc.: андохтан (андоз)
place of birth	*n*: ҷойи таваллуд
play	*vt* a game: бозӣ кардан; compete: қувва озмудан; a musical instrument: навохтан (навоз)
please	*adv*: лутфан, илтимос; *interj*: марҳамат
plum	*n*: олу
plus	*n* math: ҷамъи
pocket	*n*: киса
poem	*n*: шеър
point	*n*: нукта
Poland	*n*: Полша
police	*n*: милиса
police station	*n* generally: қароргоҳи милиса; Department of Internal Affairs: шӯъбаи корҳои дохилӣ; local: шӯъбаи ноҳиявии милиса
policeman	*n*: милиса
pomegranate	*n*: анор
poor	*adj*: камбағал, бечора
pork	*n*: гӯшти хук
pot	*n*: дег
potato	*n*: картошка
pound	*n*: фунт
Prague	*n*: Прага

pray	*vi* generally: дуо кардан; read or recite prayers: дуо хондан; desire fervently: дархост кардан, илтимос кардан (барои **for**)
prayer	*n* generally: дуо, илтимос; Muslim prayer offered five times a day: намоз
present	*adj* contemporary: ҳозира; not absent: ҳозир; *n* gift: тӯҳфа; time: ҳозира, замини ҳозир; *vt* an award: мукофот додан
president	*n*: президент, раисҷумҳурӣ
pressure	*n*: фишор
pretty	*adj*: зебо
prevent	*vt*: пешгирӣ кардан; **be prevented**: пешгирӣ намудан
price	*n*: нарх
produce	*n*: маҳсулот, тавлид
product	*n*: маҳсулот
professor	*n*: устод
profit	*n*: фоида
programmer	*n*: барномасоз
protection	*n*: ҳимоят, ҳифз
pull	*vt*: кашидан (каш)
pumpkin	*n*: каду
purple	*adj*: ҷигарӣ
purpose	*n*: ҳадаф, сабаб, мақсад
purse	*n*: сумка
put	*vt*: мондан (мон), гузоштан (гузор); in narrow space: андохтан (андоз)
put down	*vt*: мондан (мон)
put on	*vt*: пӯшидан (пӯш)
pyramid	*n*: аҳром
question	*n*: савол

Qurghonteppa	*n*: Қӯрғонтеппа
radio	*n*: радио
radish	*n*: редиска, шалғамча
rain	*n*: борон; *vi*: боридан (бор)
rainbow	*n*: тирукамон
raincoat	*n*: боронӣ
rainy	*adv*: боронӣ
raisin	*n*: кишмиш; sultana: мавиз; black: мавизи сиёҳ
raven	*n*: зоғ
read	*vt*: хондан (хон)
really	*adv*: аслан, воқеан, наход; *interj*: наход
reason	*n* aim: сабаб; mental faculty: ақл
record	*n*: сабт; *vt*: сабт кардан
red	*adj*: сурх
refuse	*vi* to do something: даст кашидан (аз from); permission: рад кардан
registration form	*n*: варақаи қайд
related	*adj*: вобаста, марбут
relationship	*n* family: хешӣ; connection: вобастагӣ, робита
relatives	*n*: табор, хеш (хешованд)
religion	*n*: дин
remarried	*adj*: азнавоиладоршуда
rent	*n* rental: иҷора; rent charge: иҷорапулӣ; *vt* as tenant: иҷора гирифтан; as owner: иҷора додан
respect	*vt*: риоя кардан (object shown with ба), ҳурмат кардан

rest	*n* relaxation: истироҳат, фароғат; remainder: бақия, монда; *vi*: истироҳат кардан, қарор гирифтан, дам гирифтан
restaurant	*n*: тарабхона, ресторан
return	*vi*: баргаштан (баргард); *vt*: баргардондан, гардон(и)дан (гардон)
rice	*n*: биринҷ; meal of cooked rice: шӯла; rice in milk: ширбиринҷ
rich	*adj*: бой (аз **in**), сарватманд, доро
right	*adj* direction: рост; correct: рост, дуруст; proper, upright: рост; *adv* direct: рост; exactly: айнан, аниқ, маҳз
river	*n*: дарё
road	*n*: роҳ
rock music	*n*: рок
room	*n* division of house: утоқ, ҳуҷра, хона; space: маҳал, ҷой
rough	*adj*: дағал
round	*adj*: доирашакл, мудаввар; *n* of game: давр
row	*n*: қатор, раста
ruble	*n*: рубл
ruby	*n*: ёқут, лаъл
rude	*adj*: дағал
rug	*n*: гилем, қолин
rugby	*n*: регбӣ
ruler	*n* straightedge: ҷадвал; sovereign: ҳукумат
Russia	*n*: Россия, Русия
Russian	*n*: рус; *adj*: русӣ
sack	*n*: борхалта, халта
sad	*adj*: ғамгин
safety	*n*: амн, амният
salad	*n*: салат, хӯриш
sale	*n*: фурӯш
salt	*n*: намак
salt-free	*adj*: бенамак
Saturday	*n*: шанбе
say	*vi*: гуфтан (гӯ, гӯй)
school	*n* before university: мактаб (макотиб); university division: факулта
scissors	*n*: қайчӣ
Scottish	*adj*: шотландӣ
season	*n*: фасл(-и сол)
second	*n* unit of time: сония; *adj*: дуюм/дуввум, сонӣ
security	*n*: амният
see	*vt*: дидан (бин)
seem	*vi*: намудан (намо)
self	*n, pron*: худ
sell	*vt*: фурӯхтан (фурӯш)
seller	*n*: фурӯшанда
sentence	*n*: ҷумла
separate	*adj*: алоҳида
September	*n*: сентябр
serious	*adj*: вазнин, ҷиддӣ
service	*n*: хизмат, хидмат
services	*n*: хадамот
seven	*num*: ҳафт
seventeen	*num*: ҳабдаҳ
seventy	*num*: ҳафтод
she	*pron*: вай, ӯ, он
sheep	*n*: гӯсфанд
shelf	*n*: ҷевон
shepherd	*n*: чӯпон
shishkabob	*n*: сихкабоб, шашлик
short	*adj* duration: кӯтоҳ; height: қадпаст
show	*vt*: нишон додан
shy	*adj*: шармгин
sick	*adj*: бемор, касал

side	*n*: самт, тараф (атроф); **both sides**: тарафайн
sightseeing	*n*: тамошо
silk	*n*: шоҳӣ; atlas: атлас
sing	*vi*: суруд хондан, сурудан (саро)
singer	*n*: сароянда; folk: ҳофиз
sir	*n*: ҷаноб
sister	*n* older sister: апа; younger sister: хоҳар
sister-in-law	*n* husband's sister: хоҳаршӯй; wife's sister: хоҳарарӯс; brother's wife: янга; relationship between wives of two brothers: авсун
sit down	*vi*: нишастан (шин)
six	*num*: шаш
sixteen	*num*: шонздаҳ
sixty	*num*: шаст
slave	*n*: банда
slice	*n*: бурида, порча; *vt*: пора кардан, реза кардан
small	*adj*: хурд, майда
smart	*adj*: боақл, доно
smoke	*n*: дуд; *vt* tobacco: кашидан (каш), тамоку кардан
snow	*n*: барф
snowy	*n*: барфӣ
so	*adv*: чандон; such, to this extent: ин қадар
soccer	*n*: футбол
som	*n*: (Kyrghyz currency) сом
some	*adj*: баъзе (precedes noun); some kind of: ягон (хел); **some people**: баъзеҳо; **some person**: фалонӣ
somoni	*n*: (Tajiki currency) сомонӣ

son	*n*: писар, писарбачча
son-in-law	*n*: домод
sorry	*interj*: мебахшед
soup	*n*: шӯрбо, собун; eaten with rice and yogurt: мастоба; **noodle soup**: угро; **pea soup**: нахӯдшӯрбо
sour	*adj*: турш
sour cream	*n*: қаймоқ
South Africa	*n*: Африқои Ҷанубӣ
speak	*vi*: гап задан
speech	*n*: гап, калом, сухан
spoilt	*adj*: пӯсида
spoon	*n*: қошуқ, чумча; slotted: кафгир
sport	*n*: варзиш
spouse	*n*: ҳамсар
spring	*n* season: баҳор; water: чашма; *adj* season: баҳорӣ
stand	*vi* as opposed to moving: истодан (ист); stand straight: рост истодан
stand up	*vi*: хестан (хез)
state	*n* condition: аҳвол; region, as in USA: иёлат; government: давлат; *adj*: давлатӣ
stop	*vi*: истодан (ист)
store	*n*: дӯкон, мағоза
storey	*n*: ошёна
story	*n*. ҳикоя
storm	*n*: тӯфон
strawberry	*n*: қулфинай
street	*n*: кӯча, гузар
strive	*vi*: кӯшидан (кӯш)
strong	*adj*: сахт, боқувват, мустаҳкам
student	*n* university: донишҷӯ; school: талаба

study	*vi* be in class: дарс хондан; go to college: хондан (хон); *vt* a subject: омӯхтан (омӯз), таҳсил кардан
sugar	*n*: шакар; **powdered sugar**: хокаи қанд
Sughd	*n*: Суғд
suitcase	*n*: ҷомадон
summer	*n*: тобистон; *adj*: тобистона
Sunday	*n*: якшанбе
sunny	*adv*: офтобӣ
sunrise	*n*: тулӯъи офтоб
sunset	*n*: ғуруби офтоб
superstition	*n*: хурофот
supply	*n*: таъмин
surgeon	*n*: ҷарроҳ
Sweden	*n*: Шветсия
sweet	*adj*: ширин, қандин
Switzerland	*n*: Швейтсария
syllable	*n*: ҳиҷо
Syria	*n*: Сурия
syrup	*n*: шира
table	*n* furniture: миз; chart: ҷадвал
Tajik	*n*: тоҷик; *adj*: тоҷикӣ
Tajikabad	*n*: Тоҷикобод
Tajiki	*adj*: тоҷикӣ
Tajikistan	*n*: Тоҷикистон
take	*vt* get: гирифтан (гир); carry: бурдан (бар)
take off	*vt* clothes: кашидан (каш)
take out	*vt* remove: бардоштан (бардор) (аз **from**); bring out: баровардан (баровар, барор) (аз **from**); produce, show: даровардан (даровар, дарор)
take place	*vi*: баргузор шудан, барпо гардидан
talent	*n*: ҳунар, истеъдод, лаёқат, табъ
tall	*adj*: қадбаланд, қаддароз
tape player	*n*: магнитофон
tea	*n*: чой; with milk: ширчой; **prepare tea**: чой дам кардан
teach	*vi, vt*: дарс додан
teacher	*n*: муаллим
teacup	*n*: пиёла
Tehran	*n*: Теҳрон
telephone	*n*: телефон
television	*n*: телевизор, теледидар
temperature	*n*: ҳарорат
ten	*num*: даҳ
tenge	*n*: (Kazakh currency) тенге
tennis	*n*: теннис, теннисбозӣ
Texas	*n*: Техас
Thailand	*n*: Тайланд
thank you	*interj*: ташаккур
that	*pron*: он; **that one**: ана он, ҳамон
then	*conj*: сипас
there	*pron*: он ҷо
there is/are	*vi*: ҳаст
they	*pron*: онҳо, вайҳо
thick	*adj*: ғафс
thin	*adj*: хароб
thing	*n*: чиз
things	*n*: ашё
third	*adj*: сеюм; *n, num*: сеяк, сулс (rare)
thirsty	*adj*: ташна
thirteen	*num*: сездаҳ
thirty	*num*: сӣ
this	*pron, adj*: ин; **this one**: мана, ин; ҳамин
this year	*n, adv*: имсол
thorn	*n*: хор
thousand	*num*: ҳазор

three	*num*: се
thunder	*n*: раъд, тундар
Thursday	*n*: панҷшанбе
time	*n*: вақт; occasion: бор, маротиба, ҳангом; **in/on time, timely, at the proper/right time**: сари вақт; **for the time being**: муваққатан
tired	*adj*: хаста, кӯфташуда
title	*n* of book: ном; term of address: унвон
tobacco	*n*: тамоку
today	*adv, n*: имрӯз
tomato	*n*: помидор
tomorrow	*adv, n*: пагоҳ, фардо
too	*adv* also: ҳам, (*literary*) низ; exceedingly: зиёд, беш аз ҳад
tooth, teeth	*n*: дандон
towards	*prep*: ба
tradition	*n*: анъана, ойин
transfer	*n*: интиқол; *vi*: гузаштан; *vt*: интиқол додан (ба **to**)
translate	*vt*: тарҷума кардан (ба **into**)
trashcan	*n*: ахлотдон
tree	*n*: дарахт
Tuesday	*n*: сешанбе
tulip	*n*: лола; **tulip garden**: лолазор
Turkey	*n*: Туркия
Turkmenistan	*n*: Туркманистон
turn	*vi* rotate: гаштан (гард); appeal: муроҷиат кардан (ба **to**); *vt*: гардон(и)дан (гардон)
turnip	*n*: шалғам; green turnip: турб
twelve	*num*: дувоздаҳ
twenty	*num*: бист
twice	*adv*: ду бор, ду маротиба
twins	*n*: дугоник
two	*num*: ду
type	*n*: гуна, намуд
ugly	*adj*: безеб
Ukraine	*n*: Украина
uncle	*n* paternal uncle: амак; maternal uncle: тағо
unclean	*adj*: нопок
under	*prep*: *зер, *таг
understand	*vt*: фаҳмидан (фаҳм)
unfortunately	*interj*: афсӯс, мутаассифона
unhappy	*adj*: хафа
United States of America	*n*: Иёлоти Мутаҳҳидаи Амрико
university	*n*: донишгоҳ
until	*conj*: то даме ки, то он вақте ки (with subordinate clause); *prep*: то
us	*pron*: мо
use	*n*: истеъмол, истифода; *vt*: истифода бурдан; **be used** [ju:zd]: истеъмол намудан; **be used** [ju:st] **to**: ба...одат кардан; **get used** [ju:st] **to**: ба...ёд гирифтан
usually	*adv*: одатан, маъмулан
Uzbek	*adj*: ӯзбак
Uzbekistan	*n*: Ӯзбакистон
various	*adj*: гуногун, мухталиф
vase	*n*: гулдон
vegetables	*n*: сабзавот
vessel	*n*: зарф
videocassette player	*n*: видеомагнитофон
videotape	*n*: видеокасета
village	*n*: деҳа, қишлоқ
violet	*n* flower: бунафша; *adj* color: бунафш
visit	*n*: сафар, аёдат

vitamin	*n*: витамин
wait	*vi* await: интизор шудан (ро **for**); be kept waiting: мунтазир шудан (ро **for**); be patient: сабр кардан
waiter/waitress	*n*: пешхизмат
wake up	*vi*: бедор шудан; *vt*: бедор кардан
walk	*n*: сайр; *vi* aimlessly: гаштугузор намудан, гардиш кардан; with purpose: роҳ гаштан; see also **stroll**. (English uses **walk** more widely than Tajiki does; the Tajiki verbs generally have the sense **go for a walk**. To indicate motion on foot with a specified destination or path, Tajiks prefer to use *пиёда* **on foot** and a verb of motion like *рафтан* **go** or *баргаштан* **return**)
wall	*n*: девор
wallet	*n*: ҳамён
walnut	*n*: чормағз
Warsaw	*n*: Варшава
wash	*vt*: шустан (шӯ, шӯй); laundry: ҷомашӯйӣ кардан; dishes: зарф шустан
Washington	*n*: Вашингтон
watch	*n* timepiece: соат; *vt*: тамошо кардан
water	*n*: об
watermelon	*n*: тарбуз
we	*pron*: мо
weak	*adj*: суст, заиф
wear	*vt* clothes: пӯшидан (пӯш)
weather	*n*: ҳаво, обу ҳаво, боду ҳаво; **weather broadcasting company**: идораи обуҳавосанҷӣ; **weather report**: иттилои обуҳаво
wedding	*n*: тӯй, арӯсӣ
Wednesday	*n*: чоршанбе
week	*n*: ҳафта
weekend	*n*: рӯзҳои истироҳат
weekly	*adj*: ҳафтаина
weigh	*vt*: баркашидан (баркаш)
weight	*n*: вазн; **lift weights**: вазн бардоштан
west	*n*: ғарб, мағриб
what	*inter.pron*: чӣ
what kind (of)	*inter.adj*: чӣ гуна, чӣ навъ, чӣ тарз
wheat	*n*: гандум
wheel	*n*: чарх
when	*conj*: вақте ки, даме ки; *inter.pron*: кай
where	*inter.pron*: куҷо, (*colloq*, at/to) канӣ
which	*inter.pron, adj*: кадом
white	*adj*: сафед
who	*inter.pron*: кӣ
why	*inter.adv*: барои чӣ, (*colloq*) чаро (чиба, чида)
wide	*adj*: васеъ
widower	*n*: бева
width	*n*: бар
wife	*n*: зан, завҷа, бону
win	*vt*: буридан (бур), ғалаба кардан, ғолиб ёфтан (бар **over**); *vi*: ғолиб баромадан
wind	*n*: бод, шамол
window	*n*: тиреза
wine	*n*: май, шароб, кагор;
winter	*n*: зимистон; *adj*: зимистона

wish	*n*: хоҳиш, орзу; *vi*: орзу кардан (ба **for**)
with	*prep*: бо
without	*prep*: бе, бидуни
word	*n*: калима, калом
work	*n*: кор; literary: асар; effort, activity: фаъолият; *vi*: кор кардан
world	*n*: ҷаҳон, олам; *adj*: умумиҷаҳонӣ
world-wide	*adj*: умумиҷаҳонӣ
write	*vt*: навиштан (навис); articles: нигоштан (нигор)
writer	*n*: нависанда
Yaghnob	*n*: Яғноб
year	*n*: сол
year before last	*adv*: паресол
yellow	*adj*: зард
yes	*interj*: ҳа, бале
yesterday	*adv, n*: дирӯз (дина)
yolk	*n*: зардии тухм
you	*pron* singular informal: ту; plural: шумо; singular formal: Шумо
young	*adj*: ҷавон
young lady	*n*: ҷавонзан
younger sibling	*n*: ука
Zaire	*n*: Заир
zero	*num*: сифр, нул
Zimbabwe	*n*: Зимбабве
zip code	*n*: индекс

APPENDIX 3 Tajiki Verbs

Infinitive	*Present Stem*	*English*
анбоштан	**анбоз**	to fill up, to store up, to hoard, to accumulate, to pack, to stuff
андохтан	**андоз**	to unload, to throw, to eject, to pull out, to bend, to shoot, to set, to delay
анҷомидан	**анҷом**	to be accomplished, to be fulfilled
арзидан	**арз**	to have worth, to cost, to be of value
афзудан	**афзо(й)**	to multiply, to increase, to enlarge, to raise, to expand
афкандан	**афкан**	to throw, to toss, to hurl, to pitch, to project
афрӯхтан	**афрӯз**	to light, to kindle
афрохтан	**афроз**	to raise, to elevate, to hoist
афсурдан	**афсур**	to depress, to deject, to discourage
афтидан	**афт**	to fall, to drop
афтодан	**афт**	to fall, to drop
афшондан	**афшон**	to sprinkle, to scatter, to spread, to sow
бастан	**банд**	to tie, to bandage
бурдан	**бар**	to take, to bring, to win, to cut
барангехтан	**барангез**	to incite, to excite, to encourage, to move, to promote
барандохтан	**барандоз**	to abolish, to overthrow, to destroy
барафрохтан	**барафроз**	to hoist
барафроштан	**барафроз**	to raise, to hoist
барафрӯхтан	**барафрӯз**	to inflame
барафшондан	**барафшон**	to scatter, to sprinkle, to spread about, to spray
барбастан	**барбанд**	to pack
баргаштан	**баргард**	to return, to come back
баргардондан	**баргардон**	to turn away, to give back, to reverse
баргирифтан	**баргир**	to take away, to carry off
бардамидан	**бардам**	to blow, to breathe into, to inflate, to sprout
бардӯхтан	**бардӯз**	to stitch together, to fix, to staple
бардодан	**бардеҳ**	to give, to pay, to offer, to present

бардоштан	**бардор**	to pick up, to raise, to elevate, to lift
барзадан	**барзан**	to roll up, to tuck up, to fold
баркашидан	**баркаш**	to weigh,
баровардан	**баровар**	to take out, to bring out, to carry out
баровехтан	**баровез**	to hang, to suspend, to dangle
баромадан	**баро**	to exit, to go out, to leave
барошуфтан	**барошӯб**	to be disturbed,
барфишондан	**барфишон**	to sprinkle, to scatter, to spread, to sow
бархезондан	**бархезон**	to stand, to raise
бархостан	**бархоҳ**	to rise, to get up, to stand up
бархӯрдан	**бархӯр**	to encounter, to bump into, to clash, to offend
барҷастан	**барҷаҳ**	to jump o leap
бахшидан	**бахш**	1.) to grant, to bestow, to give 2.) to pardon, to excuse, to forgive, to absolve
бехтан	**без**	to sieve
бӯйидан	**бӯй**	to smell, to sniff, to perceive, to breath in
бохтан	**боз**	to lose, to fail
бозидан	**боз**	to play, to ac, to perform, to jest
бозгаштан	**бозгард**	to return, to come back
бозгардонидан	**бозгардон**	to turn away, to give back, to reverse
бозгуфтан	**бозгӯй**	to repeat, to retell, to recount
боздодан	**боздеҳ**	to give
бозёфтан	**бозёб**	to recover, to regain, to recoup
бозмондан	**бозмон**	to be hindered or detained, to lag behind
бозомадан	**бозо(й)**	to come back, to return, to come again
бозовардан	**бозор**	to bring back, to return
бозхондан	**бозхон**	to be called back
бозхостан	**бозхоҳ**	to take to task, to reprove, to reprimand, to interrogate
болидан	**бол**	to be glad, to rejoice
боридан	**бор**	to rain, to snow, to pour
бофтан	**боф**	to braid, to plait, to knit, to weave
бойистан	**бош**	to be mandatory, to be necessary
бӯсидан	**бӯс**	to kiss

будан	бош	to be
бурдан	бар	to take, to bring, to win
буридан	бур	to cut
вазидан	ваз	to blow, to bluster
варамидан	варам	to swell, to inflame, to dilate, to protrude, to be inflated, to be inflamed, to bloat, to puff (up), to bulge
варзидан	варз	to cultivate, to exercise, to train, to cherish, to knead
ваҳмидан	ваҳм	to fear, to form frightful
вогузоштан	вогузор	to leave, to cede, to transfer, to abandon
водоштан	водор	to set, to appoint, to set up
ворастан	ворaҳ	to be delivered, to be saved, to be relieved
ворaҳидан	ворaҳ	to be delivered, to be saved, to be relieved
вохӯрдан	вохӯр	to meet, to come across
газидан	газ	to bite, to sting
газондан	газон	passive form of газидан
ғалтидан	ғалт	to roll, to wallow, to welter
ғалтондан	ғалтон	to roll to cause
гандидан	ганд	to rot, to putrefy, to decay, to spoil
гаравидан	гарав	to follow, to adhere to, to pursue
гардидан	гард	to ramble, to walk, to spin, to revolve
гардондан	гардон	to turn around, to revolve, to rotate
гаройидан	гарой	to have a tendency, to intend, to desire
гаштан	гард	to revolve, to rotate, to spin, to turn
ғежидан	ғеж	to slip, to slide
ғелидан	ғел	to roll down, to tumble
ғеҷидан	ғеҷ	to slip, to slide
гӯзидан	гӯз	to fart
гиристан	гирй	to weep, to cry
гирифтан	гир	to take, to deceive, to obtain, to get
гирондан	гирон	to light, to kindle
гӯрондан	гӯрон	to bury
ғӯтидан	ғӯт	to sink, to plunge, to immerse
ғӯтонидан	ғӯтон	to cause to dive, to cause to plunge
гудохтан	гудоз	to melt, to dissolve

гузаштан	**гузар**	to pass, to cross, to expire
гузидан	**гузин**	to choose, to select, to elect
гузоридан	**гузор**	to put, to serve, to pay, to perform
гузоштан	**гузор**	to place, to put
ғунгидан	**ғунг**	to buzz
ғундоштан	**ғундор**	to harvest, to gather, to amass, to pick
ғунудан	**ғанаб**	to rest, to relax, to sleep
ғунҷидан	**ғунҷ**	to hold, to be packed together, to contain
ғунҷонидан	**ғунҷон**	to collect, to gather together
гурехтан	**гурез**	to run away, to escape, to flee, to avoid
ғурридан	**ғур**	to roar, to growl
гусастан	**гусил**	to cut, to sever, to tear, to disconnect, to rupture
гусехтан	**гусил**	to cut, to rupture, to break (off), to disconnect
густурдан	**густур**	to spread, to propagate, to expand, to diffuse, to open
гуфтан	**гӯй**	to say, to tell, to relate, to speak
давидан	**дав**	to run, to gallop
дамидан	**дам**	to blow, to breath into, to sprout
даравидан	**дарав**	to harvest, to reap, to cut
дарандохтан	**дарандоз**	to unload, to throw, to eject, to pull out, to bend, to shoot, to set, to delay
дарафтидан	**дарафт**	to attack, to assault, to strike down
дарафтодан	**дарафт**	to attack, to assault, to strike down
даргирифтан	**даргир**	to catch on fire
даргирондан	**даргирон**	to set on fire, to light
даргузаштан	**даргузар**	to pass away, to die
дарёфтан	**дарёб**	to gain, to collect, to take possession
даридан	**дар**	to tear, to rip
даркашидан	**даркаш**	to retract, to pull or draw out
дармондан	**дармон**	to be stuck, to be trapped
даровардан	**даровар**	to take out, to bring out, to produce, to show
даровехтан	**даровез**	to hang, to suspend, to grapple with
даромадан	**даро**	to enter, to go in, to come in
даромехтан	**даромез**	to intermingle, to intermix, to blend, to mingle

дарпайвастан	**дарпайванд**	to join, to connect, to link
даррабудан	**даррабо**	to steal, to pilfer, to lift, to swipe, to kidnap, to hijack
даррасидан	**даррас**	to overtake, to happen, to come upon
даррафтан	**даррав**	to run away, to flee, to escape, to shirk, to fly, to avoid, to evade, to be dislocated
даррондан	**даррон**	to tear, to rip up
дархостан	**дархоҳ**	to request, to solicit, to intercede
дидан	**бин**	to see, to watch, to observe, to experience
додан	**деҳ (диҳ)**	to give
донистан	**дон**	to know
доштан	**дор**	to have, to hold
дуздидан	**дузд**	to steal
дурахшидан	**дурахш**	to shine, to sparkle, to glitter
дӯхтан	**дӯз**	to sew
дӯшидан	**дӯш**	to milk
ёзидан	**ёз**	to lie down, to stretch out
ёфтан	**ёб**	to find, to discover, to acquire
жӯлидан	**жӯл**	to become entangled, to become disheveled
жӯлонидан	**жӯлон**	to dishevel
задан	**зан**	to strike, to hit, to beat
зебидан	**зеб**	to befit, to suit
зирбонидан	**зирбон**	to fry
зистан	**зиҳ**	to live
зодан	**зой**	to give birth
зойидан	**зой**	to give birth
зудудан	**зудо**	to clean, to purify
калавидан	**калав**	to stagger, to totter
кандан	**кан**	to dig, to pick to pluck, to rip, to pull
қапидан	**қап**	to hold
кардан	**кун**	to do, to make
кафидан	**каф**	to crack, to split
кафондан	**кафон**	to chop, to split, to break up
кашидан	**каш**	to pull, to drag, to draw
кашонидан	**кашон**	to transport, to portage, to carry

кӯбидан	**кӯб**	to beat, to knock
кебидан	**кеб**	to beware, to be afraid
киштан	**кор**	to sow, to plant
коридан	**кор**	to sow, to plant
костан	**коҳ**	to lose weight
кофтан	**коб**	to look for, to search for, to dig
коҳидан	**коҳ**	to grow thin, to lose weight
коштан	**кор**	to sow
кушодан	**кушо**	to open, to untie
куштан	**куш**	to kill, to switch off, to put out
кӯфтан	**кӯб**	to beat, to knock
кӯфтан	**кӯб**	to beat, to knock
кӯчидан	**кӯч**	to move, to migrate
кӯшидан	**кӯш**	to strive, to make an effort, to try hard
лағжидан	**лағж**	to slip
лақидан	**лақ**	to chatter
ламсидан	**ламс**	to touch, to palpate
лангидан	**ланг**	to limp, to walk lamely
лаппидан	**лап**	to lap, to swish, to ripple
ларзидан	**ларз**	to shake, to tremble, to shiver
лесидан	**лес**	to lick
лофидан	**лоф**	to boast, to brag
мазидан	**маз**	to suck, to absorb, to taste
макидан	**мак**	to suck, to absorb
макондан	**макон**	to suckle, to nurse
мирондан	**мирон**	to kill
молидан	**мол**	to rub, to spread
мондан	**мон**	to put, to place, to be left, to remain, to keep, to last, to stay, to tarry, to delay, to survive
монондан	**монон**	to be kept
мукофотонидан	**мукофотон**	to award
мурдан	**мур**	to die
навардидан	**навард**	to travel, to traverse, to roll, to fold, to twist
навистан	**навис**	to write
навиштан	**навис**	to write, to compose
навозидан	**навоз**	to play a musical instrument, to strum

навохтан	**навоз**	to play a musical instrument, to strum
намудан	**намо**	to appear, to seem
нигаристан	**нигар**	to look, to glance
нигоридан	**нигор**	to write, to portray, to paint, to illustrate, to draw
нигоштан	**нигор**	to write, to portray, to paint, to illustrate, to draw
ниҳодан	**нех (них)**	to place, to put,
нишастан	**нишин**	to sit, to sit down, to take a sit, to reside, to dwell
нишонидан	**нишон**	to seat, to set, to plan, to fix, to implant, to settle down
ниюшидан	**ниюш**	to listen, to hearken, to eavesdrop, to search
нозидан	**ноз**	to boast of, to flaunt, to brandish, to plume oneself
нолидан	**нол**	to moan, to cry, to lament, to complain
номидан	**ном**	to name, to call, to nominate
нӯшидан	**нӯш**	to drink
овардан	**ор/овар**	to bring, to produce, to accept
овехтан	**овез**	to hang, to suspend
озмудан	**озмо**	1) to test, to try, to examine 2) to experience
олудан	**олой**	to contaminate, to pollute, to stain
омадан	**(би)ё/ой**	1) to come, to arrive 2) to become 3) to befall
омӯхтан	**омӯз**	to learn, to study
оромидан	**ором**	to be quieted down, to become quieted
оростан	**орой**	to adorn, to decorate
осудан	**осо**	to rest, to obtain peace of mind, to repose
ошомидан	**ошом**	to drink, to guzzle, to swig, to imbibe
пажмурдан	**пажмур**	to fade, to wither, to droop, to waste away
пажӯҳидан	**пажӯҳ**	to do research, to probe, to investigate, to search
пазируфтан	**пазир**	to accept, to receive, to approve, to admit
пазонидан	**пазон**	to cook, to cause to cook

пайвастан	пайванд	to join, to connect, to link
паймудан	паймо	to measure, to travel, to go
парастидан	параст	to adore, to worship, to idolize
парвардан	парвар	to nourish, to foster, to educate
пардохтан	пардоз	to settle accounts, to pay, to reimburse
паридан	пар	to fly, to jump, to flutter, to leap
парокандан	парокан	to scatter, to broadcast, to disseminate, to strew
партофтан	парто	to throw, to hurt, to cast
перостан	перой	to trim (off), to dress up, to embellish, to decorate
пиндоштан	пиндор	to suppose, to imagine
писандидан	писанд	to admire, to like, to select, to approve of
пӯйидан	пӯй	to search, to run after, to inquire, to look for something
пойидан	пой	to keep watch, to watch, to guard, to stop, to wait
полудан	полой	to filter, to strain, to purify, to refine
пошидан	пош	to sprinkle, to scatter, to defuse
пурсидан	пурс	to ask, to question, to beg, to inquire
пӯсидан	пӯс	to rot, to spoil, to go bad, to putrefy
пухтан	паз	to cook
пучидан	пуч	to pinch
рабудан	рабо	to steal, to pilfer, to lift, to swipe, to kidnap, to hijack
размидан	разм	to war, to fight, to battle
рақсидан	рақс	to dance
рамидан	рам	to shy, to be startled, to stampede, to buck
ранҷидан	ранҷ	to take offence, to be offended, to be annoyed
ранҷондан	ранҷон	to offend, to give offence, to annoy, to insult
расидан	рас	to reach, to attain, to get to, to arrive, to ripen
расондан	расон	to complete, to finish, to conclude, to help
растан	раҳ	to be saved, to be freed, to be delivered

рафтан	**рав**	to go, to go out/away, to leave
раҳидан	**раҳ**	to be saved
раҳондан	**раҳон**	to deliver, to save, to rescue, to set free
рахшидан	**рахш**	to shine, to glitter
резондан	**резон**	to pour, to spill, to cast away
рӯёндан	**рӯён**	to cause to grow
ресидан	**рес**	to spin, to weave
рехтан	**рез**	to pour, to cast, to flow, to fall
рӯйидан	**рӯй**	to grow
рондан	**рон**	to drive, to pilot, to conduct, to ride
рустан	**рӯй**	to grow
рӯфтан	**рӯб**	to sweep
сабзидан	**сабз**	to germinate, to sprout, to grow
сабзондан	**сабзон**	to grow, to cultivate, to cause to germinate
сазидан	**саз**	to merit, to deserve, to be worth
санҷидан	**санҷ**	to weigh, to measure, to test
саройидан	**сарой**	to sing
ситезидан	**ситез**	to quarrel, to fight,
ситонидан	**ситон**	to take by force, to seize, to wrench, to snatch
сойидан	**сой**	to pulverize, to grind, to abrade, to wear away
сохтан	**соз**	to make, to build, to construct, to produce
судан	**сой**	to rub, to grind, to pulverize, to abrade
сулфидан	**сулф**	to cough
супоридан	**супор**	to hand over, to give, to offer
супурдан	**супур**	to hand over, to give, to offer
сурудан	**саро**	to sing
сурфидан	**сурф**	to lay down
сурхидан	**сурх**	to turn red, to become red
сутудан	**сито**	to praise
суфтан	**сой**	to polish
сӯхтан	**сӯз**	to burn, to consume, to be consumed, to flame
тавонистан	**тавон**	can, to be able to, to ability

такондан	**такон**	to dust by shaking, to shake, to cause to shake
талбидан	**талб**	to demand, to request
танидан	**тан**	to spin/weave
тапидан	**тап**	to beat, to throb
таркидан	**тарк**	to burst, to explode
тарконидан	**таркон**	to blow up, to explode
таровидан	**таров**	to leak, to drip water
тарошидан	**тарош**	to shave, to clip, to shear, to plane, to scrape, to sharpen
тарсидан	**тарс**	to be afraid, to fear
тарсонидан	**тарсон**	to frighten, to scare
тафсидан	**тафс**	to become red-hot
тафсонидан	**тафсон**	to heat, to warm it up
таҷҳизонидан	**таҷҳизон**	to equip
тобидан	**тоб**	1) to shine, to shimmer 2) to resemble, to look like
тозидан	**тоз**	to gallop, to rush, to attack
тофтан	**тоб**	to twist
тохтан	**тоз**	to run, to gallop
туршидан	**турш**	to become sour, to turn rancid
фармудан	**фармо**	to order, to command
фаровардан	**фарор**	unloaded, lowered down
фаромадан	**фаро**	to get down, to climb down, to come down
фарсудан	**фарсо**	to wear down, to tire, to erode
фаҳмидан	**фаҳм**	to understand, to comprehend
фаҳмондан	**фаҳмон**	to cause to understand, to explain
фахридан	**фахр**	to brag, to boast, to vaunt
фиребидан	**фиреб**	to lie, to deceive
фирефтан	**фиреб**	deceived, fooled, tricked
фиристодан	**фирист**	to send
фитодан	**афт**	to fall
фишондан	**фишон**	to shake, to cause, to move
фишордан	**фишор**	to shake, to press, to squeeze
форидан	**фор**	to give pleasure, to please
фузудан	**физо**	to add, to increase
фуровардан	**фурор**	to unload, to bring down, to let down

фуромадан	**фуро**	to get off, to come down from
фурӯхтан	**фурӯш**	to sell
фусурдан	**фусур**	to be depressed, dejected
фишурдан	**фишор**	to press, to squeeze
хазидан	**хаз**	to creep, to grovel, to crawl
халидан	**хал**	to prick
халонидан	**халон**	to pierce, to prick
хамидан	**хам**	to bend, to stoop
хандидан	**ханд**	to laugh
хандондан	**хандон**	to make someone laugh
харидан	**хар**	to buy
ҳаросидан	**ҳарос**	to be afraid, to fear
ҳаросонидан	**ҳаросон**	to frighten, to scare
харошидан	**харош**	to scratch, to scrape
хестан	**хез**	to get up, to stand
хиромидан	**хиром**	to strut, to prance, to walk
хобидан	**хоб**	to lie down, to sleep, to nap
хобондан	**хобон**	to put to sleep
хойидан	**хой**	to chew
хондан	**хон**	to read, to study
хонондан	**хонон**	to educate
хоридан	**хор**	to itch, to scratch
хостан	**хоҳ**	1) to desire, to wish, to want 2) to ask
хӯрдан	**хӯр**	to eat
хӯрондан	**хӯрон**	to feed
хӯсидан	**хӯс**	to scare, to frighten
хуспидан	**хусб**	to sleep, to doze
хуфтан	**хоб**	to sleep, to doze
хушкидан	**хушк**	to dry up
хушкондан	**хушкон**	to dry
чайқондан	**чайқон**	to rinse
чакидан	**чак**	dripping, oozing
чакондан	**чакон**	to drop by droplets
чамидан	**чам**	to strut, to walk in a stately fashion
ҷангидан	**ҷанг**	to fight, to war, to battle
чаридан	**чар**	to graze, to pasture

чаронидан	**чарон**	to pasture, to graze
чархидан	**чарх**	to spin, to rotate, to whirl
часпидан	**часп**	to stick, to attach, to bond, to cling
часпонидан	**часпон**	to stick on, to affix
ҷастан	**ҷаҳ**	to jump,
ҷаҳидан	**ҷаҳ**	to jump
чашидан	**чаш**	to taste
чашонидан	**чашон**	to be given a drink
чидан	**чин**	to pick, to pluck, to pare
ҷӯлидан	**ҷӯл**	to soil oneself, to make oneself dirty
ҷунбидан	**ҷунб**	to move, to stir, to shake, to nod
ҷунбондан	**ҷунбон**	to move, to change the place or position of, to rock
ҷустан	**ҷӯй**	to seek, to look for, to search
ҷӯшидан	**ҷӯш**	to boil, to bubble, to stew
ҷӯшондан	**ҷӯшон**	to be boiled
шармидан	**шарм**	to be ashamed, to be modest, to be embarrassed
шикастан	**шикан**	to break
шикебидан	**шикеб**	to be patient
шикофидан	**шикоф**	to drill, to split
шикофтан	**шикоф**	to drill
шинондан	**шинон**	1) to seat someone, to offer/ give a seat, 2) to plant
шиносонидан	**шиносон**	to introduce, to acquaint, to familiarize
шинохтан	**шинос**	to be acquainted with, to recognize, to know
шиппонидан	**шиппон**	to shake out, to shiver
шитобидан	**шитоб**	hurrying
шитофтан	**шитоб**	to run quickly, to make haste, to run
шиштан	**шин**	sitting, seated
шойистан	**шой**	to be worthy, to deserve, to suit, to be fitting
шоридан	**шор**	to stream down, to flow, to trickle
шошидан	**шош**	to urinate, to pee
шӯридан	**шӯр**	to revolt, to riot, to rebel, to stir up trouble
шӯронидан	**шӯрон**	to arouse, to incite

шудан	**шав**	to become
шукуфтан	**шукуф**	to flower, to bud, to blossom, to open
шумо有идан	**шумор**	1) to count, to add 2) to consider, to reckon, to take account
шумурдан	**шумур**	to add up, to calculate, to count
шунавидан	**шунав**	to hear, to listen
шунавонидан	**шунавон**	to cause to hear, to cause to be heard
шунидан	**шунав**	to hear, to listen
шустан	**шӯй**	to wash, to cleanse

APPENDIX 4 *Харитаҳо*

Харитаи Африқо

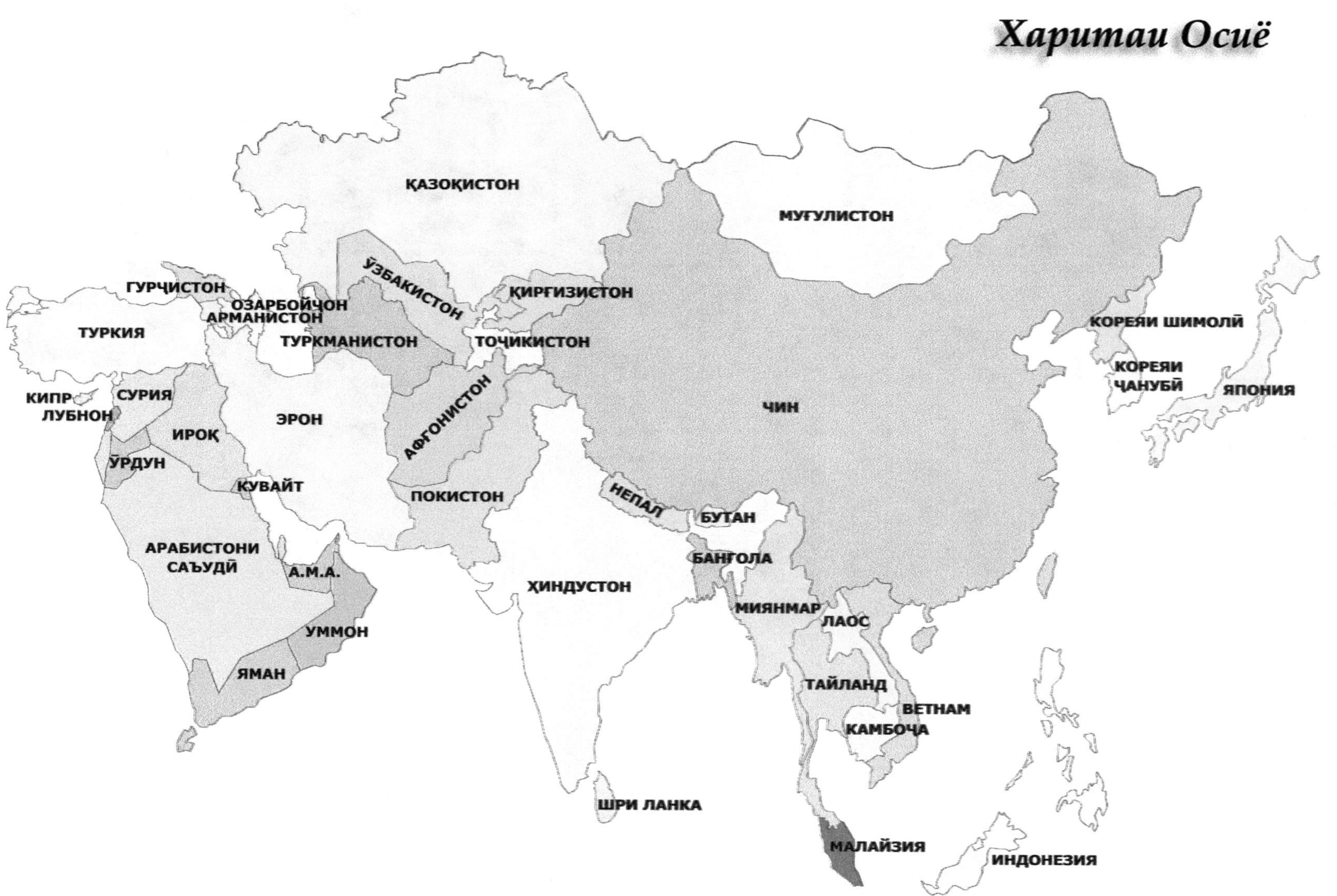
Харитаи Осиё
ҚАЗОҚИСТОН
МУҒУЛИСТОН
ГУРҶИСТОН
ОЗАРБОЙҶОН
АРМАНИСТОН
ӮЗБАКИСТОН
ҚИРҒИЗИСТОН
ТУРКИЯ
ТУРКМАНИСТОН
ТОҶИКИСТОН
КОРЕЯИ ШИМОЛӢ
КОРЕЯИ ҶАНУБӢ
ЯПОНИЯ
КИПР
ЛУБНОН
СУРИЯ
ЭРОН
АФҒОНИСТОН
ЧИН
ИРОҚ
ӮРДУН
КУВАЙТ
ПОКИСТОН
НЕПАЛ
БУТАН
АРАБИСТОНИ САЪУДӢ
БАНГОЛА
А.М.А.
ҲИНДУСТОН
МИЯНМАР
ЛАОС
УММОН
ЯМАН
ТАЙЛАНД
ВЕТНАМ
КАМБОҶА
ШРИ ЛАНКА
МАЛАЙЗИЯ
ИНДОНЕЗИЯ

Харитаи Амрикои Марказӣ
МЕКСИКА
КУБА
ҲАИТӢ
ҶУМҲУРИИ ДОМИНИКАН
ЯМАЙКА
ПУЭРТО РИКО
БЕЛИЗ
ГВАТЕМАЛА
ҲОНДУРАС
САЛВАДОР
НИКАРАГУА
КОСТА РИКА
ПАНАМА

Харитаи Амрикои Шимолӣ

Харитаи Амрикои Ҷанубӣ

Порт-оф-Спейн
ТРИНИДАД ВА ТОБАГО
Каракас
Ҷорҷтаун
ВЕНЕСУЭЛА
Парамарибо
Кайенна
ГАЙАНА
ГВНИЕЯИ ФАРО
Богота
КОЛУМБИЯ
СУРИНАМ
ЭКВАДОР
Кито
ПЕРУ
БРАЗИЛИЯ
Лима
БОЛИВИЯ
Бразилия
Ла Паз
ПАРАГВАЙ
ЧИЛИ
Асунсон
Сантяго
АРГЕНТИНА
УРУГВАЙ
Буэнос Айрес
Монтевидео

Харитаи Астралия ва Океания

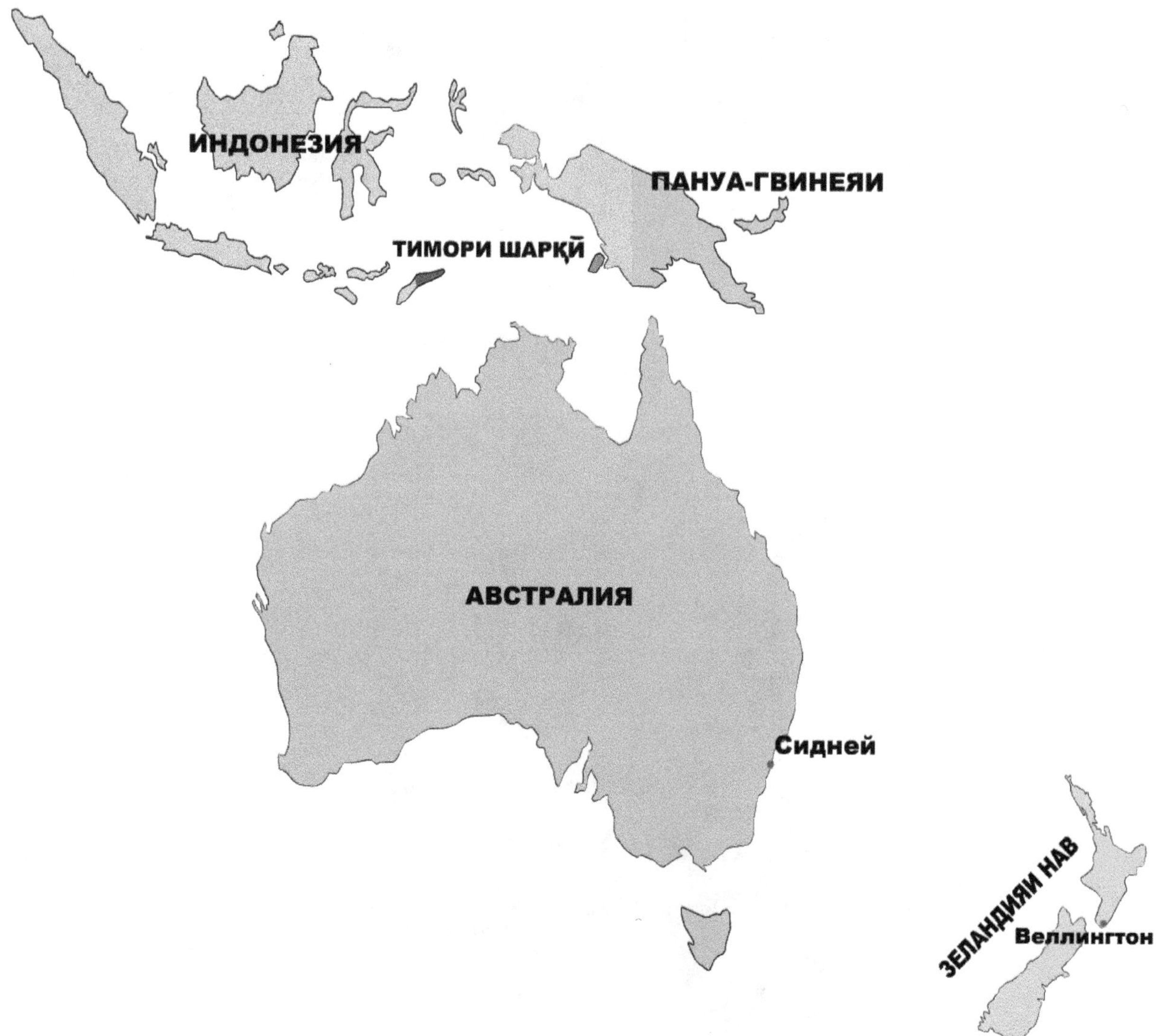

Харитаи Осиёи Миёна

Харитаи Ховари Миёна

Харитаи Аврупо

Index

Printed in the USA
CPSIA information can be obtained
at www.ICGtesting.com
LVHW050744081023
760309LV00013B/30